5/7/12

SIMPLY HISTORY

1900 to Present

Robert Taggart

WALCH  PUBLISHING

1   2   3   4   5   6   7   8   9   10

ISBN 0-8251-6994-6

Copyright © 1998, 2005, 2012

J. Weston Walch, Publisher

40 Walch Drive • Portland, ME 04103

www.walch.com

Printed in the United States of America

Table of Contents

Table of Contents, *continued*

To the Reader

Welcome to *Simply History: 1900 to Present*. This book reviews key people, places, and events from the beginning of the twentieth century to the early years of the twenty-first century.

Topic 1: A New Century and World War I introduces the changes that marked the end of the nineteenth century. These include important new inventions and scientific developments, and how the rise in imperialism and nationalism led to World War I. Finally, you will read about the end of the war and the creation of the League of Nations.

Topic 2: The World Between the Wars discusses the period between World War I and World War II including the worldwide economic depression, and how many nations became independent. We will review the rise of communism in China and Russia, the rise of dictators in Europe, and the growth of imperialism in Japan.

Topic 3: World War II addresses the events that led up to World War II. You will read about developments in Germany, Italy, and Japan during the 1930s, and how the League of Nations failed to prevent war. The course of the war in Europe, Africa, and Asia, and the changes that followed the war will be highlighted.

Topic 4: The World After World War II deals with events and developments around the world during the late 1940s and 1950s, such as the Iron Curtain and Common Market in Europe, the creation of the state of Israel, the rise of Arab nationalism, and the rise of independence in Africa and Southeast Asia.

Topic 5: The Americas presents the major events and issues in the United States, Canada, Mexico, Central America, the Caribbean, and South America from 1960 to 2004, including the Gulf War, the war in Afghanistan, and the Iraq War.

To the Reader, *continued*

Topic 6: Europe and the Former Soviet Union introduces the social, political, and economic factors that affected this region from 1960 to early 2005. You will read about the reunification of Germany, the collapse of the Soviet Union, and the changes in many nations of Eastern Europe. You will also read about the breakup of Yugoslavia, the wars that followed, and the new nations that formed in the region.

Topic 7: The Middle East and Africa discusses the geographic, religious, and economic factors that affect life in this region. We will review the many types of government found here and the sources of unrest in the area. We will also discuss how oil has affected economies in much of the Middle East and about the contrast between rich and poor nations in Africa.

Topic 8: Asia and Australasia addresses the way nations in this region adjusted to independence after colonial rule. The tensions between India and Pakistan, the war in Vietnam, and governments in Cambodia and Burma will be covered. You will read about changes in communist China, in North Korea and South Korea, and in Indonesia, the Philippines, Australia, and New Zealand.

Topic 1

A New Century and World War I

Chapter 1: The World Enters the Twentieth Century

Inventions Change the World

In the early years of the twentieth century, new inventions changed business and industry. They changed people's lives, too. Advances in science brought new understanding of the world we live in, and people gained new knowledge about human beings and human nature.

The first really big change was the use of electricity. The American Thomas Edison perfected the lightbulb in 1879. Then he found ways to transmit electric power through a system of lines. An Edison system lit up New York City in 1882. Edison developed the generator, which used electric power to run huge industrial machines. A factory could now be built anywhere, because it no longer needed waterpower. Cities became cleaner as electric trolleys replaced manure-producing horses.

Inventions helped people communicate much more easily, too. Alexander Graham Bell patented the telephone in 1876. (Bell was a Scotsman who lived in the United States.) U.S. President Rutherford B. Hayes had a telephone put in the White House in 1878. Networks of telephones spread across the country and around the world. By 1900, 1.5 million telephones were in the United States alone.

Guglielmo Marconi was a young Italian inventor. He developed a way to send messages using radio waves instead of wires. He sent a wireless telegraph or radio message across the Atlantic Ocean in 1901. In 1904, the vacuum tube was invented. Now radios could play music and human voices in people's homes. During the 1920s, radio broadcasts came into millions of homes worldwide, every day.

Transportation also became modern during this time. Different inventors in both Europe and the United States developed gasoline engines that powered the automobile. In Germany, Karl Benz and Gottlieb Daimler were auto pioneers. In France, Louis Renault was a pioneer. In America, Charles and Frank Duryea built one of the earliest automobiles in 1893. Henry Ford followed in 1896.

Ford had the biggest impact on the automobile industry. First, he designed a simple, reliable, and affordable car. It was called the Model T. (It came in one color only: black.) To make his cars, Ford created the assembly line. Car frames moved past workers as they put the cars together. Cars were made twice as quickly with assembly lines. As a result, almost anyone could afford to buy a Model T.

Another huge change in transportation began in 1903. The Americans Wilbur and Orville Wright made the first powered and sustained airplane flight that year. The airplane industry was born. Planes played a part in World War I. In the 1920s, they began carrying mail and then passengers.

These advances had an important impact on people's daily lives. Middle-class homes were now safely lit with electric lights. People played music on Edison's new invention, the phonograph. Edison added more enjoyment to people's lives when he improved motion picture technology in the 1890s. People around the world flocked to theaters to watch movies in the early 1900s. Movies became even better when sound was added to them in 1927. George Eastman brought photography to the world. He put his simple Kodak box camera on the market in 1888.

Breakthroughs in Science

During the 1800s, scientists made many discoveries. They learned that matter is made up of tiny particles called atoms. Soon, this idea became part of physics, which is the study of matter and energy. Then, in 1897, J. J. Thomson of England discovered the electron. An electron is an even tinier particle that is part of an atom. In 1898, Marie Curie and Pierre Curie of France studied radioactive elements. These elements change all the time by throwing off tiny particles.

Next, Ernest Rutherford of England found that the atom has a nucleus, or core. He also found more tiny particles within atoms. He called them protons. He studied atoms by splitting them apart with radioactive particles. This led to nuclear physics. Later, scientists learned more about the nuclear structure of atoms. They were able to create power and bombs by smashing atomic nuclei. By World War II, scientists had built the world's first atomic bomb.

Scientific discoveries did not stop there. Two other men moved physics in new directions. Max Planck of Germany showed that energy was released in definite units. He called each of these packages of energy a quantum. This was a very new concept. Another German, Albert Einstein, explained how a small mass can become a huge amount of energy. He also came up with the theory of relativity. This theory explains atomic events in terms of motion, space, and time. Other scientists used Einstein's ideas to learn more about atomic energy, which became very important later in the twentieth century.

New Knowledge About Human Beings

Scientists of the nineteenth and early twentieth centuries also studied living things. Charles Darwin developed his theory of evolution in the mid-1800s. This theory explained why living creatures changed over millions of years. A monk in Austria named Gregor Mendel wondered about this, too. He studied pea plants in the mid-1800s. Mendel learned a lot about how certain characteristics are passed on from a parent plant to its offspring.

Other scientists finally found out about Mendel's work around 1900. They found threadlike structures, called chromosomes, in plant and animal cells. Mendel had believed that these particles existed but had not been able to find them. These twentieth-century scientists also discovered that each chromosome contains many genes. They discovered that genes give a person (or other animal or plant) his or her own characteristics. Later in the twentieth century, scientists found out much more about chromosomes and genes.

Other scientists learned new things about human and animal behavior. Ivan Pavlov was a Russian biologist who studied dogs. He trained dogs to water at the mouth when he rang a bell. This is called a conditioned reflex. Pavlov had conditioned his dogs to respond in a certain way to a particular stimulus.

A new science called psychology developed in the late 1800s. Psychology is the study of the human mind. The American John Watson applied what Pavlov had learned to psychology. Watson called his system *behaviorism*. Behaviorism suggests that all human behavior is a response of the nervous system to stimuli from the world that a person lives in.

Sigmund Freud of Austria is probably the world's most famous psychologist. He developed a new idea about human behavior in the early 1900s. Freud studied the thought processes that go on without a person being aware of them. Freud called this type of study psychoanalysis. Not all of Freud's ideas are accepted today. But they had a huge impact on psychology.

The New Industrial World

It was no accident that so much new technology came out in the early twentieth century. Starting in the late 1800s, companies began setting up research centers. One of the first was in Germany. The German chemical industry wanted to find the best ways to use the latest science. Thomas Edison set up one of the first research labs in the United States. Alexander Graham Bell's telephone company soon did, too.

Science went to work for industry in these research laboratories. Companies paid scientists to work in the labs. In return, the company owned the rights to whatever a scientist might discover while at work.

The people who lived and worked in this new industrial world were much more connected to the outside world than earlier people had been. News from around the world arrived in a flash. Newspapers, radio, and telephone lines kept people informed daily.

Transportation systems also drew people together. Railroads then crisscrossed North America. In Russia, railroads carried people over great distances between Siberia and Moscow. As more and more people owned cars, networks of highways were built. Families could travel easily. Trucks could bring more goods to more places. Canals shortened shipping times. Trade between nations increased. Production was up, so manufacturers needed new markets in other nations. They also needed raw materials from other countries.

This modern industrial economy didn't grow at the same rate everywhere in the world. The countries of Western Europe, such as Great Britain and France and Germany, were very industrial. So was the United States. Southern, Central, and Eastern Europe were less developed. Much of their economy continued to be based on farming.

The same thing was true in much of Latin America, Africa, and Asia. Nations and colonies in these areas had little industry. Most of their people lived in rural areas and were poor farmers. Japan, however, had begun changing over to a modern economy in the 1880s. By 1910, it was a strong industrial country.

The lives of people in the industrial nations were quite different from those in rural nations. Western Europeans, for example, generally had more and better food, clothing, and shelter than their parents or grandparents had. They could usually change jobs if they wanted to. Rural peasants in countries such as India, however, remained tied to the land. They had few choices about how they could lead their lives. They often did not have enough food, clothing, or shelter.

The lives of women who lived in the industrial nations in the early 1900s changed in extra ways. Little by little, new jobs opened up for women after 1900. More women were able to work in medicine, the law, industry, and other areas. They were no longer as tied to the home as they once had been. They could buy ready-made clothes and other goods at department stores instead of staying home and making them. Prepared foods cut down on cooking chores. During World War I, women worked to keep war-related businesses running. They showed clearly that they were important and capable citizens. Women gained the right to vote in most western democracies during and after the war.

The industrial countries were wealthy and powerful and developed strong military forces. They wanted control of markets in which they sold their goods and where they bought raw materials. Tensions grew among these strong nations. Weaker and less powerful countries resented them. These problems eventually led to World War I.

Chapter 2: The World Moves Toward War

Imperial Rivalries and Nationalism

Starting around 1870, the powerful and industrial countries of the world began building overseas empires. They colonized foreign lands. This empire building went on until World War I stopped it in 1914.

Nations wanted overseas colonies for many reasons. Factories were producing more and more goods. Colonies provided new markets that would buy these goods. Colonies also had the raw materials, such as rubber and copper, that industries needed to keep up their high levels of production. Consumers in developed nations wanted to buy products, such as coffee and spices, from far-off places. Wealthy industrialists saw colonies as fine places to invest their large profits.

Nationalism also prompted a desire for colonies. Feelings of nationalism were very strong and nationalists said that colonies would add to their country's glory and strength. Obviously, a strong country needed a strong army. Natives of a colony were a source of new soldiers. Then, too, a country with an overseas empire and trade to protect needed a strong navy. Colonies had ports that could host navy bases and refuel ships.

There was also a desire to spread the Christian religion and Western culture around the world. Some people in developed nations had no respect for the cultures of the colonies that were being taken over, and thought that all non-Western people were "backward." They felt white Westerners had a duty to "civilize" non-Western people. Naturally, each industrial nation thought its own culture was the best one to bring to "backward" peoples.

All these reasons prompted nations to acquire colonies. So, it's no wonder that industrialized countries became intense rivals. Each developed country wanted as many colonies as possible. No country wanted a rival to take control of any unclaimed areas.

England and France had been major powers for many years. Germany and Italy had only become unified nations in the late 1800s. They worked to develop their own empires so that they would be equal with other industrial nations. Older powers worked to keep the upper hand.

The United States took control of areas in Latin America and the Pacific Ocean. Japan was a power in Asia. The world was filled with dueling nations, bumping into one another and maneuvering for position.

The Military Buildup

The inevitable result of all this rivalry between nations was a buildup of military forces. Rival countries wanted to be sure their armies and navies were as strong as those of others. They also needed strong military forces to keep control of overseas colonies and trade.

More and more, military planners were shaping the policies of European nations. This was especially true in Germany; its general staff of army officers controlled government policy.

Countries made more powerful, more destructive weapons. They spent money to build defenses along their boundaries. Germany began to create a large, modern navy. Other nations then began to build up their navies, too. Great Britain had the strongest navy in the world, yet it made its navy even bigger to keep ahead of all the other nations. This arms race cost each country a lot of money.

The Alliances

Next, the countries of Europe began looking for allies. They wanted to form alliances in case they were attacked.

Germany had defeated France in a war in 1871, and worried that France would want revenge. So in 1879, Germany formed an alliance with the powerful nation of Austria-Hungary. Italy joined the alliance in 1882. It was called the Triple Alliance. Each member promised to help any other member that was attacked.

The Triple Alliance was aimed at France. So, France reached out for its own allies. Russia and France made an alliance in 1894. In 1907, Great Britain reached an understanding with them, called an entente, or friendly understanding. An entente is less formal and binding than an alliance. This Triple Entente said that each member would come to the aid of any other member that was attacked.

This alliance system was potentially dangerous. Trouble between any two members of opposing groups could draw in all the other members. Any armed conflict would not be fought between just two countries. The conflict would involve all of Europe.

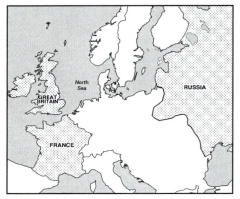

The Triple Entente   **The Triple Alliance**

Trouble in the Balkans

The Balkan area, in southeastern Europe, is the home of many different ethnic groups. For many years, these people were ruled by the Turks of the Ottoman Empire. During the 1800s, national feelings became strong among many Balkan people. They wanted self-rule. The Ottoman Empire was getting weak. Other countries in Europe supported different Balkan peoples for reasons of their own.

Throughout the 1800s, the Balkan area was filled with unrest and armed conflict. Greeks fought for and won independence in 1829, with some outside help. In the 1870s, Russia fought a war against the Turks. Other European powers then met with Russia to redraw national boundary lines in the Balkans. By the early 1900s, Serbia, Bulgaria, Romania, and Montenegro were independent. The Balkan countries fought wars against the Ottoman Empire in 1912 and again in 1913.

The major nations of Europe stayed involved in the Balkans. Russia supported the Slav people of Serbia and Bulgaria. Russians were fellow Slavs. Also, Russia wanted access to the Aegean Sea through the Balkans. Great Britain and other European countries wanted to hold Russia back. The Balkan area was so unstable, it was called "the powder keg of Europe."

Serbia had gained its independence in 1878. Serbians were not satisfied, though. They wanted to unite all the Slavs in eastern and east central Europe. They wanted to form a much bigger nation that would include Slavs in nearby areas, such as Bosnia and Herzegovina. Austria-Hungary had taken control of them in 1908. A bitter Serbia wanted them back. It looked to Russia for support.

* Bosnia was part of the Austro-Hungarian Empire

The Balkans in 1908

The War Begins

The "powder keg" blew up on June 28, 1914. Archduke Franz Ferdinand of Austria and his wife were visiting Sarajevo, the capital of Bosnia and Herzegovina. A Serbian terrorist shot and killed both of them. Austria-Hungary blamed the Serbian government. It declared war on Serbia on July 28. In response, Russia called all the soldiers of its army to active duty. Russian soldiers massed on the German border. On August 1, Germany declared war on Russia.

Two days later, Germany declared war on France, its longtime enemy. In a surprise move, German troops swept across Belgium to attack France. Belgium's borders were unprotected, because Belgium was a neutral country. It had pledged not to take sides in any war. In return, other nations of Europe had promised not to attack it. Great Britain was outraged at Germany's action in Belgium. The day German forces entered Belgium, Great Britain declared war on Germany.

The world war had begun. Here is how the fighting nations lined up: France, Russia, Great Britain, and Italy were the Allied Powers. (Italy had left its alliance with Germany and Austria-Hungary.) Japan joined them also. Germany, Austria-Hungary, the Ottoman Empire (Turkey), and Bulgaria were the Central Powers.

Chapter 3: The Great War

The Opposing Sides

The Central Powers and the Allied Powers each had certain strengths and certain weak points at the beginning of the war.

The Central Powers were located side by side. So, it was easy to move troops from place to place and keep in touch. Germans and Austrians spoke the same language. They were natural allies. Also, Germany was very ready for war. It had a fine army, good plans and supplies, and a united people.

At the same time, the Central Powers had far fewer people than the Allies. This meant fewer soldiers and fewer workers to produce war supplies. Germany had a superb navy but limited sea access.

The Allied Powers were separated from one another. The Central Powers were between Britain and France on the west and Russia on the east. Great Britain was an island. Also, the Allied Powers were not natural allies. They had only recently agreed to help one another. They spoke different languages. Keeping in touch and moving troops was difficult. Only France had a large and well-prepared land army. But France had far fewer people than Germany had, so its army was smaller than Germany's. Russia had a large army, but it wasn't well run. Also, Russia was a huge country, and its railroad system wasn't good. So, Russian troops couldn't move quickly.

The Allied Powers did have some important strengths. They had 1.25 million more people than the Central Powers. They were able to produce more war materials. Also, they controlled the seas. This meant that they could keep their troops and home populations supplied, and deny shipments of supplies to the Central Powers.

A New Kind of War

World War I used new weapons that were far more destructive, and involved civilians in a major way for the first time.

The machine gun was among the new weapons. Its ability to fire many bullets, one after the other rapidly, was unprecedented. Machine gun and artillery fire kept soldiers pinned down in trenches for weeks at a time. Another new weapon was the tank. This armored vehicle carried soldiers and broke through enemy lines. The airplane first became a military weapon in this war. Planes dropped bombs and scouted out enemy troop movements. Germany used submarines to nearly cripple Allied shipping. A horrifying new weapon used by both sides was poison gas. Gas masks were developed to make poison gas less useful.

This war also involved civilians. Earlier armies had been made up of professional soldiers, men who fought in exchange for pay and food. The soldiers of World War I were mostly ordinary citizens fighting for their country.

Civilians at home were also affected. They worked in war industries. They endured shortages of goods and food. Many were caught up in the artillery fire and bombing and were injured and killed. This had not happened on a large scale in earlier wars.

War propaganda was also a big part of World War I. Governments used a lot of this to keep up popular support for the war. Posters and pictures in each country showed the enemy as brutal. The Allies won the propaganda war. They convinced many neutral nations to support their cause.

The Course of the War

As with many other wars, both sides in World War I expected a quick win. Instead, the war raged all around the world from 1914 to 1918. It involved so many nations and people that it was known in its time as the Great War. Most of the battles were fought in Europe. But Africa and the Middle East saw fighting as well. Navies fought in seas everywhere.

The Western Front

Germany had hoped for a swift victory by attacking France after moving through Belgium. It nearly succeeded. But French troops stopped the

Germans at the first Battle of the Marne, near Paris, in 1914. After this, the war in the west became a stalemate. Germany and France dug long lines of trenches along their shared border, the western front. Troops settled into the trenches, which were deep enough for a person to stand up in. From time to time, groups of soldiers tried to break through to the enemy trenches. No one made much progress, and thousands were killed trying.

A sad example of the human costs of this type of warfare was the Battle of Verdun (1916). The Germans attacked the French at this town not to win, but to kill great numbers of defending French soldiers. They did, but many German soldiers died as well. The battle ended in a stalemate. Each side lost over 300,000 men.

The Eastern Front

The eastern front was along the border between Russia and the Central Powers—Germany and Austria-Hungary. Russia began by moving into enemy territory in East Prussia and Austrian Poland. Then the Germans pushed the Russians back. War on this front went from hard-fought battles to periods of winter stalemate. The Russians suffered many defeats in this fighting. But they kept many Central Powers troops tied up, away from the western front.

Great Britain and France, to get much-needed supplies to Russia, landed troops at Gallipoli, in Turkey. They hoped to win access to the Black Sea. This campaign failed, with a cost of many Allied dead and wounded.

War on the Seas

Both sides used their navies to blockade the enemy. Britain blockaded the North Sea to keep military supplies from reaching Germany's armies. It also kept food supplies from reaching German people at home.

Germany set up a submarine blockade off Great Britain. Germany's submarine attacks on British shipping worked well. Many merchant ships sank. British food supplies got very low. But antisubmarine attacks kept some supplies flowing.

Germany had done much to build up its navy of surface ships before the war. This buildup caused a great deal of tension with Great Britain.

Yet during the war, Germany's surface navy saw little action. The Battle of Jutland in 1916 was the war's only large naval battle. After it, the German navy pulled back to the Baltic Sea and stayed there.

The War in Asia, the Middle East, and Africa

In Asia, Japan captured a German naval base in China. The base was at the tip of the Shandong Peninsula. Japan went on to take the whole peninsula. At the war's end, Japan took over all of Germany's Pacific Ocean lands.

In the Middle East, Arabs helped British forces fight the Turks. The British Arab troops were led in part by Lieutenant Colonel Thomas E. Lawrence. His exploits earned him the name "Lawrence of Arabia." The Arab and British forces ended Turkish rule in the Middle East. After the war, the independent Arab nations as we know them today were formed. Among them were Syria, Iraq, Jordan (then called Transjordan), Lebanon, Saudi Arabia, and Egypt. In 1917, the British government issued a statement now known as the Balfour Declaration. It expressed British sympathy for "the establishment in Palestine of a national home for the Jewish people." In time, the state of Israel was created. The resulting conflict between the Arab nations and Israel has continued to today.

In Africa, Germany managed at first to hold onto German East Africa. But at the war's end, Germany lost its colonies in Africa along with all of its other colonies.

The United States Enters, and Russia Bows Out

When World War I began, the United States had declared itself neutral. Most Americans wanted nothing to do with war in Europe. But U.S. industries traded with both sides in the war, supplying needed food and war materials. The United States insisted on the freedom of its people to trade and travel in safety as neutral parties. German submarines made such travel unsafe.

In May 1915, a German submarine sank the British passenger liner the *Lusitania* off the coast of Ireland. Among the nearly 1,200 dead were more than 100 Americans. People in the United States were outraged. U.S. President Woodrow Wilson warned Germany not to sink another civilian ship. For two years, Germany held back on its submarine warfare. It did not want to draw the United States into the war.

By early 1917, Germany was struggling with severe shortages at home, including food shortages. German leaders worried about losing the war. They decided to go back to submarine attacks against ships going to Britain. The hope was to starve Britain into defeat. By now, most American trade was with Britain, thanks to the British blockade of Germany. The Germans took a chance that they could starve Britain into defeat before attacks on ships pulled the United States into the war. Soon, German submarines had sunk three U.S. ships.

Also in early 1917, Americans found out about a secret German plan to get Mexico into the war. They promised to give back to Mexico parts of the southwestern United States in return. The German foreign minister, Arthur Zimmermann, had outlined the plan in a secret telegram. British spies obtained the telegram and decoded it. U.S. newspapers made it public. This Zimmermann telegram made Americans very angry.

Meanwhile, the Russian tsarist government fell. The tsar had ruled Russia as an autocrat, but in March 1917, the Russian Revolution toppled the tsar. The Bolsheviks, or Communists, took over in November 1917. Soon, Russia was out of the war. With Russia out, all the Allies were democracies. Americans were now more able to see the war as a fight between democracy and nondemocracy.

All these factors combined to make Americans agree to join the war. The United States entered World War I in April 1917. Its troops finally began arriving in Europe in the spring and summer of 1918. They provided a badly needed freshness and vigor. They greatly boosted the morale of the tired Allied soldiers. They probably made the difference in ending the war with victory for the Allies.

The War Ends

Germany launched a last great offense in the spring and summer of 1918. The German army almost broke through the British and French forces on the western front. But the Allies, helped by fresh American troops, stopped them. The Allies pushed the German army back to the German border. The ruler of Germany, the kaiser, was forced to step down. The new republic of Germany signed an armistice on November 11, 1918. (An armistice is an agreement to stop fighting. It is in effect until a formal peace treaty is written up and signed.)

■ OF NOTE

Veterans Day honors all those, living and dead, who served with the U.S. armed forces in wartime. Veterans Day began as Armistice Day on November 11, 1919. It commemorated the end of World War I at 11 A.M. on November 11, 1918, when the armistice ending the fighting was signed. It became a holiday honoring the soldiers of World War I in the United States, France, Great Britain, and Canada (where it is known as Remembrance Day).

World War I was incredibly expensive. More than 8 million people were killed in battle. Many more were wounded. Almost as many civilians died, from fighting, hunger, and disease. (A worldwide flu epidemic killed around 20 million people in 1918.) Property losses amounted to about $400 million. The war left European nations in an unsettled state. A lasting peace was hard to achieve. It was also hard to make societies stable again.

Chapter 4: Searching for Peace

The Fourteen Points

In 1917, U.S. President Woodrow Wilson declared that the United States should enter World War I. "The world must be made safe for democracy," he stated. Most countries were fighting the war to advance their own selfish interests. But most ordinary people wanted to think of the war in Wilson's terms. People saw this as "the war to end all wars." They longed for peace and democracy around the world.

In January 1918, Wilson made a speech that outlined the now famous Fourteen Points. These points expressed what Wilson saw as the foundation for a lasting peace. The peace agreement at the end of the war should include these terms, Wilson said. Eight of the Fourteen Points were related to specific land areas.

Six of the Fourteen Points were more general. This is what they said all countries should agree to:

- no secret treaties among nations
- freedom of the seas for all countries, in war and in peace
- free trade among all nations
- cutbacks to the lowest possible levels in military arms for all nations
- fair decisions on all claims about colonies and all claims of native people in colonies
- an association of nations to keep peace

The Fourteen Points said what people around the world felt. Even people in the Central Powers agreed that a peace based on these terms would be acceptable. That did not happen, however.

The Paris Peace Conference

The fighting ended after Germany signed the armistice. For a lasting end to the war, the nations who took part had to sign a peace treaty.

The peace conference at the end of World War I was held in 1919 in Paris, France. Right from the start, there was a serious problem. Members of the Allies were angry and bitter about the war. It had lasted a long time and had caused a huge loss of life and property. The Allies decided to write the terms of the peace themselves. The members of the Central Powers could only sign the final terms.

Nearly 30 nations took part in the Paris Peace Conference. But the peace terms were worked out by the Big Three—Great Britain, France, and the United States. Italy was part of a Big Four for a while, but the Italian representative left when Italy's demands for territory weren't met.

Peacemakers faced many problems. Every member of the Allied Powers wanted new territories. Some wanted control of the same areas. The political situation was confused in central and eastern Europe. Austria and Hungary were now separate nations. Ethnic groups in eastern Europe wanted their own countries, but different ethnic groups mingled in the same areas. Colonial peoples who had helped in the war wanted self-rule; colonial powers wanted to keep control of the colonies.

Reparations were another difficult question. The war had been costly. Much of Belgium and parts of France—the western front—had been destroyed. Veterans, widows, and children needed support. Many people thought that Germany should have to pay for these damages, or some of them.

Many people also wanted Germany to pay reparations because they blamed Germany for starting the war, and they wanted revenge. They also wanted to take land away from Germany and other Central Powers. They hoped to teach Germany and Austria a lesson about going to war.

Woodrow Wilson was the leader of the opposite view at the peace meeting. He and people like him wanted a fair peace. A peace based on the Fourteen Points would give justice to everyone. A peace based on revenge would keep bad feelings among the countries of Europe very much alive. Wilson was correct. The world went to war again 20 years later.

The Peace Treaties

The Paris conference made a separate treaty with each member of the Central Powers. All had to pay reparations for war damages. The treaty with Germany was the harshest.

The Versailles Treaty

The treaty with Germany was signed at the French palace of Versailles in May 1919. Under the Versailles Treaty, the Germans agreed to pay for all civilian damage during the war. That payment was a huge sum. Also, Germany had to transfer large chunks of its land to other nations. It lost all of its overseas colonies. It had to shrink its military forces to a fraction of what they had been. Finally, Germany had to admit that the Central Powers were responsible for starting the war.

The Germans were not allowed to change any part of this treaty. They were just ordered to sign it. They did so because they had no choice. But the German people were deeply angry about the treaty. They were bitter about being forced to admit "war guilt." They felt the high payments were unfair. These feelings helped pave the road to the next world war.

The Versailles Treaty also created a League of Nations. This was an organization of many of the world's countries somewhat like today's United Nations. Members met and discussed issues. Countries were supposed to bring their disputes to the League. The League was then supposed to help find a peaceful answer. But the League had no way to enforce its advice or decisions. So it had little effect on the way nations acted.

The Other Treaties

The monarchy of Austria-Hungary had split up in 1918. Austria-Hungary became two new nations, Austria and Hungary. Both were much smaller than either had been before the war. Most of the lands they had lost became the new countries of Yugoslavia and Czechoslovakia.

Bulgaria lost land to Greece in its treaty. The Ottoman Empire lost most of its lands, both in Europe and in Asia. Then the empire itself disappeared. A young army officer named Mustafa Kemal led a revolt against the Ottoman ruler. Kemal set up a new Turkish republic, which finally signed the peace treaty in 1923.

Problems with the Peace

After so much wartime suffering and death, the world looked forward to peace. But the problems with the peace process left a lot of tension among nations. Germans were angry about the treaty they had been forced to sign, and deeply resented the nations that had forced the treaty on them.

The peace process had drawn new borders for many countries in Europe. Many people on both sides of the old and new borders didn't like the results. Some people found themselves suddenly part of a nation in which their ethnic group was in a minority. German-speaking Austrians were part of Czechoslovakia. Some sections of Germany were now part of Poland. Former sections of Russia were, too.

Also, new countries had been formed that included many different ethnic groups. Czechoslovakia, for example, had Czechs, Slovaks, Sudeten Germans, and others. The formal name of Yugoslavia was the Kingdom of Serbs, Croats, and Slovenes. It was unclear whether multiethnic nations, such as Yugoslavia and Czechoslovakia, could hold together.

■ OF NOTE

Yugoslavia and Czechoslovakia held together only as long as they were ruled by nondemocratic communist regimes. When communism fell, Yugoslavia and Czechoslovakia came apart. In the early 1990s, Yugoslavia dissolved into the warring and separate nations of Slovenia, Croatia, Bosnia and Herzegovina, and a new Yugoslavia consisting of Serbia and Montenegro. In 1993, Czechoslovakia dissolved peacefully into the two separate nations of the Czech Republic and Slovakia.

The huge and important nation of Russia hadn't even taken part in the peace conference. As you learned earlier, Russia had had a revolution in 1917. The new Russian leaders had taken their country out of the war late that year. These new leaders were Bolsheviks, or Communists. Russia's former allies in the war were alarmed by communism. They were afraid that it would spread west and upset their democracies. So the treaty makers took lands away from Russia. They created new states in eastern Europe between Russia and the new republics of Germany and Austria. They also created the three new Baltic states of Estonia, Latvia, and Lithuania. Like the Germans, the Russians had no say in all this.

Finally, the United States failed to agree to the Versailles Treaty. In the United States, the U.S. Senate must approve all treaties. The people of the United States had gladly supported Wilson's Fourteen Points. The treaties to end the war had very little of the Fourteen Points in them. The treaties were not based on ideals. They were based on nations' self-interest. Many in the United States objected.

Also, Republicans controlled Congress. President Wilson was a Democrat. He had not included Republicans in the peace process. Some senators didn't like some of the peace terms. Others disliked the League of Nations. The U.S. Senate refused to approve the treaties. (The United States finally signed peace treaties with the Central Powers in 1921.) The United States turned its back on the problems of Europe once again.

Topic 2

The World Between the Wars

Chapter 5: The Western Democracies

The years between World War I and World War II were anything but peaceful and secure. Many people felt a sense of despair. All the death and violence of World War I had taken away their faith in a future filled with good things. Now, their fears for the future seemed to be justified. Democracy was failing in many countries. A worldwide economic slump was hurting people, banks, and businesses. Dictators were making threats toward other countries.

The countries with the fewest severe problems in the 1920s and 1930s were the established democracies of the West—Great Britain, France, and the United States.

Great Britain

Problems at Home

Postwar Great Britain had many problems to cope with. Great Britain had not suffered much direct material damage during the war, since the war had not been fought on British soil. Still, Great Britain had huge losses. About 750,000 of its soldiers had been killed. Another 1.5 million were wounded.

Great Britain had economic losses as well. To pay the costs of the war, it had borrowed money from people at home and from the United States. Now it had to pay back this debt. High taxes helped raise the needed money. The taxes came out of the income of the British people.

Great Britain was a country that depended on trade for its wealth. It needed to produce goods to sell overseas. Money earned by these sales paid for goods Great Britain had to import (ship into the country). Postwar conditions were not good for British trade and industry. Many of Great Britain's merchant ships had been sunk. Its coal mines were no longer very productive. Its factories were not modern. Other nations had moved into world markets that Great Britain used to control. Tariffs kept British goods out of other countries.

These problems with the economy meant that many British workers were unemployed. They lived on "the dole"—small payments from the government. Workers turned to labor unions for help. They also supported the Labour Party, which became much stronger during the 1920s. The Conservatives (also called Tories) were the other major party. Their support came mostly from the middle and upper classes.

During the 1920s, the Labour party ran the British government. It passed some modest reforms that took the edge off of worker unrest. During the 1930s, the Conservative Party was mostly in control. Great Britain was hit hard by the worldwide depression of these years. The Conservatives made some economic moves that helped ease the impact of the depression. By the mid-1930s, the British economy had improved.

The Irish Question

England had ruled Ireland for hundreds of years. The Irish had always resented this rule. While Great Britain was absorbed in fighting World War I, the Irish acted. Irish nationalists staged an armed uprising in Ireland's capital city of Dublin in 1916. It was called the Easter Rebellion. British troops put it down. But Irish rebels kept up guerrilla warfare.

In 1921 southern Ireland became the Irish Free State. It was self-governing and Catholic. The largely Protestant counties in the north remained part of Great Britain, called Northern Ireland. Catholics and Protestants in Northern Ireland fought each other for years.

■ OF NOTE

Northern Ireland suffered from violence and terrorist actions from the 1950s on. Catholic extremists in the Irish Republican Army (IRA) used terror attacks to try to force Northern Ireland to join the Republic of Ireland. Protestant extremists used terror attacks against Catholics to prevent any such union. British troops arrived in Northern Ireland in 1969 to try to keep peace. In 1994, the IRA declared a cease-fire and serious peace talks began. In 1998, a peace accord was signed. The agreement held hope of a peaceful future for Northern Ireland.

Radicals in the south continued to fight for a single, independent Ireland. But gradually the violence in the south ended. In 1937, the Irish Free State became the Republic of Ireland (Eire).

The Commonwealth

The British Empire had been made up of both colonies and dominions. Great Britain completely controlled the colonies. The dominions, though, were almost entirely self-governing. By law, Great Britain could control their foreign policies. It could also affect their economic policies. In practice, Great Britain did not interfere.

The British dominions included Canada, Australia, New Zealand, and South Africa. After World War I, they wanted a change in status. They demanded the total right of self-government. In 1931, Great Britain agreed to their demands. The dominions were no longer part of the British Empire. Instead, they were free members of the British Commonwealth of Nations. This is a group of nations that were once part of the British Empire. Great Britain had no say over their laws or policies. But the Commonwealth nations pledged loyalty to the British ruler.

Great Britain kept close ties with Commonwealth members by giving them special trading rights. Later, some former British colonies joined the Commonwealth.

France

Costs of the War

France faced worse problems at the end of World War I than Great Britain did. France lost a large proportion of its young men, killed in the war's fighting. Buildings and land needed major restoring. So did roads, bridges, and railroads. The costs of rebuilding were enormous.

France faced other costs as well. Like Great Britain, it had huge war debts to pay off. It didn't dare to disarm for fear that Germany might attack again. So, France had high military expenses. Tariffs and turmoil had disrupted world trade. The amount France earned from exports went down. All these expenses created inflation, which was very hard on France's lower middle class, workers, and peasants.

In the treaty ending the war, Germany had promised to make reparations to France—payments for war damages. This could have helped France out of its economic problems. But Germany could not afford to make all the payments it was supposed to.

French Politics

Politics in France were very fluid. The country had many political parties and groups. In order to govern in a parliament, or law-making body, you needed a majority. No party could get a majority in the French parliament. So groups of parties got together to form governing coalitions. The problem was that these coalitions kept coming apart. Many lasted less than a year. This made long-range planning difficult. It also made France seem like a poor ally to other nations.

Politics in France were also unsettled because of conflicts between the French Left and Right. People on the Left favored social services provided by the government. People on the Right opposed such services. Each side had many subgroups. Extreme Leftists supported communism. Extreme Rightists wanted the French monarch back on the throne.

In 1934, extreme groups on the Right staged riots over a financial scandal. The Left opposed the riots and formed a new coalition, the Popular Front. In 1936, its leader, Léon Blum, a Socialist, became the French premier. Blum's government enacted many reforms that benefited workers. But when the Popular Front collapsed, the new government canceled the reforms.

By the late 1930s, France was bitterly divided. Workers were on one side, and conservative antilabor forces were on the other. This was a dangerous situation. France needed unity to face the growing German threat.

The United States

Isolationism and the Roaring Twenties

The United States had entered World War I late. The number of killed and wounded U.S. soldiers was much lower than the numbers in Great Britain and France. Material damage to the United States was not great, either. American industry had made large profits producing war supplies. Farming had also thrived on wartime demand for food products.

Most Americans had been willing to enter the war in 1917. It had seemed necessary then. But by 1919, many Americans were sick of the war and of Europe's problems. They disliked the deal-making of the peace conference. Guided by these feelings, the U.S. Senate refused to approve the Treaty of Versailles. (That was the treaty dictating peace terms to Germany.) During the 1920s, the United States pulled back into a policy of isolationism. It would isolate itself from international affairs.

Instead, Americans enjoyed the period of peace and prosperity called the Roaring Twenties. People chased both money and pleasure at a roaring pace. Women won the right to vote. Daring young "flappers" cut their hair short and wore their skirts equally short. An amendment to the U.S. Constitution outlawed the making and sale of alcohol, so people flocked to illegal bars called speakeasies. They made "bathtub gin" at home. The new music form of jazz perfectly matched its times. Amid all the glitter, the standard of living for ordinary people rose steadily.

The Great Depression

A lot of wealth in the United States during the 1920s was created by the stock market. Prices of stocks on the New York Stock Exchange on Wall Street kept rising. You could buy a stock at one price and resell it weeks or months later for a big profit. This brought millions of Americans into the market. They bought shares "on margin"—that is, on credit. They expected to resell the stock quickly for a huge profit. Then they would repay the cost of buying the stock out of those profits. So, the stock market was driven largely by borrowed money.

One day in October 1929, a wave of selling hit the stock market. As stock prices fell, more and more people tried to sell. People who had bought stocks on margin couldn't sell them for a profit. They couldn't pay back the money they had borrowed to buy the stocks. The stock market collapsed. Wealthy people became penniless. Businesses and banks crumbled. Soon the U.S. economy fell into a depression.

It wasn't just the stock market that took down the U.S. economy. Farming was in trouble. Farmers had increased their output greatly to meet wartime demand. They had gone into debt to buy the machinery they needed to do this. After the war, farmers produced more than the market could absorb. Farm prices fell, and farmers couldn't pay their debts. Likewise, workers bought things like houses and cars on credit. They expected to be able to pay in installments over a long term.

Also, the ability of U.S. business to sell its goods overseas was blocked by high tariffs. Many countries had high tariffs to keep prices high for foreign goods that might compete with similar goods made at home. But this also meant that goods made in the native country would cost too much in foreign countries. These blocks to international trade also hurt the U.S. economy.

The depression that started in the United States soon spread around the world. Banks in Europe failed. Germany stopped making reparation payments as it had promised to do. Countries stopped paying back their war debts to the United States. Bad economic times spurred the rise of dictators across Europe.

The Great Depression, as it was called, hit hardest in the United States. At its worst, 16 million U.S. workers were without a job. Around the world, 30 million people were unemployed.

The New Deal

When the Great Depression hit, the United States had very few social service programs. Workers who had no jobs had no unemployment payments. People with no money had nowhere to turn except private charities. The Republican president, Herbert Hoover, thought it was best to let the situation take care of itself.

Americans disagreed. They elected Franklin D. Roosevelt, a Democrat, as president in 1932. Roosevelt jumped right in. He started a wide-ranging program of reforms—government programs that would make the country better. Some were aimed to fix problems right away. Others were designed to make long-lasting changes in American social policy. All of these reforms taken together are called the New Deal.

Under the New Deal, a series of laws regulated U.S. banks and stock exchanges. Unemployed people got jobs in a big public works program building bridges and roads. They improved public lands. The Social Security Act set up benefits for retired and unemployed people. Other laws protected workers and labor unions. Farmers received price supports. The Tennessee Valley Authority built dams that changed an entire region.

The New Deal changed American society and politics. Business had run mostly on its own. Now it had to operate according to various government rules. People were not entirely on their own any more when bad times came. The government gave them a "safety net" of social services to help. Some people were very much against these changes. They said it was socialism. Others thought these changes were needed to make the United States a fairer society. In any case, the United States was recovering from the effects of the Great Depression by the late 1930s.

Chapter 6: Changes in the Middle East, Asia, and Latin America

Even before World War I, native people in colonies around the world were beginning to demand self-rule. Events during the war increased those demands. The Allies had said one aim of the war was to protect the right of all people to self-government.

After the war, former German and Ottoman colonies came under the mandate system. Each territory was assigned to one of the Allies. The Allies had a mandate to prepare the colonies for eventual freedom. (No deadline was set for independence.) The League of Nations was to oversee the Allies' governing of the colonies.

All of these factors gave a large boost to nationalist feelings in many colonies. The era of imperialism was coming to an end.

The Middle East

When World War I began, the Ottoman Empire ruled much of the Middle East. (The Middle East is western Asia. It includes the lands from Iran—then called Persia—west to the Mediterranean Sea.) At the end of the war, Ottoman lands in the Middle East became mandate territories. Great Britain got the mandates for Iraq, Transjordan, and Palestine. France got mandates for Syria and Lebanon.

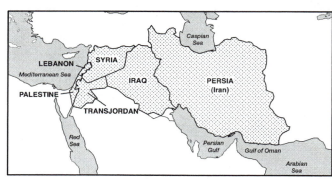

The Middle East

The Arab States

During World War I, Arabs in the Middle East had fought for the British against the Ottoman Empire. In return, Britain had promised support for a free Arab state. This state would be in the area that included Palestine. After the war, Arab nationalists began demanding the promised self-rule.

However, Britain had a conflict. In 1917, it had issued the Balfour Declaration. This was a statement expressing sympathy for setting up a "national home for the Jewish people." During the 1920s and 1930s, Jews began moving to Palestine. Heated conflicts occurred between Jews and Arabs. Both peoples thought they had the right to the same lands. This bitter conflict continued to disrupt the Middle East for the rest of the century and on into the twenty-first century.

Iraq lies to the east of the disputed land. It has rich oil fields in its river valleys. (This was the ancient land of Mesopotamia.) Great Britain allowed Iraq to become an independent kingdom in 1932.

France had less interest in granting freedom to its mandate lands. French forces bombed Damascus, the capital city of Syria, to put down revolts there in 1925 and 1926.

■ OF NOTE

The Arab-Jewish conflict is a problem that developed in the early years of the twentieth century and continues to plague the world today. The Jewish home in Palestine became the nation of Israel. Arab nations around Israel became independent. But the Arabs of Palestine never got a country of their own. Arabs and Jews in the Middle East have fought each other constantly since Israel came into existence in 1948. During the 1990s, Israel and the Palestine Liberation Organization (PLO) held ongoing peace talks. Israel recognized the PLO as the representative of Palestinian Arabs. The PLO finally recognized Israel's right to exist. Some continue to hope that a lasting peace between Arabs and Jews will come.

Turkey

Turkey is an ancient land. It was taken over by Ottoman Turks in the 1400s. As the Ottoman Empire, it controlled huge areas of Asia and Europe. Its defeat in World War I left it much smaller than it had been before the war. Of its lands in Europe, only a small strip along the Dardanelles Straits remained. It also lost control of the Arab lands of the Middle East. The remaining core of the country was a section of Asia Minor known as Anatolia.

The Ottoman Empire was ruled by a sultan (a Muslim ruler). In 1908, nationalists called Young Turks had rebelled against the sultan. They wanted the old empire to become a modern, Western-style nation. The losses of World War I sharpened discontent with the old government. The unrest became a revolution. Its leader was a very capable army officer named Mustafa Kemal. Under Kemal, the Ottoman Empire became the Republic of Turkey. The capital moved from the ancient city of Constantinople to the modern city of Ankara. The Allies agreed to return to Turkey some of the lands it had lost right after the war.

Kemal made sweeping changes in Turkish society. Turkey changed from a traditional Muslim nation to a modern, Western-style democracy. The Turkish language adopted the Western alphabet. Women received the right to vote. People wore Western dress. They took last names. Kemal became Mustafa Kemal Atatürk, which means "Father of the Turks."

Persia/Iran

Persia was another ancient nation in the Middle East. Persia was also independent. However, Britain and Russia had what are called spheres of influence in the country, or regions in which they had special rights. After World War I, Persia was torn by conflicts. Wealthy landowners opposed the interests of the poor peasants. Britain and Russia each struggled to get more power than the other, especially with regard to Persia's rich oil reserves.

In 1925, Reza Shah took over the throne. He renamed himself Reza Shah Pahlavi. Like Atatürk, he was a capable army officer. He also modernized his nation along Western lines. However, he was a less effective leader than Atatürk. He ruled as a monarch with limited powers. The name of Persia was officially changed to Iran ("Land of the Aryans") in 1935.

Egypt and India

Egypt is an African nation. It is also closely linked with the Middle East, which it lies beside. Egypt was part of the Ottoman Empire for hundreds of years. But its rulers operated independently of the Ottoman sultan. In the late 1800s, the rulers of Egypt were brought under British control. The British wanted no threats to its use of the Suez Canal, which borders Egypt on the east.

The British directed many changes in Egypt. Public health improved. A large dam at Aswan made more land productive for farming. The court system was improved. An educated middle class developed.

In World War I, the Ottoman Empire opposed Great Britain. So in 1914, Great Britain declared that Egypt was no longer part of the Ottoman Empire. Then in 1922, Great Britain declared Egypt independent. However, British troops remained there.

In 1936, Great Britain and Egypt reached a new agreement. British troops would keep control of the Suez Canal for another 20 years. Great Britain would sponsor Egypt for membership in the League of Nations. Both nations would help each other in time of war. The last part of the agreement was important for Great Britain. Italy had invaded Ethiopia in 1935. Now Great Britain had an ally in the region near Ethiopia.

India was an Asian colony of Great Britain. India had given important help to Great Britain during World War I. The claims about the war being fought for democracy had a strong effect on educated Indians. Demands for increased self-rule grew.

Several problems stood in the way of independence for India. Native rulers liked the system as it was because they had a lot of power in their own areas. Supporters of the British Empire did not want to give up this large colony. The Indian people were not unified. The two main religious groups were Muslims and Hindus. They had major differences and did not get along well together. Also, the Hindus were divided into classes called castes. There were deep divisions among these castes.

Because of these differences, the Indian independence movement was split. The Muslims gathered in the All-India Muslim League. The Hindus formed the Indian National Congress. The head of the Congress Party was

Mohandas Gandhi. Gandhi was a charismatic and skilled political leader. He inspired the Indian masses with his spiritual nature. The people called him Mahatma, "the saintly one."

Gandhi developed a type of political protest that he called "nonviolent non-cooperation." Today, we call this passive resistance. Gandhi got his people to refuse to cooperate with government policies and orders. For example, he led a boycott of British goods. His followers refused to pay British taxes. Gandhi himself went on hunger strikes. The mass resistance wore down the British. Bit by bit, they gave more and more self-rule to India.

■ OF NOTE

Gandhi's tactic of passive resistance was very effective. Dr. Martin Luther King, Jr. used it in the 1960s during the civil rights struggle in the United States. He taught civil rights activists to use nonviolent forms of protest. The activists sat in at segregated lunch counters. They marched peacefully. They refused to ride on segregated buses. As it had in India, the tactic worked. Segregation in the South eventually ended.

China

In the early twentieth century, China was under the control of various imperial powers. Like Egypt, it was independent in name. But foreign powers had spheres of influence all over the country. A nationalist rebellion in 1900 had tried to break the foreign grip on China, but it had failed.

A second rebellion started in 1911. This revolution was aimed against the Chinese Manchu rulers. It succeeded. The last Manchu emperor, six-year-old Henry Pu-yi, gave up the throne in 1912. The leader of this revolution was Sun Yat-sen. He headed the Kuomintang, or Nationalist Party. Sun and many of his followers had gone to school in the West. They tried to make China into a Western-style republic. However, much of the country was ruled by various warlords.

Before and during World War I, Japan tried to gain control of large parts of China. As part of the peace treaty after the war, Japan had to promise to respect China's independence.

Now things in China began to get very complex. Sun Yat-sen died in 1925. The new Nationalist leader was a general, Chiang Kai-shek. He led the Nationalists in battles against the warlords. More and more of China came under Nationalist control.

In 1927, Chiang ejected the Communists from the Nationalist Party. Mao Zedong became the leader of the Chinese Communists in 1931. The Communists promoted land reform and gathered support from workers and peasants. Mao and his followers set up their own communist government, called the Chinese Soviet Republic. The Nationalists then drove them out of southern China. From 1934 to 1936, the Communists made their 6,000-mile "Long March" to northern China. There, they set up their Soviet-style government again.

Chiang, meanwhile, set up his Nationalist government in southern China. He worked to make the country more Western and more industrial. He ruled as a dictator and did not allow political opposition.

The struggle between the Nationalists and the Communists was not settled until after World War II. Meanwhile, China had to deal with Japan. In 1931, Japan attacked Manchuria and took it over. Then, in 1937, Japan invaded the rest of China. Chiang, his army, and his government had to retreat to central China. They held out there until the end of World War II. During the war, Chiang's Nationalists and Mao's Communists stopped fighting each other and fought the Japanese instead. Japan's defeat in the war ended its occupation of China.

Mexico

Since 1876, Mexico had been ruled by the dictator Porfirio Díaz. Under Díaz, Mexico was stable and orderly. However, Díaz was most interested in the needs of foreign investors and large landowners. The Mexican peasants and Indians were poor and oppressed. Discontent and rumblings of revolt grew among them.

These feelings against Díaz erupted into a revolution in 1910. Competing rebel leaders took power, one after another. The struggle alarmed people in the United States who had invested money in Mexico. U.S. troops took over the Mexican city of Vera Cruz in 1914.

In 1916, the Mexican bandit leader and revolutionary Pancho Villa raided a town in New Mexico and killed several people. U.S. troops went into Mexico after him. Talk of war mounted. But it eased off when the U.S. troops withdrew in 1917. Villa kept up his raids in rural Mexico until 1920.

The Mexican Revolution went on through the 1930s. During these years, Mexico was ruled by an ever-changing series of leaders. Mexican governments took over foreign businesses. Labor unions gained much power. Big estates were broken up, and the land went to peasants. Education became widely available to all social classes.

In the late 1930s, the Mexican government began taking over important private industries. The Mexican railroads were nationalized in 1937. In 1938, the Mexican government took over the valuable foreign-owned oil companies. This angered the United States and Great Britain, who cut back sharply on their purchases of Mexican oil. Mexico turned to Japan, Germany, and Italy for markets for its oil.

World War II closed those markets and brought Mexico and the United States back together. The two nations worked closely together during the war. In 1944, Mexico agreed to pay U.S. oil companies for the properties it had taken in 1938.

The United States and Latin America

In 1903, the United States signed a treaty with the new Central American nation of Panama. The treaty gave the United States the right to build the Panama Canal across the new country. The United States needed a canal so its navy ships could get quickly from the Pacific Ocean to the Caribbean Sea. The Canal also was to be a boost to trade, since shipping times would be much shorter. The Canal was built between 1903 and 1914, when it opened.

Many years before, U.S. President James Monroe had announced the Monroe Doctrine. The United States would not allow any European meddling in the affairs of countries in the Americas. Now the United States had a vital interest in the Caribbean area: protecting the Panama Canal.

In 1903, the Dominican Republic, an island nation in the Caribbean, had said it could not pay back money it had borrowed. Europeans called on their governments to use force to get back the money they had loaned. U.S. President Theodore Roosevelt stepped in. He announced what is called the Roosevelt Corollary to the Monroe Doctrine.

The Roosevelt Corollary said that the United States had a right to take "police action" in Latin America. If a Latin American nation became unstable, foreign nations might want to step in. The United States would not allow this. Instead, it would act as a "police force" to bring the nation back in line.

That's just what the United States did—in the Dominican Republic and in a number of other Latin American nations. In 1905, the United States took over the Dominican customs system. The foreign debts were repaid. From 1916 to 1924, U.S. marines occupied that nation. Disorder broke out in the Dominican Republic in 1916. The United States sent in a force of marines to restore calm.

In 1911, Nicaragua also stopped paying its foreign debt. U.S. bankers tried to reorganize Nicaragua's finances. Disorder broke out, and U.S. marines came in. They stayed from 1912 to 1933. Haiti had a similar experience. U.S. Marines landed there in 1915 to put down disorder. They stayed until 1934.

This pattern of U.S. interference in Latin America became known as "dollar diplomacy." U.S. businesspeople and bankers loaned money to a Latin American country. The country became unable to pay back the loan as agreed. So, the United States stepped in, with or without marines, to control the nation's policies. The process caused many Latin Americans to resent the United States deeply.

Chapter 7: The Rise of Dictators in Europe

One rallying cry for World War I was that it would make "the world safe for democracy." Events after the war in Italy, Germany, Spain, and the nations of Eastern Europe showed that this slogan did not prove to be true. Dictators came to power in those countries in the 1920s and 1930s.

After the war, nations suffered from high inflation. Many people had no jobs. The worldwide depression dragged down the economy in all countries. Different groups demanded different things from governments. Life seemed to be full of chaos.

Dictators tend to rise in troubled times. People often want a strong leader who takes charge and starts to fix things. A democracy puts many limits on the power of even a strong leader. In a totalitarian state, a strong leader takes nearly absolute power. The people lose the right to vote, to speak freely, to oppose the leader. The army and the police control the country and its people. The people are urged to love and support the state—in other words, the leader. The leader and the state have nearly total control.

Governments like this arose in many nations of Europe between the world wars. Many of the same elements were involved in each country's events.

Italy and Mussolini

Italy was a constitutional monarchy. Its head of state was a king, but the government was run by a parliament and a prime minister. Italy had some serious basic problems. It had many people and not much good farmland. It had few raw materials to support industry. It had more problems when World War I ended. Italian industry slumped badly. Workers and former soldiers had no jobs. War debt was high, and prices kept rising.

Many Italians were angry with their leaders. Violent labor strikes broke out. Armed groups supporting various political positions fought one another. The Italian government was run by a coalition. It didn't seem to be able to do anything to restore order to the country.

A strong leader named Benito Mussolini emerged. He was the head of the Fascist Party. Mussolini and his Fascists stirred up fears in Italy of a Bolshevik (communist) uprising. Armed groups of Fascists began attacking people who opposed them, especially socialists and communists.

In October 1922, Mussolini was ready to take power by force. To stop this, the king appointed Mussolini premier. The parliament gave Mussolini wide powers to restore order. Mussolini used these powers to make himself a dictator, in stages.

Fascists took over all positions in the central and local governments. A new Fascist parliament let Mussolini issue decrees that were enforced as law. Freedom of the press ended. Opposition parties were outlawed, as were free labor unions and strikes. The Fascist government controlled all parts of the Italian economy. Italy became a police state—the police spied on all aspects of people's lives. Mussolini gave himself a new title: *il Duce,* "the leader."

Mussolini also built up Italy's army and navy, a common program for a dictator. The military buildup and the other programs cost a lot of money. They helped offset the effects of the worldwide economic depression. But they put a strain on Italy's economy.

Italy's Foreign Policy

Mussolini's foreign policy was one of the factors that led to World War II. Mussolini was a nationalist and a militarist. He looked beyond Italy's borders to expand the nation's power and wealth, setting his sights on Ethiopia.

Ethiopia was an independent African nation. It was ruled by an emperor, Haile Selassie I. Ethiopia had beaten back an Italian invasion in 1896. Now Mussolini decided to try again. In late 1934, patrols along the border between Italian Somaliland and Ethiopia clashed. Mussolini used this clash as an excuse to invade Ethiopia. In 1935, Italian troops moved in. By 1936, Ethiopia was part of the Italian Empire.

Haile Selassie had gone to the League of Nations for help when Italy threatened to invade. The League had done nothing. After the invasion, the League placed economic sanctions on Italy. But the sanctions had large loopholes. Valuable items of trade, such as oil, were still allowed. The trade sanctions that were in effect were only partly observed. They worked so poorly that the League called them off in the summer of 1936. Italy quit the League in 1937.

The League's failure to do anything effective about Ethiopia was a big blow. Rulers who thought about moves against other lands saw that the League wouldn't act to stop them. Powerful nations, such as Britain and France, seemed unwilling or uninterested in acting. Militarists in Italy, Germany, and Japan took note.

After Ethiopia, in October 1936, Mussolini developed ties with the German dictator Adolf Hitler. They formed the Rome-Berlin Axis. In this agreement, Italy and Germany said they would support each other. The German Nazi Party's policy of racism soon spread to Italy. New laws cut Italian Jews out of many aspects of Italian life.

Mussolini also got Italy involved in the Spanish Civil War. He sent Italian troops to Spain to fight in support of General Franco's forces.

Germany and Hitler

Germany agreed to stop fighting World War I in November 1918. In 1919, an assembly created a new democratic government called the Weimar Republic. The outlook for its survival was shaky from the start.

The Allies had forced German civilian leaders to sign the harsh Versailles Treaty at the war's end. In that treaty, the leaders had agreed that Germany was responsible for the war, and that Germany would pay reparations. These parts of the treaty made the German people especially angry.

After the war, many Germans simply didn't believe their armies had lost; instead, they felt that their civilian leaders had sold their troops out. They blamed socialists, liberals, communists, and Jews for what had happened. The Weimar Republic struggled against attacks on many sides. A communist revolt broke out in Bavaria. A right-wing group tried to overthrow the government in Berlin. Private armies of former soldiers, the *Freikorps* (free corps), formed.

At the time, the economic situation in Germany was bad. Many people were out of work. Inflation reached unbelievable levels. The German gold supply was gone. Germany had to make the reparations. The government answered by printing more and more paper money. This drove prices up, while the value of the money went down considerably. By 1923, Germany was printing billion-mark bills. Each billion-mark bill was worth about 25 cents.

In this chaos, many political parties and groups formed. One was the National Socialist German Workers' Party. It was called the Nazi Party, from the German word for "National." Its leader, or *Führer*, was Adolf Hitler. Hitler and the party were very much against communists, liberals, and Jews. The Nazis attracted people of all kinds who were hit hard by Germany's economic problems. In 1923, Hitler tried to spark a Nazi revolt in a beer hall in Munich. The revolt failed. Hitler spent nearly a year in jail, where he wrote his Nazi handbook, *Mein Kampf ("My Struggle")*.

After 1923, Germany's economic problems got better. Inflation leveled off. Industry became productive again. Germany joined the League of Nations in 1926. In 1929, the reparations Germany had to pay were reduced. But then the worldwide economic depression hit. Middle-class people lost their savings. Workers lost their jobs. Once again, Germans turned to the Nazi Party. Hitler was a gifted public speaker. He drew people in with promises to restore Germany to strength, honor, and glory. He blamed the country's problems on Jews and communists.

Hitler was appointed chancellor of Germany in 1933. Right away, he called for new elections. His supporters, called Brownshirts or storm troopers, used terror tactics against non-Nazis. The new legislature gave Hitler the power to act as a dictator.

As Mussolini had done in Italy, Hitler turned Germany into a police state. Nazi officials controlled the state governments. All political parties other than the Nazis were banned. Political opponents were sent to concentration camps. Freedom of speech and of the press disappeared. Nazi youth groups formed. Labor strikes were outlawed. Jews were no longer allowed to be German citizens. They were barred from many jobs. They had to wear yellow stars on their clothing. Other laws took all kinds of civil and property rights away from Germany's Jews.

As in Italy, the German government controlled all aspects of the economy. The Gestapo (secret police) and the SS (Hitler's special soldiers) controlled the people.

Hitler's Foreign Policy

Hitler's aims in foreign policy were also like Mussolini's. Germany had twice in the past been an empire, or *Reich*. Hitler intended to create another empire. So, he called his period of rule the Third Reich. He insisted that Germany had a right to expand. First, he said, it was natural for Germany to absorb all areas in other nations in which mostly Germans lived. Second, he said, the racially pure Germans needed more space in which to live. Hitler said they had a right to take this *Lebensraum* (living space) from non-German areas.

Hitler followed a clever policy to expand Germany's borders. He moved gradually. He threatened, pretended to negotiate, then acted. Sometimes he just acted. He was more than willing to use force. He had seen that Great Britain and France would do a lot to avoid violence. So Hitler moved step-by-step to accomplish his aims. To Hitler's opponents, no single step seemed worth waging war over.

In 1935, Hitler began openly building up his country's military forces. The Versailles Treaty forbade this. The League of Nations condemned Germany. But Germany had left the League in 1933. Untroubled by the League, Germany continued to rearm.

Next, in March 1936, Hitler sent troops marching into the Rhineland. This was German territory on the west side of the Rhine River, bordering France. The Versailles Treaty said this area was supposed to remain disarmed. As Hitler expected, Britain and France did nothing about this move.

Now Hitler reached out for some allies. He and Mussolini signed an alliance in October 1936. This tie between Italy and Germany became known as the Rome-Berlin Axis. Later, in 1940, Hitler also signed an anticommunist pact with Japan. This made Italy, Germany, and Japan into the Rome-Berlin-Tokyo Axis.

Hitler's next targets were Austria, Czechoslovakia, and Poland.

Spain and Franco

In the first part of the twentieth century, Spain was a constitutional monarchy. A king ruled but shared power with a parliament. The country was very rural, with a large class of poor farmers. Workers in industry were not well off, either. The Catholic Church was a powerful force in Spanish life. It was allied with the wealthy large landowners.

Spain went through years of turmoil in the early 1900s. Many farmers and workers were anarchists, wanting an end to all government. Other workers supported socialism. Conservatives wanted the monarchy to remain. Groups in the provinces wanted self-rule. Yet others promoted the idea of a republic. All these groups clashed. Workers went on strike.

During World War I, Spain remained neutral. The economy boomed during the war years but then got worse. Violence became common. During most of the 1920s, General Miguel Primo de Rivera ruled Spain as a military dictator. He started public-works and labor-reform programs. Primo de Rivera lost popular support and had to resign in 1930. The middle class elected supporters of a republic in 1931. The king left the country. The new government started a program of major social reforms.

Conservatives won the 1933 elections. They took back some of the social reforms. Leftists objected. They wanted even more radical reforms. Anarchists and communists stirred up strikes and armed protests. In 1936, Leftists united in a Popular Front and won the election. Street battles spread, and soon Spain was plunged into civil war.

The revolt against the Popular Front was spearheaded by a fascist group called the Falange. Their leader was General Francisco Franco. The rebels were called the Nationalists. Their supporters were the army, the Church, and the large landowners, plus fascists and conservatives in general.

The supporters of the elected government were called Republicans or Loyalists. They included workers and peasants and people who wanted regional self-rule. They also included anarchists, socialists, communists, and other leftists. This diverse group was not nearly as unified as the Nationalists.

The Spanish Civil War raged from 1936 to 1939, when the Loyalists finally gave up. This was much more than a civil war, though. It pulled in many other nations of Europe. German and Italian troops fought alongside Spanish Nationalists. German and Italian planes dropped bombs on Loyalist towns and cities. Russia sent planes and military advisers to help the Loyalists. Britain and France did little. Idealistic volunteers from the United States and some nations of Europe fought, too. They formed the International Brigade.

After the war, Franco set up a fascist dictatorship in Spain. Loyalists were jailed and killed. Only one party, the Falange, was allowed. The government controlled the economy, as in Italy. The army, the Church, and the landowners remained powerful. Franco was *el Caudillo,* "the leader."

Eastern Europe

The peace at the end of World War I set up a number of democracies in eastern Europe. Few of these succeeded. The major problem was that these countries had not lived with democracy before. The different social classes were not used to working for a common purpose. Most land was held by wealthy aristocrats. The economies were mostly rural.

Lower-class people did not have much chance to get an education. The social classes—peasants, nobles, the military, and the small middle class—did not have much in common with one another. During the 1920s and 1930s, only the Baltic states (Latvia, Lithuania, and Estonia) and Czechoslovakia stayed democratic.

Austria was a much smaller nation after the war than before. It was split between socialist and conservative parties. During the 1930s, Austria was ruled by fascist dictators.

In Hungary, the military and the nobles grabbed power in 1920. They set up a military dictatorship. In the 1930s, the leaders of Hungary became more and more pro-Nazi and pro-Hitler.

Yugoslavia, created in 1918, faced ethnic conflict. The Serbs wanted to rule the country. The Croats wanted self-rule. In 1929, King Alexander became the royal dictator. He renamed the country Yugoslavia, supposedly uniting Serbs and Croats. But Alexander was a Serb. So, the Croats resented his rule. He was assassinated in 1934 by Croat separatists.

During the 1930s, Yugoslav leaders became more and more pro-Hitler. But the Yugoslav people did not. They fought hard to keep the Germans from taking over their country, which happened in 1941. The Germans then let an extreme Croat leader take over Croatia. The Croats took revenge for Alexander's Serb dictatorship. They massacred many Serbs, and also Jews.

Poland started out as a democracy after the war. As in other postwar nations, the new Polish government faced keen opposition from both the right and the left. The pattern was repeated. In 1926, Marshal Josef Pilsudski became a military dictator. His support came from the large landowners, industry leaders, and the army.

■ OF NOTE

In 1991, a bloody civil war broke out when Yugoslavia dissolved. Serbs, Croats, and Bosnian Muslims all fought and killed one another. The Serbs started a policy of "ethnic cleansing," forcing millions of Croats and Muslims to move out of Serb-held areas. The Serbs also deliberately killed many Croats and Muslims. In part, this was revenge for the killings of Serbs by Croats during World War II. The cycle of revenge is difficult to stop.

Romania was torn by Nazi groups who used terror against opponents. King Carol II set up his own fascist dictatorship in 1938 to stop a coup.

Bulgaria had an especially violent political life. Murders and coups replaced its authoritarian ruler with others. King Boris III created a royal dictatorship in 1936.

Chapter 8: Military Japan and Communist Russia

Japan

By the early twentieth century, Japan had become a modern industrial nation. But Japan was an island. It needed to bring in raw materials from overseas. It needed foreign markets to buy its goods. It needed territories in which its growing number of people could go to settle.

During World War I, Japan had taken over German-controlled lands and islands in the Pacific Ocean area. After the war, it gave a peninsula back to China. At home, the parliament passed a few social reforms. More people had the vote. Labor unions and political parties formed.

However, Japan was not a democracy. The emperor had absolute power. In 1926, Hirohito became the new emperor. He allowed the Japanese military to run the government. The military leaders restarted a foreign policy of expansion. Leaders of industry agreed. Overseas lands would give them the markets and raw materials they needed. These needs were even stronger now that the worldwide economic depression had upset world trade.

Japan set its sights on Manchuria, the northern area of China. Japan was already doing some business there. In September 1931, an explosion occurred on a Japanese railroad in Mukden, Manchuria. The Japanese army in that area blamed the Chinese for the explosion. This army soon took over all of Manchuria. Japan then set it up as an "independent" state called Manchukuo. Its head of state was Henry Pu-yi, who at the age of six had been the last emperor of China.

In 1933, the League of Nations decided that Japan should withdraw from Manchuria. Japan's answer was to withdraw from the League. This was the first great blow to the prestige of the League. Nations could see that the League would not back up its decisions with any kind of force.

In 1937, Japan expanded its moves into China. With this invasion, Japan tried to take over all of China. Warring factions in China were fighting a civil war. Now they united to try to stop the Japanese. They were partly successful. Japan took over large parts of northern and eastern China. Yet, the Chinese forces held on in central and western parts of the country. They harassed the Japanese with guerrilla warfare. The war reached a stalemate by 1938.

Japan's aggressive moves in China were one of the steps that led to World War II. After that war began in 1939, Japan moved aggressively to take over more of Asia.

The Russian Revolution

For centuries, Russia was under the absolute rule of an emperor called the tsar (or tsarina, for a woman). Starting in 1894, the tsar was Nicholas II. He was against any kind of liberal reforms or civil rights for his people. He used the police to put down protests.

In the early 1900s, though, many people in Russia were discontented. Most Russians were poor peasants who didn't even own their land. Russia had very little industry. People who did work in factories earned very little. Socialists wanted reforms. In 1905, a group of workers marched peacefully to the tsar's palace. They wanted to present their demands for change. Instead, the army fired on them, killing and wounding many.

This sparked a revolution. Strikes, riots, and rebellions broke out everywhere. The tsar's army managed to put down the revolt. The tsar then allowed the election of an assembly, called the Duma. But it had little power. Secret groups in Russia kept pushing for revolution.

World War I was a disaster for the Russian army. It was poorly led and poorly supplied. Russian soldiers fought bravely. But millions of them died, were wounded, and were captured. Food was scarce both on the front lines and back home. Soldiers and civilians alike lost all faith in the war and their government.

In March 1917, workers went on strike in Moscow, demanding bread. The tsar ordered his troops to fire on the workers. Instead, the soldiers joined them. This revolution of workers and soldiers spread. Tsar Nicholas had no choice but to give up his throne.

The Leadership of Lenin

The revolution that overthrew the tsar was known as the March Revolution. After the overthrow, power in Russia passed to two rival groups. One was the provisional government. It was supposed to rule until a new, permanent form of government was chosen and set up. The provisional government was only temporary. So it had no real power. It put off decisions on reforms and other urgent matters. Meanwhile, it kept Russian troops fighting in the world war.

The other ruling group was the Petrograd Soviet of Workers' and Soldiers' Deputies. (A soviet was a revolutionary council of workers and soldiers.) The Bolsheviks (who later called themselves the Communist party) soon took control of this and other soviets.

The Bolshevik leader was V. I. Lenin. Lenin's original name was Vladimir Ilyich Ulyanov. He also used the name N. Lenin. The "N" stood for "nobody," because Lenin was a made-up name. Lenin had lived in exile for many years. He returned to Russia in April 1917, traveling in a sealed railroad boxcar.

Lenin developed a new type of communism. The basic ideas of communism came from a German thinker, Karl Marx. Marx said that industrial nations would fall when the workers rose up. They would take over the means of production. However, Russia was not an industrial nation. It did not have many workers. So, Lenin adapted Marx's ideas to Russia's realities. Lenin said that, in Russia, a small group of Marxists would lead the workers to revolution.

This is just what happened. In November 1917, the Bolsheviks overthrew the provisional government. They immediately set up a communist government. This government took ownership of all land in Russia. It also signed a peace treaty with Germany early in 1918. The war-weary Russian people were glad to be out of the war. This was known as the November Revolution.

In 1917, there were two revolutions in Russia, one in March and one in November. But these revolutions are sometimes called the February Revolution and the October Revolution. This is because, in 1917, Russia did not use the same calendar as most other European countries. Their calendar was 13 days behind other countries. According to that calendar, the day that people in Moscow demanded bread was in February, not March. The Bolshevik uprising later that year took place in November, not October. In 1918, after the Revolution, Russia switched to the calendar used in other countries.

Many forces inside and outside Russia did not want the Bolsheviks in power. A number of groups began fighting them: conservatives who wanted the tsar back, moderates who were against communism, and even foreign forces from the Allies (including the United States), Japan, and Poland. The Bolsheviks were called the Reds. The anticommunists were the Whites. The civil war lasted from December 1917 until 1921. Millions of Russians died. The Bolsheviks won.

After the civil war was over, the Communists needed to restore Russia. All resources had gone to the army during the war. Now people were starving. Industry was almost destroyed, as were the transportation networks.

In 1921, Lenin launched his New Economic Policy (NEP). He allowed some private enterprise so the economy would recover. Peasants could run their own small farms. People could own and operate small businesses. The major industries, though, were state-owned—for example, oil and steel—and also the banks.

In 1922, Russia was renamed. It became the Union of Soviet Socialist Republics, or U.S.S.R. The soviets were the revolutionary councils of workers and soldiers. The republics were the separate regions of the nation. Russia was one of them. The republics had some self-rule. But the central Soviet government, headquartered in Russia, strictly controlled all things it considered important. The Communist party controlled the government, and Lenin controlled both of them.

The Leadership of Stalin

Lenin died in 1924. His death set off a bitter struggle for power. The loser was Leon Trotsky, who had been an important Bolshevik leader. He was exiled and later murdered in Mexico. The winner was Joseph Stalin, the secretary general of the Communist Party. Stalin was not much interested in worldwide communist revolution. Instead, he wanted to make the Soviet nation an important industrial power.

Under Stalin, the communist government took complete control of the economy. It ran according to plans. The first, begun in 1928, was the Five-Year Plan. A second Five-Year Plan followed in 1933. Industry had to modernize. Factories had to stop making consumer goods, such as refrigerators and clothing. Instead, they made such things as machinery and steel.

Also, Soviet farming now became collective. Small farms were combined (collected) into large ones run by the government. This allowed farmers to share mechanical farm tools, such as tractors, which were scarce. Many peasants were very much against giving up their lands. They killed their animals and burned crops in protest. Faced with death or prison, the peasants had to give in. Most farms became collectives.

Stalin also made the Soviet Union into a police state. People could not express any thought that the Communist Party did not approve of. Secret police and party spies kept most people in line. But during the 1930s, some opposition to Stalin became noticeable. Stalin's answer was a series of purges. Vast numbers of party members and army officers were swept away. Victims were tried, put in prison, exiled to Siberia, or killed.

The Soviet Communist Party supported a group called the Comintern, or the Third International. It worked with communist parties in other nations to help spark communist revolutions all around the world. It also directed these outside communist groups to support Soviet foreign policy goals.

The Soviet Union and other nations in Europe felt uneasy with one another. Britain and France were democracies. Communism as it was practiced in the Soviet Union called for revolution to overturn democracy. The U.S.S.R. supported the Comintern to reach that goal. Germany and Italy were fascist. Fascists were totally anticommunist.

However, Stalin saw threats to Soviet security developing in the 1930s. Japan held Manchuria, along the Soviet border. Hitler ruled Germany, and he wanted more lands and an end to communism. So the U.S.S.R. joined the League of Nations in 1934. As a League member, the U.S.S.R. urged strong action against the aggressions of Italy and Germany.

The Soviet Union (Stalin) also tried to develop defensive pacts with Britain and France. All three nations worried about possible war with Germany. But Britain and France mostly wanted to prevent Germany from moving west, toward them. Stalin wanted to stop any German move to the east. So the U.S.S.R., Britain, and France didn't reach an agreement. Instead, Stalin made a pact with Hitler in 1939. The Soviet Union and Germany pledged to stay neutral toward each other if war should break out.

Topic 3

World War II

Chapter 9: The Road to War

Early Steps Toward War

Many people had called World War I "the war to end all wars." Certainly most people had hoped that would be true. Yet, in many ways the 1920s and 1930s were merely a long truce, a lull between two storms. The peace agreements that ended World War I had left many problems unsolved. They had created other, new problems.

The 1920s were a period of postwar adjustment. During the 1930s, clashes between nations began to break out again. Looking back, we can see that these clashes were the first steps on the road to World War II.

First, Japan invaded Manchuria in 1931, taking it from China. The League of Nations and the United States protested. But, they took no real action against Japan.

Next, Germany began to rearm itself in 1935. This violated the Versailles Treaty, which Germany had signed at the end of World War I. The League of Nations condemned the rearmament. Germany ignored the League. Adolf Hitler, Germany's ruler, followed up by sending German troops into the Rhineland, next to France, in 1936. This, too, violated the Versailles Treaty. Britain and France did nothing.

Benito Mussolini, Italy's ruler, sent Italian troops into Ethiopia in 1935. The African nation became part of Italy in 1936. The League imposed economic sanctions on Italy. The sanctions didn't work and weren't enforced well.

Spain fought a civil war from 1936 to 1939. It became a kind of mini-European war. Fascist Italy and Nazi Germany helped one side in the war. Communist Russia helped another. Democratic Great Britain and France mostly kept their distance.

In 1937, Japan invaded more parts of China. Japanese and Chinese troops fought to a stalemate. The United States and the European nations did not step in.

The final steps were soon to come. They were final because of all these earlier steps. The conflicts built on one another until war could hardly be avoided.

Attempts to Keep the Peace

Not everything in the 1920s and 1930s led to war. The nations of the world took some positive steps to try to keep peace in the world.

In 1921 and 1922, the United States and European nations took part in the Washington Naval Conference. Out of this came the Five-Power Treaty. It set up a ten-year "holiday" during which the United States, Great Britain, Japan, France, and Italy agreed not to build any warships. That treaty also set limits on the navies of those five nations. The Washington meeting also produced the Nine-Power Treaty. In this pact, the major powers promised to take no more lands or rights from China.

Another move toward peace was the Locarno Pact of 1925. A number of European nations met at Locarno, Switzerland. They agreed to settle any future disputes among themselves peacefully. Several nations signed mutual help pacts. Germany was invited to join the League of Nations, which it did in 1926. Germany, France, and Belgium agreed to honor their existing borders. Other countries that were part of the Locarno Pact were Great Britain, Italy, Czechoslovakia, and Poland.

In 1928, 23 nations signed the Kellogg-Briand Pact. More nations signed on later, for a total of over 60. This treaty condemned war as a way of settling disputes between nations. (It was named for the men who wrote it: U.S. Secretary of State Frank Kellogg and French Foreign Minister Aristide Briand.)

The League of Nations was not able to stop aggressions by Italy and Germany. However, the League did have some successes. It settled some disputes between nations. Also, it provided loans and expert advice to some nations.

In the end, though, the growing tensions among nations overcame the efforts to keep the peace.

Austria and *Anschluss*

Adolf Hitler wanted to expand Germany's borders. He claimed that his aim was simply to unite all Germans in a larger German state. Various German-speaking people lived in nations that were on Germany's borders.

One such nation was Austria. The treaty that ended World War I left Austria a very small country. The country could hardly survive economically. Many Austrians wanted their country to be joined with Germany. When one country joins another one to itself, it is called annexation. In German, it is *Anschluss*. However, it didn't matter what Austrians wanted. The peace treaties forbade *Anschluss*.

As usual, Hitler took matters into his own hands. German troops marched into Austria in March 1938. Instantly, the country became part of Germany.

Again, the League of Nations did not act. Great Britain and France made official protests. Italy did not protest, even though Austria was on its northern border. Benito Mussolini and Hitler had made an alliance in 1936.

Czechoslovakia

Next, Hitler turned to Czechoslovakia. This was a new nation created by the treaties at the end of World War I. Alone among the countries of eastern Europe, it was a successful democracy.

The western end of Czechoslovakia was known as Sudetenland. More than three million Germans lived here. The Czech government tried to treat them fairly. Still, most Sudeten Germans wanted to be part of Germany.

Hitler followed his usual tactics. He made sure that a vocal Nazi Party developed in Sudetenland. His agents circulated a lot of propaganda. They spread untrue stories about the terrible ways the Czechs mistreated the Sudeten Germans. Violent protests broke out in Sudetenland. Hitler openly prepared his army to invade.

Czechoslovakia had an alliance with France. This pact called on each country to protect the other one in case of attack. Great Britain was friendly to Czechoslovakia, too, although not an ally. In September 1938, Hitler called a conference in Munich, Germany. He and Mussolini met with British Prime Minister Neville Chamberlain and French Premier Edouard Daladier. Czechoslovakia was not invited to attend. Neither was its other ally, the U.S.S.R.

The goal of the British and French leaders was to avoid war. So at Munich, they agreed to let Hitler annex the Sudetenland. He did. Hungary and Poland then grabbed other parts of Czechoslovakia. In March 1939, Hitler's armies invaded and took over what remained of the country.

In dealing with Hitler, Great Britain and France followed a policy of appeasement. When he returned home from Munich, a smiling Chamberlain had announced that the agreement he had made "means peace in our time." He was wrong. The agreement at Munich stands as a famous reminder that appeasement may tell aggressors that they can do whatever they want.

The Hitler-Stalin Pact

By now, the leaders of Great Britain and France could see that war with Germany was likely. They began building up their military forces. They could also see that Poland was likely to be Hitler's next victim. Great Britain publicly pledged to help Poland. France was already Poland's ally.

Great Britain and France also tried to make an alliance with the U.S.S.R. However, the Soviet leader, Joseph Stalin, did not trust Great Britain and France to change their policy and stand up to Hitler at last. Instead, Stalin made a pact with Hitler in August 1939. The Soviet Union and Germany agreed not to attack each other. Secretly, they also agreed to split up lands in the nations of eastern Europe between them.

The Hitler-Stalin Pact shocked leaders in the West. Nazi, fascist Germany was extremely anticommunist. The communist U.S.S.R. was highly antifascist. But self-interest won out. Hitler now did not have to worry about fighting a war to both the east and the west. This had been a big problem for Germany during World War I. Stalin could use parts of Poland as a buffer between the U.S.S.R. and Germany. War between these two nations might still come. But at least it was put off for now.

Poland—The Final Straw

Hitler finally made a move that touched off a world war. As the Western leaders had expected, Poland was his next target.

Poland was a large country that lay just to the east of Germany. The treaties ending World War I had created an odd situation there. A "Polish corridor" of land separated Germany from East Prussia, which was a part of Germany. The corridor gave Poland access to the Baltic Sea. Also, the treaties had made the seaport of Danzig a free city. It was run by the League of Nations. Before the war, both the Polish corridor and Danzig had been part of Germany. Danzig, especially, was still very German.

Hitler now followed his usual pattern. A strong and vocal Nazi Party took control of Danzig. Propaganda stories told of how Poland mistreated Germans in the Polish corridor. The party insisted that Poland give Germany rights in the corridor and that the League return Danzig to Germany.

Then Hitler moved to take what he wanted. On September 1, 1939, the German army marched into Poland. Great Britain and France finally decided they had to act. On September 3, they declared war on Germany. World War II had begun.

Chapter 10: The War Begins and Spreads

The Nature of the War

World War I involved most of the world. Battles were fought in Africa and the Middle East, as well as in Europe. Naval actions took place in both the Atlantic Ocean and the Pacific Ocean.

World War II, though, was truly more worldwide. Battles in the Pacific area were as critical to the outcome as battles in Europe. So were actions in North Africa and the U.S.S.R.

World War I had seen the use of many new weapons, such as the machine gun and poison gas. Airplanes, too, had taken a limited part in war for the first time. In World War II, airplanes played a very important role. Attack planes launched from ships became a strong new weapon of the world's navies. War planes helped support the movements of armies on land.

Planes also brought civilians directly into the war. Both sides bombed enemy cities, with civilians as their targets. The idea was that civilians could not stand up to such an assault. They would force their leaders to give up and ask for peace. This did not happen, though. Great numbers of civilians died in the bombings. But the survivors held on.

World War II did feature the use of one deadly new weapon: the atomic bomb. In 1945, a U.S. plane dropped one atomic bomb on the Japanese city of Hiroshima and one on the city of Nagasaki. More than 200,000 people were killed instantly, and the cities were flattened. The world had never before seen a weapon capable of so much destruction.

World War II was very different from World War I in the way it was fought. On the western front, the first world conflict had been a war of stalemate. Troops had dug into opposing lines of trenches. Military planners in the 1920s and 1930s assumed the next world war would be fought in the same way. So, both France and Germany built a chain of fortifications along the border between them. In effect, they replaced the mud trenches with trenches of concrete and steel.

The French chain was called the Maginot Line. The German chain was the Siegfried Line. These fortified lines were strong. But when war came, they were not nearly as useful as the military planners had expected. World War II turned out to be a war of quick troop movements. Armies didn't hunker down into trenches. They fought in the open, on the move.

In some ways, World War II did resemble World War I. Many of the same nations were involved. France and Great Britain were once again allied against Germany (and Austria, which was now part of Germany). The United States again stayed out at first, then came in on the side of France and Great Britain. This time, though, Italy fought on the side of Germany. So did Japan.

Both World War I and World War II started in Eastern Europe. In both wars, Germany fought on two fronts. It invaded both Russia on the east and France on the west. And in both wars, Germany lost.

Here's how the main players in the war lined up. The Allies were Great Britain, France, the Soviet Union, and (starting late in 1941) the United States. The Axis Powers were Germany, Italy, and Japan. They got their name from the 1936 pact between Italy and Germany, called the Rome-Berlin Axis.

War in the West
Hitler's Blitzkrieg

The early years of World War II brought a lot of success to the Axis Powers. Hitler's army and air force moved swiftly to take over western Poland. The Germans called this type of speedy action blitzkrieg, or "lightning war."

Once Hitler had made his move into Poland, Stalin made his. Soviet forces took over eastern Poland. For the rest of the war, the nation of Poland no longer existed. Next, the U.S.S.R. invaded the Baltic countries of Estonia, Latvia, and Lithuania. Soon, they became part of the Soviet Union.

The U.S.S.R. also invaded Finland in 1939. The Finns held the Soviets off for a while, but had to give up in March 1940. From Finland, the Soviets got bases in the Baltic Sea and some eastern lands along the Russian border.

During this time, Britain and France had called up their armies. France massed troops along the Maginot Line. Great Britain sent troops across the English Channel to northern France. But all the action was to the east of Germany. Hitler was making no moves to the west. People in the Western nations called this a "phony war" or "sitzkrieg." The inaction did not last long.

In April 1940, German forces suddenly invaded Denmark and Norway. These neutral nations were to the north of Germany. Denmark and Norway gave Hitler's military both air and submarine bases within striking range of Great Britain. They also gave the German navy good access to the Atlantic Ocean.

The German blitzkrieg next overran the Low Countries—the Netherlands, Belgium, and Luxembourg. These tiny nations were no match for the powerful German army. They fell quickly, in May 1940.

Dunkirk and the Fall of France

From Belgium, German troops poured into northern France. The Maginot Line did not extend along this border. The Germans quickly cut off French, British, and Belgian troops from the rest of the French army. They were trapped at Dunkirk, a small seaport in the north of France.

The Belgian troops surrendered. The British people pulled off an amazing rescue of the French and British troops. Boats of all sizes and types crossed the English Channel and began ferrying the soldiers back to Great Britain. Navy ships, yachts, sailboats, small motorboats—English people used any seaworthy vessel to save their troops.

German forces now pressed farther south into France. Seeing his chance, Mussolini declared war on France and Britain. Italian troops invaded southern France.

The German army took Paris, the French capital, in June 1940. The Germans then divided France into two parts. They occupied and ruled most of the country, including the coast along the Atlantic Ocean and the English Channel. They allowed a Frenchman, Philippe Pétain, to rule southern France, strictly under Nazi control. Pétain ruled from the town of Vichy. So his regime was called Vichy France.

Some French people kept up a fight against the Nazis. Inside France, they worked secretly and were called "the Resistance." Outside France, they were headquartered in North Africa and called the Free French. Their leader was General Charles de Gaulle.

Great Britain and the United States

Now Hitler turned his sights on Great Britain. His plan was to bomb Great Britain into surrender. German planes began dropping bombs on British cities, railroads, and factories. The four-month period of the heaviest bombing, in 1940, is called the Battle of Britain.

The bombing did not break the spirit of the British people, as Hitler had hoped. In fact, it made them more determined to resist. They were helped a lot by fighter pilots of the Royal Air Force. British warplanes downed many German bombers. Great Britain's prime minister, Winston Churchill, expressed the thanks of the British people when he said, "Never was so much owed by so many to so few."

As had happened in World War I, the United States chose to remain out of this war at first. Still, most Americans favored the Allies. Anti-German feelings grew stronger after the fall of France and the Battle of Britain. But the United States was officially neutral. It was not supposed to do anything to help either side in the war.

U.S. President Franklin D. Roosevelt, though, wanted to help Great Britain. He turned over 50 old navy destroyers to Great Britain in exchange for leases on British naval bases. In March 1941, the U.S. Congress passed the Lend-Lease Act. It allowed Roosevelt to supply arms and other supplies to Great Britain, and other nations, on credit. The U.S. navy helped protect ships carrying these supplies across the Atlantic Ocean from German submarine attacks.

The United States was still officially a neutral nation. But its actions were not at all neutral. Hitler, though, did not want to get the United States into the war. U.S. public opinion did not support U.S. entry into the war yet, either. So the clashes between German submarines and U.S. navy ships in the Atlantic remained an unofficial war.

War in the East and South

The Axis Powers were also taking control of Eastern Europe and the Mediterranean area. Italy had invaded and conquered Albania in 1939. In 1941, Germany invaded and took over countries in Eastern Europe: Romania, Bulgaria, Hungary, and Yugoslavia. Italy had attacked Greece in 1940, and Germany completed the conquest in 1941.

Italian and German troops also took over large parts of North Africa. Most of Egypt remained under British control. Turkey was neutral. The rest of the Middle East was in the Allies' control.

Germany Invades Russia

In the spring of 1941, Hitler decided to invade the Soviet Union. This attack surprised Stalin, and many other people as well. It was not a big surprise that Hitler had chosen to ignore his nonaggression pact with Stalin. Hitler had a history of breaking promises.

But Hitler had intended to avoid fighting a war on both the east and west sides of Germany. On the west, though, France was already under German control. Now, Hitler thought, German troops could take the U.S.S.R. in a quick attack during the summer and fall of 1941. Germany would gain rich farming areas, and more land for its people to expand into.

At first, the German blitzkrieg was successful. German armies took Ukraine. They were nearly to Leningrad and Moscow. Hundreds of thousands of Soviet soldiers were killed and wounded. But the Soviets held out until a new ally arrived—the Russian winter. Winter in Russia is bitterly cold. Hitler decided to keep his troops in the U.S.S.R. through the winter. They were not equipped for the brutal conditions. The United States was sending supplies to the Soviets, so they were able to hold out and fight back. The United States and Great Britain had decided that any country under attack by Germany was an ally of theirs, even if it was, like Russia, communist.

The "Final Solution"

Part of Hitler's Nazi code was a warped concept of "racial purity." Hitler believed that "pure" Germans (blonde and blue-eyed types) were members of an "Aryan race." Members of other groups were "racially inferior." So it was natural, according to this thinking, for Germany to conquer nations where "inferior" people lived. This included Eastern Europe and Russia. Mostly Slavs lived there, and the Nazis thought Slavs were quite inferior.

The Jewish people were the special target of Hitler's ethnic hatred. During the 1930s, the Nazi government of Germany had passed many laws taking away Jewish rights and property. Nazi thugs had beaten up and killed Jews at will.

OF NOTE

Hitler misused the term *Aryan*. Aryans were actually people who settled in Iran and northern India in 1500 B.C.E. *Aryan* also refers to a family of languages called Indo-European, and to groups of people who speak one of those languages. In fact, the name *Iran* means "Land of the Aryans."

Nazi policy began forcing Jewish people to relocate to special sections of German cities. These Jewish sections were called ghettos. It was hard to earn a living in a ghetto. Many people starved to death there. Not many Jews were able to escape from Germany.

In 1941, Hitler came up with a "Final Solution" to the "Jewish problem." All Jews in Germany, and in German-occupied lands, were to be killed. Nazi police and soldiers rounded up Jews from all across Europe. They packed the Jews into railroad cattle cars. The journeys ended at concentration camps in eastern Germany and Poland. There, millions of Jews died by poison gas. Their bodies were burned in huge ovens that ran night and day.

The Jews of Europe were not the only victims of Hitler's concentration camps. The Nazis also sent "racially impure" Slavs, Gypsies, and others to their deaths at the camps. Resistance fighters and homosexuals also died there. By the end of World War II, the Nazi government had killed six million European Jews, and nearly as many of these other victims.

The German government also used slave labor to run some of its factories and industries. The slaves were concentration camp inmates and prisoners of war (POWs). This was a violation of international law about the treatment of POWs by the nation who captured them.

Chapter 11: The War Goes Global

Japan's Moves in Asia

While Germany and Italy were making their moves of conquest in the West, Japan was doing the same thing in the East. Japan officially became a member of the Axis Powers in 1940. That's when it signed an alliance with Germany and Italy.

Japan had big plans for expansion in Asia. It saw World War II as a good time to put those plans into action. The European powers were busy fighting in the West. France and the Netherlands had fallen to Germany. So, Japan took over French Indochina and the Netherlands' East Indies. This was in accord with Japan's slogan for expansion, "Asia for Asians."

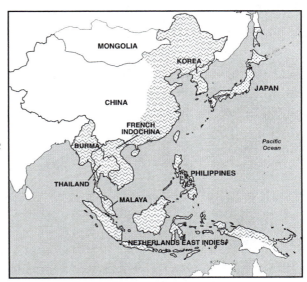

Japanese Conquests During WWII

Japan had invaded China in the 1930s. Japanese troops continued to hold large areas of China during the world war. One of these areas was Manchuria, in northern China. It shared a border with the Soviet Union. To make sure there would be no trouble along this border, Japan signed a nonaggression pact with the U.S.S.R. in 1941.

Pearl Harbor: The United States Enters the War

Japan's moves in Asia did not please the United States. It stopped shipments of war-related raw materials to Japan. Late in 1941, officials from Japan and the United States met in Washington, D.C. They talked about possible changes in Japanese policy.

While these talks were going on, Japanese warplanes suddenly bombed the U.S. navy base at Pearl Harbor, Hawaii. The American forces were caught completely off guard. U.S. ships sank at anchor, and thousands of U.S. sailors died.

The date was December 7, 1941. U.S. President Franklin Roosevelt called it "a date that will live in infamy." The very next day, the United States and Great Britain declared war on Japan. Several days later Germany and Italy were also formally at war with the United States. The war now reached entirely around the globe.

The United States was officially at war. But its military forces were not ready to fight a war. So, Japan still had a free hand in the Pacific area and Asia. Japanese forces quickly took U.S. islands in the Pacific, including the Philippines. They seized Burma, Thailand, and Malaya from the British. Dutch Indonesia also fell to the Japanese. Next, Japan took New Guinea and the Solomon Islands. The vast continent-country of Australia was now in real danger.

The Tide Turns: The War in the West

North Africa

The years of the war through 1941 had seen a series of Axis victories. The tide began to turn in favor of the Allies during 1942. In November of that year, Allied forces landed troops in North Africa. U.S. General Dwight Eisenhower commanded these forces. Their aim was to defeat the strong German army in the region led by General Erwin Rommel. Rommel's skill at fighting here had earned him the nickname "The Desert Fox."

Eisenhower led his troops eastward toward Rommel. British General Bernard Montgomery led his army westward from Egypt. Rommel and his forces fought hard, but they finally had to give up in May 1943. This was an important victory for the Allies. The Axis powers no longer held any part of North Africa. The Suez Canal was safely in Allied hands.

Stalingrad

Another turning point was the Battle of Stalingrad, in the Soviet Union. During the winter of 1941–1942, the Soviets had held back the German army from Leningrad and Moscow. In the summer of 1942, the Germans in the U.S.S.R. moved south toward Soviet oil fields. For six months, the Germans and Soviets fought fiercely over the city of Stalingrad. Early in 1943, the German troops at Stalingrad had to surrender.

This was a huge victory for the Soviets and a huge defeat for the Germans. Soviet troops now began to force back the rest of the invading German army toward Poland and Germany.

The Battle of the Atlantic

The tide of battle also began to turn on the high seas in 1942. German submarines, called U-boats, had been sinking Allied ships since early in the war. The rate of sinkings was very high right through early 1943. This put the Allies in great danger. They depended on the ships for supplies from the industries of the United States to fight the war. This conflict was called the Battle of the Atlantic.

Gradually, the Allies worked out ways to cut down on the number of sinkings by U-boats. Their best weapon was sonar. This new development used sound waves to find and track submarines underwater. The Allies also used navy vessels and warplanes on aircraft carriers to protect their merchant ships. By 1943, the U-boats were no longer a big threat.

The Invasion of Italy

By the summer of 1943, the Allies were ready to attack an Axis power itself. They took the island of Sicily, just off the coast of Italy, in July. A group of Italians forced Mussolini, Italy's dictator, to resign. The Allied army invaded mainland Italy in September. The new Italian government fought on the side of the Allies. But the German troops in Italy fought the Allied advance strongly. The struggle continued until the end of the war in 1945.

Victory in Europe

The Allied leaders met in Tehran, Iran, in December 1943. Stalin, the Soviet dictator, had often asked Britain and the United States to attack Germany. This would take some of the military pressure off the U.S.S.R. At Tehran,

U.S. President Roosevelt and British Prime Minister Churchill told Stalin that the time had finally come. Allied forces would sweep into France in 1944.

The invasion began on June 6, 1944, known as D-Day. Allied armies came ashore on the beaches of Normandy, in northern France. The Germans hadn't expected the Allies to land there, so they weren't well prepared. The Allied forces began to push the German troops back to the east. More Allied forces landed on the southern coast of France. Paris was freed from the Nazis in August. The Germans had moved back to the Siegfried Line on the German border by September.

Meanwhile, the Soviet army was pushing westward. The Soviets took back the Baltic and Eastern European nations in 1944. Early in 1945, they entered Germany itself. The Allies broke through the Siegfried Line and moved into Germany, toward the Soviets. Hitler committed suicide. The Allies agreed to let the Soviets officially take Berlin, which they did on May 2, 1945. The German army surrendered on May 8, 1945. This was called V-E Day—Victory in Europe Day.

In Italy, the German army had surrendered in April 1945. Antifascist Italians caught Mussolini and shot him. Neither fascist dictator—Hitler nor Mussolini—had survived the war.

The Tide Turns: The War in the Pacific

Japan's tide of victory, like Germany's, began to turn in 1942. The major turning points in the Pacific were two naval battles in May and June of that year. The first was the Battle of the Coral Sea. This sea lies just off the coast of northeastern Australia. A Japanese naval fleet was moving across the sea to attack Australia. U.S. and Australian navy and air forces stopped this advance.

Next, U.S. forces stopped an even larger Japanese fleet that was trying to take over the Midway Islands. This kept Hawaii safe from a Japanese invasion.

The U.S. forces now worked their way west across the Pacific Ocean. U.S. and Japanese forces fought fierce battles over small, strategic islands. Each one that the United States captured was a stepping-stone toward Japan itself.

Meanwhile, U.S. forces moved northwest through the larger islands of the Pacific. Troops from Australia and New Zealand took part in this campaign, too. First the Japanese were forced out of the large islands from which they had threatened Australia. Then the United States, under General Douglas MacArthur, took back the Philippines.

Soon the Americans held island bases from which they started bombing the home islands of Japan itself. U.S. navy ships moved into bases near Japan, too. Japanese fighter pilots flew suicide missions, or kamikaze attacks, against these ships. They crashed their planes into the U.S. vessels, blowing up themselves and at least parts of the ships as well.

Japan's fighting ability was by now greatly weakened. But the Japanese were still fiercely determined to resist. It seemed that only a U.S. invasion of Japan would cause the Japanese to surrender. U.S. military leaders, including President Harry Truman, thought the loss of Allied life in such an invasion would be too high. They reached a momentous decision.

The Allies ordered Japan to surrender. It refused. On August 6, 1945, a U.S. plane dropped an atomic bomb on the Japanese city of Hiroshima. This single bomb killed 80,000 people and destroyed more than half of the city. Two days later, Russia declared war on Japan and invaded Manchuria. On August 9, the United States dropped a second atomic bomb, this time on the city of Nagasaki. On August 14, Japan agreed to end the war. Japan and the Allies signed the formal surrender papers aboard the U.S. warship *Missouri* in Tokyo Bay on September 2, 1945. This was called V-J Day—Victory in Japan Day. World War II was officially over.

■ OF NOTE

At the time the first atomic bombs were dropped, scientists didn't know how deadly radiation is to human health. In the weeks and months after the bombs went off, many Japanese people died of radiation poisoning. Years later, many more Japanese people died of leukemia and other cancers caused by exposure to the bombs' radiation. More recently, in 1986, there was an explosion at a nuclear power plant in Chernobyl, Ukraine. People are still dying from the effects of radiation exposure from that accident.

Chapter 12: The World After the War

The Price of the War

Like World War I, World War II was extremely expensive. More than 20 million people died, both soldiers and civilians. Much of Europe was left in ruins. Bombs had destroyed many cities and factories, railroads and highways. People driven from their homes were living in refugee camps. Food was scarce, and jobs were gone.

When Allied forces moved through Germany, they discovered another dreadful price of the war. They found the Nazi concentration camps. People outside Germany were shocked to learn that the Nazis had shot and gassed to death millions of Jews and other people in these camps.

Many civilians had died in the war because of bombings and battles near their homes. But the planned killing of most of an ethnic group— genocide—was not an accepted part of war. So from 1945 to 1946, Nazi leaders were tried for war crimes in a special court at Nuremberg, Germany. Twelve of these men received death sentences. Others were sentenced to life in prison.

Japanese wartime leaders were also tried for war crimes. Armies under their command had deliberately killed many civilians in the Asian countries that they had captured. Japanese soldiers had also badly mistreated prisoners of war. The Tokyo war crimes trial sentenced seven Japanese leaders to death.

■ OF NOTE

The destruction of European Jews during the Nazi era is called the Holocaust. In 1993, the U.S. Holocaust Memorial Museum opened in Washington, D.C. This museum documents the events of the Holocaust, using videos, photographs, and other exhibits. More information can be found at http://www.ushmm.org.

Postwar Europe

Europe Divided

Early in 1945, the Allied armies were starting to invade Germany. It seemed clear that the war would soon be over. So, the leaders of the three most powerful Allied nations met to make final plans. They gathered at Yalta, in the U.S.S.R. Present at the meeting were Joseph Stalin of the Soviet Union, President Franklin Roosevelt of the United States, and Prime Minister Winston Churchill of Great Britain.

The three men decided to divide Germany into four parts. They expected this division to last for only a short period of time after the war ended. Each major ally—the U.S.S.R., Great Britain, the United States, and France—would occupy and govern one of the four parts. Berlin, the capital of Germany, would also be divided into four zones. Nations liberated from German control would hold free elections.

When the war in Europe ended, the Allies divided Germany as they had planned to. Part of the division lasted until 1990. That had not been part of the plan. Eastern Germany made up the postwar Soviet occupation zone. Soviet officials made this into the new communist nation of East Germany. The zones occupied by the United States, Great Britain, and France became the democratic nation of West Germany.

The Divided Germany

East Germany was a Soviet satellite. Its economy and government ran the way the Soviet Union said they should run. Its leaders said and did what Soviet leaders told them to say and do.

The U.S.S.R. made other nations of Eastern Europe into Soviet satellites, too. This was a direct violation of the Yalta agreement. But

Soviet troops had occupied most of Eastern Europe when they drove the Germans out. So the U.S.S.R. had control of these countries. Poland, Hungary, Romania, Bulgaria, Czechoslovakia, and Albania all became communist countries tied to the Soviet Union. As in East Germany, the economy, government, and leaders of each of these nations followed the Soviet model.

Yugoslavia was also communist. But its dictator, Marshal Tito, refused to stay closely tied to the U.S.S.R.

Western Europe Rebuilds

At the end of World War II, Europeans needed a lot of help to get back on their feet and rebuild. In 1943 the Allies had set up an agency to provide emergency aid to areas liberated from the Axis powers. It was called UNRRA (United Nations Relief and Rehabilitation Administration). It gave people food, clothing, and medical care. It also rebuilt some roads and bridges and factories.

However, Europe needed a long-term plan for help. U.S. Secretary of State George Marshall came up with one. Under the Marshall Plan, the nations of Western Europe got together and drew up a long-range recovery plan. The United States then gave large amounts of economic aid to help those countries put the plan into effect.

The Marshall Plan was a big success. It helped the democratic countries of Europe become strong again. This fit U.S. goals for several reasons. The democracies of Europe didn't have to use socialist or communist methods to fix their economies. Also, a strong Western Europe would be a good barrier to the spread of communism. And the growing European economies provided much-needed markets for U.S. goods. (The Soviet Union and its satellites turned down any Marshall Plan assistance.)

East Versus West

Europe was now split into two opposing groups: the mostly communist nations of Eastern Europe and the mostly democratic nations of Western Europe. Tensions grew.

Berlin

One problem spot was Germany's capital of Berlin. Like Germany itself, Berlin was divided into four occupation zones. The city was also well within the Soviet occupation zone of East Germany. The Western powers controlled three of Berlin's zones. That part of the city was democratic and was recovering well from wartime damage. The communist eastern section of the city was not thriving.

In 1948, the Soviets tried to force Great Britain, France, and the United States to turn all of Berlin over to them. Their tactic was to set up a blockade. It would cut off all land and water routes across East Germany to the city. Without supplies, the people of Berlin would starve. The Allies would have to give up the city.

Instead, the Allies set up an amazing airlift. Planes flew in everything the people of Berlin needed every day. The airlift went on for six months. It worked so well that the U.S.S.R. gave up the Berlin blockade.

Greece, Turkey, and the Truman Doctrine

The Soviet Union controlled almost all of Eastern Europe. It wanted to extend that control and expand communism. Greece and Turkey were logical targets.

Communists had tried to take over the Greek government during World War II. Great Britain had helped snuff out that attempt. After the war, the Greek Communists tried again. This time, they had help from nearby Soviet satellites. At the same time, the U.S.S.R. put pressure on Turkey to become more friendly to Soviet policies.

U.S. President Harry Truman was alarmed by these attempts to expand Soviet control. In March 1947, he announced a new U.S. policy. It came to be known as the Truman Doctrine. It said that the United States would help any country that faced a threat by communists. This included communists within or outside of a country. Truman put the policy into effect by sending military help to Greece. With this aid, the Greek government was able to end the communist rebellion. The U.S.S.R. left Turkey alone after this, too.

Post-War Japan

When World War II ended, Japan lost all the overseas lands it had taken control of. All it had left were the home islands that made up the nation of Japan itself. The U.S. army occupied and controlled the country. General Douglas MacArthur commanded the army and, in effect, ruled Japan.

U.S. policy in Japan had several aims. The country was disarmed. Its industry had been focused on producing goods for war. Now it was rebuilt for peacetime output to benefit the Japanese people. Huge amounts of U.S. aid made this rebuilding possible.

Also, U.S. policy turned Japan into a democracy. Military leaders no longer controlled the government. A new constitution set up a parliament, with a prime minister to run the government. The emperor kept his throne, but he had almost no power. Women were now allowed to vote. The constitution also stated that Japan was giving up war "forever." Education became more open to all people. Land reform made it easier for farmers to buy their own land. The Japanese people did not resist any of these U.S.-imposed changes on their society. In fact, they seemed very willing to cooperate with U.S. policy.

In 1951, Japan and many other nations signed the peace treaty for World War II. In it, Japan officially gave up all its claims to lands beyond its borders. A United States-Japanese pact allowed U.S. troops to stay in Japan to defend the disarmed nation. In 1952, Japan took back full control of its own affairs from the United States.

A New International Order

Before World War II, the most important and powerful countries in the world had been the nations of Western Europe. Great Britain, France, and Germany had controlled empires and world trade. After World War II, two different nations commanded the scene: the United States and the U.S.S.R.

These two nations were very different. The United States was an open democracy. People could speak their minds and vote freely for their choice of leaders. The economy was capitalist—mostly controlled by private citizens and companies, not by the state. The Soviet Union was a communist state run by a dictator. The economy was state controlled. The country did not have free elections, free speech, or a free press.

The United States wanted countries around the world to become or remain democratic. The Soviet Union wanted the world's nations to become communist. In fact, one basic idea of communism was that capitalism would, sooner or later, fail. Workers would rise up in revolutions. They would reform their capitalist nations into communist ones. This didn't actually happen. But the U.S.S.R. did back communist movements in any country wherever it could.

The United States–Soviet struggle didn't become a war in the usual sense. The U.S. and Soviet armies didn't fight each other the way they had fought the German armies in World War II. Instead, the two nations fought for allies. This struggle was known as the Cold War. It continued to disrupt the world until the 1990s.

The United Nations

The Allies in World War II had called themselves "the United Nations." They were united in their fight against Germany. During the war, the Allies started making plans to form a new organization of nations. Many countries attended a 1945 meeting in San Francisco. They created a new United Nations, united to keep peace and help one another. This new United Nations officially came into existence in October 1945. It moved to permanent headquarters in New York City.

The United Nations provides a place for the world's countries to talk to one another about issues and needs. Its main purpose was, and is, to keep peace in the world. Another purpose is to protect human rights. The United Nations also gives valuable medical, educational, technical, and economic help to countries that need it.

The United Nations has several main parts. Delegates from all the member nations make up the General Assembly. It is like a legislature, where members discuss their concerns. The General Assembly elects a secretary-general to lead the United Nations. This person heads the Secretariat, all the employees who keep the United Nations running on a daily basis.

The Security Council is in charge of the United Nation's most important job, to keep peace in the world. The Council has 15 members. Five of these members are permanent—they are always members of the Council. The five are the United States, Great Britain, Russia (formerly the Soviet Union), France, and China. If any one of these five votes against a Council decision, that vote counts as a veto. That is, the decision is overruled.

The Security Council can impose economic sanctions on nations. For example, the Council can block a nation from selling its goods to other countries. It can stop other countries from selling their goods to that nation. The Council can also form armed military units. Soldiers from U.N. members make up these armed forces. The Council can send its military units into any country to keep the peace and stop armed conflicts. This is a big advantage over the old League of Nations. The League had no way to enforce its decisions.

The United Nations faced a big problem right from the beginning. The United States and the Soviet Union were starting to face off in the Cold War. Their rivalry was reflected in the United Nations. The democratic and noncommunist nations tended to side with the United States. The communist nations sided with the U.S.S.R. This split sometimes made it hard for the General Assembly to work in a cooperative way.

Also, the Security Council made the critical decisions about peacekeeping actions. The Western nations on the Council could veto decisions the Soviet Union favored. The U.S.S.R. could veto decisions favored by the Western nations. Sometimes this veto power prevented the Council from acting.

Topic 4

The World After World War II

Chapter 13: Europe: Democracy and the Iron Curtain

The Cold War

At the end of World War II, world leadership passed to two nations that were new to this role: the United States and the U.S.S.R., or Soviet Union. These two countries had been allies—countries that support each other—during the war. But friendly relations between the two nations began to dissolve even before the war was over.

By 1945, Soviet armies had swept German forces out of Eastern Europe. (Eastern Europe included the nations between the borders of the U.S.S.R. and Germany/Austria.) Joseph Stalin, the Soviet ruler, had promised the United States and other allies that he would allow free elections in the countries of Eastern Europe after the war. He did not. Instead, he put these nations under Soviet control.

A struggle then developed between the United States and the U.S.S.R. The Soviet Union wanted to expand communism beyond the borders of Eastern Europe. It worked actively to promote communist activity and communist governments in countries all over the world. The United States opposed the spread of communism and tried to promote democracy in countries worldwide. In 1947, U.S. President Harry Truman declared that the United States would send aid to any country that was threatened by communists. This was called the *Truman Doctrine.*

Unlike wars in the past, this struggle was not fought by armed troops of the U.S.S.R. and the United States. Instead, it was an economic and political war. Each side gave other nations financial and political support. They hoped that this aid would persuade nations to become or stay democratic or communist, or at least to support the United States or U.S.S.R. Because the war wasn't fought with military weapons, it was called the Cold War. The Cold War was the controlling feature of world politics from 1945 through most of the rest of the twentieth century.

One big reason the United States and the U.S.S.R. didn't get into a military war was the atomic bomb. In 1945, the United States had become the first nation in the world to drop an atomic bomb on a civilian target—the Japanese city of Hiroshima. The world had seen with horror the huge destructive power of the atomic bomb. Soon, even more powerful bombs based on atomic energy, called nuclear bombs, were developed. The U.S.S.R. developed its own atomic and nuclear bombs, too.

The concept of world war was now completely changed. By the 1950s, the United States and the U.S.S.R. had built enough nuclear weapons to totally destroy each other. A third world war could mean the end of the world. Neither the United States nor the U.S.S.R. wanted to start such a war. So they did not fight their war of ideas and politics with nuclear weapons. Instead, they fought with the "cold" weapons of money and political support. Competing groups of cooperating nations were one of those "cold" weapons.

NATO and the Warsaw Pact

When the Soviet Union took over Eastern Europe, Western leaders got very worried. They were afraid the Soviet armies would invade Western Europe next. So in 1949, the United States, France, Great Britain, Italy, and eight other nations formed NATO, the North Atlantic Treaty Organization. They all agreed to help any one of them that was attacked. In 1954, the NATO nations drew up plans for armed forces.

The Soviet Union responded by calling its satellites to a meeting in 1955. They created the Warsaw Pact. The U.S.S.R. and the Eastern European countries agreed to provide troops for mutual use in case of war.

The Common Market and Comecon

The Western and Eastern blocs also created economic alliances. In 1949, the Soviet Union and the Eastern European satellites created Comecon, the Council for Mutual Economic Assistance. The council's purpose was to coordinate economic activities within the states of the Soviet bloc.

In Europe, some leaders felt that the only way to be sure of continued peace was to bring their nations closer together. They felt that closer economic ties might be the key. So in 1952, six nations—Belgium, Italy, France, Luxembourg, the Netherlands, and West Germany—formed a group. They agreed to stop making individual decisions about two of their most important industries, coal and steel. Instead, an independent body would make the decisions with the aim of benefiting all of the group's nations.

This first step was a great success. So in 1957, the six nations created the European Economic Community, or EEC. It was best known as the Common Market, and it combined other parts of these nations' economies. Over time, the Common Market took away rules that made trade among their nations difficult. Instead of having six separate markets, they formed one common market. Later, other European nations joined the Common Market. Over time, it became known as the European Union, or EU.

The Soviet Union

Joseph Stalin had been the dictator of the U.S.S.R. since the 1920s. Stalin had made the communist nation into a police state. He allowed no opposition and ruthlessly got rid of anyone he thought might be against him. He directed the Soviet takeover of Eastern Europe as World War II ended.

Stalin died in 1953. A power struggle followed his death. Top communist leaders shared power for a while. Nikita Khrushchev became the new Communist Party secretary. By 1958, he was also firmly in charge of the Soviet government, as premier.

The Soviet Union saw some changes under Khrushchev's rule. The most startling was a program of attacks on many of Stalin's policies. Khrushchev denounced Stalin for having created a cult of himself. Statues and pictures of the dead leader disappeared from public places. Buildings and streets named for Stalin got new names. Prisoners in labor camps came home.

Khrushchev continued the Soviet policies of controlling Eastern Europe and pressing the spread of communism worldwide. But under Khrushchev, relations with the United States were sometimes less tense. He met several times with the leaders of the United States, Britain, and France. These meetings were called summit conferences, because the highest leaders of each country came to them.

Also, the Soviet Union under Khrushchev adopted a policy of peaceful coexistence with the United States. The U.S.S.R. no longer insisted that a worldwide communist revolution was sure to happen. Instead, it said that it could accept that East and West could exist side by side without war.

In spite of "peaceful coexistence," United States–Soviet relations were extremely poor at times. A summit conference was scheduled to be held in 1960 between Khrushchev and U.S. President Dwight Eisenhower. Just before the meeting, the U.S.S.R. shot down a U.S. spy plane over Soviet territory. Khrushchev canceled the meeting. In 1962, the United States discovered that the U.S.S.R. had set up missiles in Cuba that could reach the United States. The United States and the U.S.S.R. teetered on the edge of nuclear war. Then U.S. President John F. Kennedy got Khrushchev to back down and remove the missiles.

At home, Khrushchev steered the Soviet economy toward heavy industry, as Stalin had done. Consumer goods remained hard to get for the Soviet people. Khrushchev's economic and farming policies weren't very successful. But Soviet advances in rocket science were impressive. In 1957, the U.S.S.R. launched the world's first earth-orbiting satellite, called *Sputnik*. A Soviet rocket reached the moon in 1959. And in 1961, Soviet air force officer Yuri Gagarin became the first person to circle Earth in space.

Eastern Europe

The nations of Eastern Europe became Soviet satellites. The U.S.S.R. called them "people's republics." In each, a communist government ruled with absolute power. The economy, politics, and society followed the Soviet model. Opposition parties were banned. Free speech and a free press disappeared. Industries became state-owned.

The Eastern European people's republics included Poland, East Germany, Czechoslovakia, Hungary, Romania, Bulgaria, and Albania. The Soviet Union kept them closely tied to itself. Most contacts between these nations and Western Europe were cut off. Prime Minister Winston Churchill of Great Britain said that "an iron curtain has descended across Europe."

However, each of these nations had once been independent countries. So from time to time, dissent against Soviet control erupted.

Yugoslavia

Yugoslavia kept some distance between itself and the U.S.S.R. Fighting among several groups here during the war ended with a communist victory. The communist leader was Josip Broz, known as Marshal Tito. Tito insisted on following an independent course in his country instead of doing what the Soviet Union ordered. In 1948, the U.S.S.R. and its satellites broke off relations with Yugoslavia. Seeing a cold war opening, the United States and its allies gave economic aid to Tito.

Yugoslavia and the U.S.S.R. became friendlier during the 1950s. Still, Tito loosened state control of the economy. He also let most peasants keep their own individual farms. Yet the country remained communist, and Tito ruled as a dictator until his death in 1980.

East Germany

The Allies had divided Germany into occupation zones at the end of World War II. The Soviets made their zone into a people's republic called the German Democratic Republic in 1949. It was better known as East Germany. Its communist leader from 1946 to 1971 was Walter Ulbricht. He ruled as strictly as Stalin had in the U.S.S.R. The state took total control of the economy, which focused on heavy industry.

Overworked and hungry East German workers revolted in 1953. Soviet troops and tanks put down the rebellion. But unhappy East Germans kept trying to leave for West Germany. Ulbricht blocked the border. But the German capital of Berlin was divided into East Berlin and West Berlin. Skilled East German workers kept flowing into West Berlin, which had a free economy and a free political system. Ulbricht stopped that flow in 1961 by building the Berlin Wall. It ran between East and West Berlin. People could get through the wall only at a few heavily guarded entryways. People who tried to sneak across the wall were shot and often killed by East German border guards.

Poland

Poland was a very faithful Soviet satellite at first. Then, after Stalin's death, demands for reforms grew. In 1956, workers demonstrated. Troops put down the protest. But Poland's new ruler, Wladyslaw Gomulka, made some changes. For example, elections became open to some opposition candidates. Most collective farms were dissolved. The press gained some freedoms.

Hungary

The greatest threat to Soviet control of its satellites in the 1950s came from Hungary. Hungary's communist government had become less rigid after Stalin's death. In 1956, students and workers demonstrated and demanded more reforms. Imre Nagy, as premier, agreed and promised free elections. Soviet troops and tanks once again moved in. The rebels were killed, exiled, and imprisoned. Nagy was executed. The communist government took strict control again.

Western Europe

The main business of the countries of Western Europe after World War II was economic recovery. Great Britain, France, and Italy had all suffered huge losses in the war. Roads, buildings, factories, and bridges had been damaged and destroyed. The Marshall Plan, a U.S. program of massive aid, helped make this recovery possible.

The Western European countries were also involved in the cold war. They acted with the United States to resist communist pressures in Europe and elsewhere.

Great Britain

Winston Churchill, leader of the Conservative Party, had been a great wartime leader. But he and his party lost the election of 1945. Voters chose the Labour party and its leader, Clement Attlee. The Labour Party followed a policy of moderate socialism. The government took over important

British industries. Nationalized businesses included the railroads, the coal industry, and utilities like electric power companies.

Also, medical care was socialized—every British person became entitled to free medical care provided by the government. When Churchill and the Conservatives came back into power in 1951, they left these Labour Party changes in place.

France

A new French government was set up in 1946. But it was unstable, with governing groups changing often. France lost its colonies in Southeast Asia to Asian nationalists after a nine-year war. War also broke out in Algeria, a country in North Africa that France had taken over. General Charles de Gaulle then emerged as a strong French leader. As president of France, he used the powers in a new 1958 constitution to bring stability to French politics and to move Algeria to independence.

West Germany

The three zones occupied by the Allies at the end of World War II became the postwar nation of West Germany. It was a strong, democratic country allied with the other nations of Western Europe. It helped block the spread of Soviet communism to Western Europe. By 1955, West Germany had become fully independent. It was allowed to rearm, and it joined NATO.

From 1949 to 1963, West Germany's elected leader was Konrad Adenauer of the moderate Christian Democratic Union. Adenauer oversaw a remarkable recovery of the German economy, called Germany's "economic miracle." At first, this miracle was threatened by the millions of refugees who poured into West Germany from Eastern Europe. But many of the refugees were skilled workers. They added to the productive nature of West Germany's workforce.

Italy

Italy in the postwar years had a strong Communist Party that clashed often with the more moderate parties that formed ruling coalitions. The Communists lost much influence in the mid-1950s.

Spain

In Spain, a dictator ruled. Francisco Franco and his fascist and conservative followers had won the Spanish Civil War in 1939. The other Western powers would have nothing to do with Franco until the 1950s. Then the United States saw Franco's Spain as a possible ally against the Soviet Union. The United States began giving Franco aid in return for the use of Spanish military bases. Spain was allowed to join the United Nations in 1955.

Chapter 14: The Middle East and Africa

Before World War II, many countries in Asia, Africa, and the Middle East were colonies. They were governed and controlled by Western European nations. Independence for many of these colonies came quickly after the world war.

The war inspired a new wave of nationalism among the colonies of the world. People in Asia, the Middle East, and Africa saw the white colonial powers defeated. Germany conquered France. Great Britain and the United States ejected Germany and Italy from Africa and the Middle East. The Japanese took Asian colonies away from Western powers.

It was clear to nationalist leaders that the Europeans' hold on their colonies was now greatly weakened. Also, many Africans and Asians had served in the armies of the colonial powers during the war. They returned with the feeling that they had now earned the right to self-rule.

Several colonial powers fostered the drive for self-rule by the way they governed their colonies. They spread education among the native population. They also trained natives to work in colonial governments. Trained, educated native people naturally felt they were perfectly capable of self-rule.

Egypt

Egypt is one of the Arab nations of North Africa. It also lies next to the Middle East. Its links to Middle East politics and interests are very close. So, Egypt is often considered a Middle Eastern nation as well as an African nation.

Egypt had been a fully independent nation since 1936. However, Great Britain still had a lot of influence over the Egyptian government in the 1940s and early 1950s. The country's ruler was King Farouk I. The Egyptian people were becoming angry about Farouk's expensive living style and his corrupt officials.

A group of young army officers led a revolution against Farouk in 1952. The king had to give up his throne. Egypt became a republic in 1953. The country's new leader was Gamal Abdel Nasser, who was elected president in 1956. He ruled with complete power. He worked to bring economic and social welfare reforms to Egypt's mostly poor population.

Nasser refused to take sides in the Cold War. He courted both the West and the East in order to get needed aid for Egypt. When he couldn't buy arms from the West, he got them from Czechoslovakia. He tried to get loans from the West to build the Aswan High Dam. This was a huge project that would vastly increase the amount of land available for farming in Egypt. When the West turned down the loans, Nasser got help from the Soviet Union.

The last British troops were due to leave Egypt in 1956. In July 1956, Egypt took over the Suez Canal. The canal had been run by a British-French company. It was a vital link in British-French trade, especially for oil. In October, Israel invaded Egypt's Sinai Peninsula. Great Britain and France landed troops at the canal and drove Egyptian forces back. This caused a great world crisis. The United States spoke out against the invasion. The Soviet Union made threats to send troops to help Egypt. The United Nations quickly sent a peacekeeping force to the canal area and arranged for a cease-fire. The crisis ended. But Egypt and Israel clashed again in later years.

Palestine and Israel

During World War I, the British had promised both Jews and Arabs a homeland in the Middle East region of Palestine. The Jews saw this area as their homeland from biblical times. The Arabs had lived there for centuries and claimed it as their homeland.

In the years between the world wars, many Jews moved to Palestine. Many more flowed there because of Hitler's war of genocide against them. Alarmed Arabs wanted the influx stopped. Great Britain, unable to solve the problem, turned it over to the United Nations. In 1948, the United Nations split the land. It gave western Palestine to the Jews and eastern Palestine to the Arabs. As a result, more than 700,000 Palestinian Arabs had to leave their homes and land. Many of them ended up in refugee camps in nearby countries, such as Jordan and Syria.

The Jews declared their part to be the new independent nation of Israel. As soon as British troops withdrew, war broke out between Arabs and Jews. Syria, Iraq, Transjordan, Lebanon, and Egypt attacked Israel. The young nation fought them off and even made some gains. The United Nations arranged a truce to end the war in 1949.

However, the Arab nations remained committed to making Israel disappear. They refused to recognize it as a legal nation. They refused to trade with it. Egypt refused to allow ships carrying Israeli goods to pass through the Suez Canal.

Another big and continuing problem concerned the Palestinian Arabs. Eastern Palestine had not become an Arab state of Palestine. Instead, it had become part of the Arab kingdom known since 1949 as Jordan. Palestinian Arabs lived as refugees in Jordan and other Arab states bordering Israel. They remained determined to regain their Palestinian homeland in Israel. Israel remained determined to hold on to what it had. The problem had not yet been solved by the early twenty-first century.

The Suez crisis of 1956 created another Israeli-Arab armed fight. When Egypt took the canal, Israel invaded Egypt and took the Gaza Strip. This was an Egyptian district along the coast between Israel and the canal. Israel was about to take the Sinai Peninsula from Egypt when the United Nations halted fighting.

Israelis and Arabs continued to clash along their borders. Meanwhile, Israel built a successful economy, with modern cities and farms in former desert areas. Jews from all over the world continued to migrate to Israel.

The Arab Nations of the Middle East, Iran, and Turkey

Arab nationalism was a very strong force during and after World War II. It resulted in many newly independent nations in the Middle East in the 1940s and 1950s. It also gave rise to calls for Arab unity. This produced mergers and joint groupings among Arab nations.

The earliest of these was the Arab League. It was formed in 1945 by Egypt, Iraq, Transjordan, Syria, Lebanon, Saudi Arabia, and Yemen. Its general purpose was to promote cooperation among these Arab nations. Its focus was to prevent the formation of a Jewish state in Palestine. When Israel came into existence in 1948, members of the Arab League quickly went to war with the new nation.

■ OF NOTE

Arab is a term that describes people who speak the Arabic language. Many Arabs practice the religion of Islam. Most Arabs live in North Africa, the Middle East, and the Arabian Peninsula. Arab nations that joined the Arab League after its founding in 1945 were Morocco, Algeria, Tunisia, Libya, Mauritania, Sudan, Somalia, Djibouti (all in Africa), Kuwait, Bahrain, Qatar, United Arab Emirates, and Oman (all on the Arabian Peninsula).

Nasser, Egypt's leader, had a strong belief in Arab unity. In 1958, he arranged for the union of Egypt and Syria. The new joint state was called the United Arab Republic (UAR). The Syrians soon came to feel that Egypt controlled the United Arab Republic. Syria took back its individual independence in 1961.

Iraq and Jordan responded to the formation of the United Arab Republic with a union of their own in 1958. The kings of Iraq and Jordan formed a federation called the Arab Union. It was pro-Western, so the United Arab Republic waged a propaganda campaign against it. A coup later in 1958 overthrew the king of Iraq. The new Iraqi government ended the Arab union with Jordan.

Another factor that affected Arab nations during these years was the Eisenhower Doctrine. It was a policy announced by U.S. President Dwight Eisenhower in 1957. It was similar to the 1947 Truman Doctrine. The United States pledged to give military help to any country in the Middle East that was threatened by communists. Pro-Western governments in the Middle East supported the new doctrine. Neutral and anti-Western governments did not. They saw it as an excuse for Western meddling in their internal affairs.

Here is a brief summary of developments in individual Arab nations of the Middle East in the 1940s and 1950s.

Iraq

During World War II, Iraq had a series of governments. They went from pro-British to pro-German and then back to pro-British. After the war, Iraq's leader, Nuri as-Said, kept the country pro-Western. He got agreements with foreign-controlled oil companies to pay Iraq large royalties. With this money, he paid for development programs and public works. The United States provided military aid. In 1958, a military coup overthrew Said. Iraq now became a strongly pro-Arab republic. Its foreign policy favored the U.S.S.R. more than the United States. However, Iraq kept up its production of oil and its profitable sale to Western nations.

■ OF NOTE

In 1960, British control of Kuwait ended. Iraq immediately claimed Kuwait, saying that this country had once been part of Iraq. The Kuwaiti ruler asked Great Britain to send in troops to prevent an Iraqi invasion and takeover. Great Britain did, and the crisis ended. In 1990, Iraq revived its claims to Kuwait, invading and taking over the country. A U.S.-led coalition forced Iraq out of Kuwait. This was called the Gulf War.

Syria

Syria had been under French control since the 1920s. It became fully independent in 1946. It was very unstable politically in the postwar years. In 1949 alone, it went through three military coups. During the 1950s, Syrian and Israeli troops often clashed along the countries' borders. Also during those years, Syria became more and more anti-Western and pro-Soviet. It began receiving aid from the U.S.S.R. for large development projects. The Syrian government took over many private industries. From 1958 to 1961, Syria was united with Egypt in the United Arab Republic. The socialist Baath party took power in 1963.

Lebanon

Like Syria, Lebanon had been controlled by France. It also achieved full independence in 1946. France had joined two different peoples and regions to create the country. The coast and plain were mostly Muslim. The mountainous area was mostly Christian. This created much political instability in the new nation. The upper classes, largely Christian, did well with a thriving economy. They also held most of the power. The lower classes, largely Muslim, remained poor and mostly powerless. The Christians favored ties with the West. Muslims favored ties with neighboring Arab states. They expressed their views at times with protests and riots. By the 1970s, these conflicts had escalated into a full-scale civil war.

Jordan

After World War I, Jordan was a mandate territory called Transjordan, under British control. It became a fully independent kingdom in 1946. As a result of the 1948 Arab League war against Israel, Transjordan annexed the Arab portion of Palestine. The nation's name became Jordan. During the 1950s, Jordanian and Israeli troops often clashed along the countries' borders. Jordan received aid from Western nations. Its relations with the United Arab Republic were not very friendly after Iraq dissolved the Arab union with Jordan.

Iran

Iran, formerly Persia, was a non-Arab nation. It was ruled by a pro-Western shah. In the early 1950s, the nationalist Mohammed Mossadegh became prime minister. His government nationalized Iran's foreign-owned oil companies. This created a crisis until the shah reasserted power. He made agreements that allowed the foreign interests to operate the oil industry and pay Iran large royalties. The shah used the royalty payments to promote social and economic reforms and benefits for the Iranian people. He also banned political opposition and became a near-absolute ruler.

Turkey

Turkey was another non-Arab nation of the Middle East. Turkey's nationalist leader, Kemal Atatürk, had modernized the country along Western lines in the 1920s and 1930s. Under his successors in the 1940s and 1950s, the country's economy kept making good progress. Western aid helped to spur this progress. Turkey became a close ally of the Western powers in response to Soviet attempts to force its influence on the country. Turkey joined NATO in 1952.

Africa

At the end of World War II, the vast continent of Africa was almost entirely controlled by Western imperial powers. By the mid-1960s, only a few African nations remained colonies. The rest had become independent in rapid order, beginning in the late 1950s.

As elsewhere in the world, some African nations became independent with little trouble. For others, freedom came only with conflict.

Many independent African nations south of the Sahara faced common problems. The Western nations had created many colonies with a mix of different peoples. They spoke different languages, had different customs. Often, a colony included peoples who were traditionally at odds with one another. Also, the economy in most of these new nations was based on subsistence farming. Some of these nations had many raw materials; others had few. There was not much industry, because the colonial powers had used the African colonies as sources of raw materials for their home industries. In some African nations, white settlers tried to stop or interfere with native rule. And not all colonial powers had trained many Africans in the skills needed to run a modern, independent nation.

In seeking solutions to these problems, most new African governments turned to some form of socialism. The governments owned or directed at least some of the factories and other important industries. The idea was to guide the development of a nation in a way to benefit the people. However, some leaders used socialism to benefit themselves and their supporters more than to benefit the welfare of the nation as a whole.

Also, democracy on the Western model often broke down in the new African nations. African governments had to turn poor, divided countries into modern, industrial, unified nations. This often led to one-person or one-party rule.

The nations of North Africa were Arab. The rest of the continent was inhabited by many different ethnic groups, mostly black, with different languages and customs. North Africa was separated from central and southern Africa by the vast Sahara Desert. It had developed quite differently from the rest of the continent. Its Arab peoples were traders and desert nomads.

Morocco and Tunisia

Arab nationalism became strong in this region, as it did in the Middle East. Growing native unrest in Morocco and Tunisia forced France to grant independence to these colonies in 1956. A sultan ruled the new kingdom of Morocco. Tunisia ended its kingdom in 1957. The independence leader Habib Bourguiba served as president of the nation until 1987.

Libya

Britain and France took over Libya from Italy during World War II. They granted Libya independence in 1952 as a constitutional monarchy. It seemed destined to remain a poor desert nation. But in the late 1950s, great oil fields were discovered. The new oil wealth raised the standard of living for many Libyans during the 1960s. But much of the wealth went to the ruling families and high government officials. This sparked a revolution in 1969.

Algeria

Algeria did not achieve independence easily. France considered Algeria not a colony, but an actual part of France itself. The European settlers there were called *colons.* They completely opposed independence. But most Algerians were Arab and Berber Muslims. They demanded independence or at least home rule. Radical nationalists started a guerrilla war against

France in 1954. France was not able to defeat the nationalists. France's new president, Charles de Gaulle, arranged for a peaceful settlement of the war. Algerians voted in large numbers for independence in 1962.

Ghana

Ghana was the first of the sub-Saharan British colonies to gain independence. Nationalist feelings in Ghana became very strong after World War II. Britain responded by giving Ghana more and more self-rule. Independence came in 1957. Ghana's first prime minister, then president, was Kwame Nkrumah. Although Ghana was a republic, Nkrumah became more and more of a dictator.

Guinea

Guinea and other sub-Saharan French colonies pressed for independence in the 1950s. France held elections in these colonies in 1958. The people of each colony could choose to have their country become part of a French community. They could keep economic and political ties with France. Or they could break all ties with France and become fully independent. Guinea was the only colony that chose full independence. It became a free nation in 1958 with Sékou Touré as its president. France cut off all aid to the country. Touré turned to Eastern European nations for economic help. He also set up a one-party state and a socialist system.

Kenya

Kenya was a British colony in East Africa. Its fertile highlands had attracted a number of white settlers. British policy favored these settlers and saved the highlands for white rather than black settlement. The main native group of this area was the Kikuyu. The reserves set aside for them weren't big enough. Angry Kikuyu rebels formed a secret society called the Mau Mau in the early 1950s. They waged an attack-and-kill campaign, against European settlers, and Kikuyu who did not support them. The British colonial government put down the Mau Mau. But Great Britain also changed its policy of favoring whites. Instead, it prepared Kenya's black population for independence. That came in 1963. Kenya's first president was Jomo Kenyatta, who had been involved in the Mau Mau uprising. Kenya became a one-party state, but with political freedoms allowed. Kenyatta followed moderate and pro-Western policies.

South Africa

South Africa was very different from the rest of Africa. It was not a colony of a European nation. Instead, it was ruled by whites who had settled there. The Afrikaners were whites of Dutch, or Boer, ancestry. Fewer in number were white settlers of British ancestry. Nonwhites in South Africa outnumbered whites by about four to one. Yet the whites firmly controlled the country.

In 1948, Afrikaners took charge of the government. They put into place a policy of strict separation of the races called apartheid. Blacks lost all political rights. They had to live in special restricted areas. Whites controlled the economy and the nation's mining wealth. South African blacks opposed apartheid, but had little power to change it. Other nations opposed apartheid, too. More and more, the policy led to South Africa's isolation from other countries of the world. Apartheid in South Africa did not end until the 1990s.

Chapter 15: Asia After the War

Japan and China

Japan

From 1945 to 1952, U.S. occupation forces controlled Japan. Under U.S. direction, Japan became a democracy. In 1952, Japan became fully independent again. Under the terms of the war-ending peace treaty, Japan had been disarmed. With the Cold War underway, the United States wanted Japan to be able to defend itself against communist expansion. The two countries signed a military aid and rearming treaty in 1953 and a mutual defense pact in 1954.

Meanwhile, Japan's economy grew steadily. Japanese industry turned out high-quality products and sold them around the world at affordable prices. Japan's role in world trade expanded. The Japanese standard of living rose.

China

Before World War II, China had been torn by a civil war. The Chinese communists were led by Mao Zedong. The nationalists, or Kuomintang, were led by General Chiang Kai-shek. During the war, Japan invaded and took over large parts of China. The communists and nationalists put aside their civil war to concentrate on fighting the foreign foe, Japan.

During World War II, the communists gained strength. They secured the support of China's vast peasant population. Their Red Army and Communist party grew. Soviet forces gave the Chinese communists military arms they had captured from the Japanese in Manchuria. The nationalist forces were divided and tired. When the world war ended, the communists and nationalists turned back to their civil war.

In 1949, the nationalists gave up and retreated to the island of Taiwan (also called Formosa then). There, Chiang set up what he called the Republic of China. This was supposed to be a democracy. But Chiang actually ruled as a dictator.

The Chinese communists under Mao also set up a dictatorship. The Communist Party, headed by Mao, controlled all aspects of Chinese life. Chinese society had been rural, traditional, and loosely organized. Now the communists directed people's loyalties to the state and the party rather than to the family. Religion and independent thought were very much put down. Women, though, gained new rights.

China had suffered many years of civil war and Japanese occupation. So, the first job of the communist government was to get the economy restarted. Factories were rebuilt, farms were restored, and inflation was checked. During the 1950s, the government directed the economy through several Five-Year Plans of total control. The state took ownership of the land and then organized farms into large collectives and communes. Heavy industries were built up. The second Five-Year Plan, known as the Great Leap Forward, was not a success. The economy faltered, and production was down by the end of the 1950s.

The Chinese leaders believed in aggressively pushing the spread of communism. China sent troops to North Korea to help those communists in the Korean War. China gave a lot of military aid to communists who were fighting the French for freedom in Indochina. China also took over the mountain country of Tibet in 1950. All through the 1950s, mainland (communist) China made threats to invade and capture Taiwan (nationalist China).

The Soviet Union, another large and powerful communist nation, seemed like a natural ally of China. During the 1950s, China and the Soviet Union signed several mutual-help and friendship pacts. However, the cooperation between these two communist nations began to erode in the late 1950s and the 1960s. The Chinese communists held on to their policy of pushing for communist revolutions around the world. The Soviets, though, turned to a policy of peaceful coexistence with the West. Relations between the two countries became strained and competitive.

The Korean War

Like Germany, Korea was divided into occupation zones at the end of World War II. The United States occupied southern Korea. The U.S.S.R.

occupied northern Korea. The country, located on a peninsula, was divided in two along the 38th parallel of latitude. The Soviet zone became the communist country of North Korea. The U.S. zone became the democratic country of South Korea. Many people on both sides wanted to see the two nations united as one Korea. The area became a focus of the struggle between democracy and communism.

In 1950, North Korea invaded South Korea. Its purpose was to unite the two countries under one communist rule. The United Nations Security Council quickly raised a combat force to oppose the North Korean aggression. The United States provided most of these troops, along with South Korea. Nineteen other U.N. members sent some forces as well.

The war moved back and forth between North and South Korea. At first, North Korean forces moved deep into South Korea. Then more U.N. troops arrived. The U.N. army, commanded by U.S. General Douglas MacArthur, drove the North Koreans back above the 38th parallel. The U.N. forces pushed all the way to the Yalu River, which divides North Korea from China. China responded by sending in large numbers of its own soldiers. They and the North Koreans drove the U.N. forces back deep into South Korea. The U.N. troops fought back.

By the spring of 1951, the opposing armies were lined up roughly along the 38th parallel. The battle line stayed there until both sides reached an armistice—an agreement to stop fighting—in 1953. No peace treaty was ever signed to end the war. Korea has remained divided along the 38th parallel ever since.

India and Pakistan

India was a British colony that had gained a lot of self-rule in the years before World War II. It helped Great Britain during the war with both troops and expenses. Indian soldiers were a big factor in pushing back Japanese troops that invaded India in 1944. However, India was officially a neutral state during the war.

The leader of India's independence movement was Mohandas Gandhi. He was the head of the Indian National Congress, the Hindu independence league. Gandhi and the congress insisted on immediate self-government in return for

India taking full part in the war. But India had another major religious group, the Muslims. Their independence group was called the Muslim League. The Muslims and their league didn't want to be part of a Hindu-run India. So, they insisted on having their own separate independent nation.

The British tried to work out a form of government that both Hindus and Muslims could agree on. Meanwhile, riots broke out across the country. The only solution seemed to be a division of India along religious lines. So in 1947, the independent nations of India and Pakistan came into being. The Hindus of India were to make up the new nation of India. Most people in this region were Hindu. So India became a very large nation. Pakistan was made up of two areas to the north of India where mostly Muslims lived. The two parts were widely separated. (The eastern part later became the separate nation of Bangladesh.)

The split between India and Pakistan was not peaceful. Along border areas, Hindus and Muslims fought bitterly. Masses of people moved from their homelands to become part of the nation that matched their religion. Pakistan and India fought for many years over the region of Kashmir.

Indian independence began on a tragic note. Gandhi was assassinated in 1948. India's new leader was an associate of Gandhi's named Jawaharlal Nehru. He led India as its prime minister from 1950 to his death in 1964.

Nehru adopted a neutral foreign policy for India. He refused to align the country with either the United States or the Soviet Union in the Cold War. Instead, he became a spokesman for independent, neutral nations of the Third World—the underdeveloped, non-Western countries of the world. At home, Nehru steered India toward a "mixed economy." The government owned some industries. Private individuals owned other businesses. The government remained democratic.

Pakistan was a republic at first. In the 1950s, it was very pro-Western. This brought much-needed economic aid to the country. In 1958, General Ayub Khan became military dictator of Pakistan. He ruled until 1969.

Both Pakistan and India faced—and continue to face—the problem of extreme overpopulation. They had many more people than either country could support other than in poverty. Pakistan had the extra problem of not enough natural resources to support industry.

Because of the conflicts between them, both nations had to spend too much money on their military forces. Also, although they had been formed along Muslim-Hindu lines, both nations were very diverse. Each had a bewildering variety of peoples, cultures, and languages. These problems were very difficult to overcome, and both countries continue to struggle with these problems today.

Southeast Asia

World War II had a large impact on the nations of Southeast Asia. Those nations are shown on the map on the next page. They were all colonies of, or controlled by, Western imperial powers.

During the war, Japan took over most of Southeast Asia from the Western colonial nations. People in the colonies could see now that the white ruling nations could be beaten—by Asians. When Japan lost the war, it wasn't easy for the Western colonial powers to take back their colonies. Asians in those colonies began making strong demands for self-rule.

Also, as the world war ended, the Cold War began. Southeast Asia became a field of battle—sometimes hot, sometimes cold—in that war. Chinese communists offered support to native movements for self-rule. The Western powers opposed the spread of communism. They used that as a reason to oppose native independence movements in some countries. These conflicts began in the 1950s and became even more widespread in later years.

Indochina

During the late 1800s, the French had gained control of the area of Southeast Asia called Indochina. This area included the countries of Vietnam, Laos, and Cambodia. Japan had taken over French Indochina during World War II. After the war, France wanted to take back control of these nations. The native people objected. The Indochina war broke out. It was centered in Vietnam.

Vietnam

While Japan occupied Vietnam, the communist leader Ho Chi Minh organized an independence league. It was called the Viet Minh (in Vietnamese, short for the League for the Independence of Vietnam).

After World War II, the French and the Viet Minh couldn't agree on terms for independence. War started between them late in 1946.

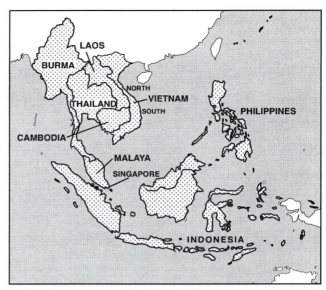

Southeast Asia

Ho Chi Minh's forces waged a guerrilla campaign against the French for eight years. Finally, the Viet Minh defeated French troops defending the fortress of Dien Bien Phu. France reached a settlement with the Viet Minh. Vietnam was divided into two countries along the 17th parallel. North Vietnam was a communist nation ruled by Ho Chi Minh. South Vietnam was a republic ruled by the Vietnamese and supported by France and the United States. The South Vietnamese government was not very effective or popular. Its anticommunist leader, Ngo Dinh Diem, refused to hold promised elections. In 1959, as unrest grew, communist guerrillas called Viet Cong restarted the war. That war pulled in the United States and continued until 1973.

Laos

France allowed Laos to become independent in 1949. During the Indochina war, the Viet Minh invaded Laos and took control of parts of the country. Procommunist Laotians, called Pathet Lao, helped the Viet Minh. When the Indochina war ended in 1954, all foreign troops left Laos. But the Pathet Lao kept control of northern areas of the country. From 1958 to 1961, Laos was torn by a civil war. The Pathet Lao (supplied by the U.S.S.R.) fought right-wing forces (supplied by the United States). Neutralists tried to reach agreement with both sides. A provisional government of pro-Western, Pathet Lao, and neutral factions was set up in 1962. Chaos continued through the 1960s and 1970s.

Cambodia

France took back control of Cambodia from the Japanese at the end of World War II. The country became independent in 1953. Its leader, Prince Norodom Sihanouk, kept Cambodia neutral through the 1960s. He was able to play China, the U.S.S.R., and the United States against one another to get aid for his country.

Philippines

The only U.S. possession in this area was the Philippines. The United States had started the independence process for this island nation before the war. The Philippines gained independence in 1946. The nation adopted a United States-style government.

Burma, Malaya, Singapore

Great Britain quickly saw that it could not hold on to its Asian possessions after World War II ended. Burma became an independent republic in 1948. Independence for Malaya was delayed until jungle warfare by communist rebels was ended. Malaya became independent in 1957. Singapore got a special semi-independent status in 1958. Malaya, Singapore, and northern Borneo became the Republic of Malaysia in 1963. Singapore was populated mostly by city-dwelling, business-oriented Chinese. Malaya had mostly rural Malay farmers. In 1965, Singapore withdrew from Malaysia.

East Indies

Before the war, the Netherlands had held a scattered colony called the Dutch East Indies. It was made up of a group of thousands of islands. Japan occupied these islands during World War II and left after its defeat in 1945. The nationalist Achmed Sukarno then declared the islands to be independent. The Dutch, though, wanted their colony back. The two sides fought bitterly. The United Nations stepped in, and Indonesia became an independent republic in 1949.

Thailand

Alone among the nations of Southeast Asia, Thailand was never taken over by a Western colonial power. It was occupied by Japan during the war but regained its independence afterward. A pro-Western military government took power in 1958.

Chapter 16: The United States and Latin America

The United States

Foreign Policy

U.S. foreign policy in the late 1940s and the 1950s was focused on the Cold War struggle with the Soviet Union. U.S. leaders felt it was important to contain the spread of communism around the world. So, in the years after World War II, the United States played a role as a world leader.

This was a big change in U.S. policy. Before World War II, the United States had preferred to remain uninvolved as much as possible in the affairs of foreign nations. Even when the world wars erupted, the United States had tried to stay out of the conflicts. Now the United States became involved in nations around the world. It tried to promote democracy and keep countries from becoming communist or allies of the Communist bloc.

In the late 1940s, the United States sponsored the Marshall Plan. That aid program helped the nations of Europe recover from World War II. The United States helped form the NATO alliance to counter the threat of communism in Western Europe. It also took part in the Berlin airlift to keep that city functioning when the U.S.S.R. cut off all its land routes to the outside world. U.S. President Truman announced the Truman Doctrine in 1947. He said that the United States would send help to any country that faced a threat by communism.

During the 1950s, the United States and the U.S.S.R. were very active in the newly independent nations of the world. Each superpower used aid and politics to persuade these new countries to line up on its side of the Cold War. Also in the 1950s, the United States played a major military and political role in the Korean War. The United States also promoted the formation of SEATO, the alliance aimed to prevent the spread of communism in Asia. U.S. President Eisenhower announced the Eisenhower Doctrine in 1957. He said that the United States would send help to any Middle Eastern nation that was threatened by communism.

Tensions between the United States and the Soviet Union rose and fell during the 1950s. In the mid-1950s, the U.S.S.R. adopted the policy of "peaceful coexistence." East and West were supposed to be able to exist side by side in peace. Still, both sides kept missiles aimed at each other, and tensions persisted.

Domestic Policy

The fear of communism led to a period of communist-hunting within the United States itself. The hunt was led by U.S. Senator Joseph McCarthy. He called many people before Congress. There, he grilled them about their supposed ties to the U.S. Communist Party and worldwide communism. McCarthy and his followers accused many government workers and people in the Hollywood film industry of disloyalty to the United States. Americans finally began to see McCarthy's actions as a fraud, a "witch-hunt." As people lost belief in McCarthy's charges, his influence disappeared.

In 1954, the U.S. Supreme Court started a huge change in American society. It made a landmark decision in a case called *Brown v. Board of Education of Topeka.* The Court said that segregation of schools by race was illegal. Black children could no longer be forced to attend all-black public schools. White public schools must be open to black students.

Southern states resisted the Supreme Court's ruling. Black children who tried to attend white public schools faced violence. President Eisenhower sent federal troops to places such as Little Rock, Arkansas. The troops made sure that black students were able to go to the white schools.

The Supreme Court's decision, and the fight to enforce it, sparked a general movement for black civil rights. At this time, the U.S. South was very segregated. Blacks and whites had to use separate facilities in public places. Blacks and whites had their own drinking fountains, restrooms, and benches in public parks. Blacks were not served at many restaurants and could not stay at many hotels. Most southern states also had found ways to keep blacks from voting.

Now blacks, and some whites, began to take action against segregation. Students sat in at lunch counters that refused to serve blacks. African

Americans in Montgomery, Alabama, boycotted (refused to use) the city buses because they were segregated. A black minister, Dr. Martin Luther King, Jr., became a leader of this boycott. He went on to become the most outstanding leader of the civil rights movement. Real successes came in the 1960s, after the movement grew and captured the attention of the nation. But the change began in the 1950s after the *Brown v. Board of Education of Topeka* decision.

Latin America

During the 1930s, the United States had changed its policy of constantly interfering in the affairs of Latin American nations. Under the new Good Neighbor Policy, the United States would promote cooperation with Latin American countries. The United States didn't always live up to this ideal. But it did play much less of a role in Latin America after World War II than it had previously.

One cooperative move was the formation of the Organization of American States (OAS) in 1948. Twenty-one American nations joined this alliance. They met regularly to discuss mutual policies and problems in the Americas. Special agencies of the OAS helped members deal with their economic and social needs.

After World War II, Latin America continued to face many common problems. Some nations relied on just one cash crop for most of their income. Many nations had little industry and little money to build industry. They looked to the World Bank and foreign investors for the cash they needed. Often, they were unsuccessful. Not much U.S. foreign aid was directed toward Latin America.

Economic problems brought political instability. Coups were common features of Latin American politics. Often, a military group, called a junta, would overthrow an elected government. This was especially likely when a democratic government seemed to favor the common people rather than the wealthy elite.

Argentina

Argentina was largely populated by people of European background. It had modernized in the first half of the twentieth century. During the 1930s and early 1940s, it went through a series of military coups. In 1946, General Juan Perón was elected president. He ruled as a popular dictator, helped by his actress wife, Eva Perón. Perón appealed to the common people. He passed labor reforms and spent money on public works and welfare programs. His spending ran the country into a lot of debt, and his government abused human rights. When Eva Perón died of cancer in 1952, many people stopped supporting her husband.

The military came to fear Perón's power. Army officers threw him out of office in 1955. A series of civilian and military governments ruled for the next 18 years. None could control inflation or improve the poverty of the people.

Guatemala

Guatemala was ruled for many years by the dictator Jorge Ubico. A liberal elected government replaced him in 1945. As it often did, the United States saw the liberal government as communist, or leaning toward communism. When a coup overthrew this elected government in the 1950s, the United States was accused of helping. After this coup, Guatemala went through a number of civilian and military governments. Violence and civil war marked life in Guatemala from the 1960s on.

Cuba

In 1959, rebels led by Fidel Castro overthrew Cuba's dictator, Fulgencio Batista. Batista had taken control of Cuba in 1952 and suppressed people's freedoms. Castro's rebel band began fighting Batista in 1956. As Cuba's ruler, Castro set up Latin America's only communist government. The government took ownership of all land and industry. Peasants got some land. Many farms became large collectives. Personal freedoms remained shut down.

The United States was very hostile to Castro's Cuba. The Cuban government had not paid U.S. businesses for the property it took from them. Also, Castro tried to spread communism to other Latin American countries. He developed close ties to the Soviet Union. In response, the United States stopped all trade with Cuba. It broke off diplomatic relations. It prevented U.S. citizens from going to Cuba. It even helped a group of Cuban exiles who tried to invade the island in 1961 at a place called the Bay of Pigs. The invasion was a complete failure.

Cuba's close ties with the U.S.S.R. led to a Cold War crisis. The United States found out that the Soviet Union was sending nuclear missiles to Cuba and building missile sites on the island. From these sites, the U.S.S.R. could easily launch a nuclear attack against the United States. U.S. President John F. Kennedy demanded that the Soviets remove the missiles and tear down the bases. U.S. navy ships moved in to block Soviet ships bringing the missiles to Cuba. U.S. troops gathered in Florida, ready to invade Cuba and seemed that World War III might be about to start. But the Soviets backed off. They agreed to remove the missles when the United States promised not to invade the island.

Castro remained in power in Cuba into the twenty-first century. The United States remained hostile and kept the embargo in force, although there were some moves toward renewing relations with Cuba.

Topic 5

The Americas

Chapter 17: The United States and Canada

After World War II, people in the United States wanted to improve their standard of living. They wanted better jobs, better homes, and better educations. U.S. citizens also wanted changes in government programs that would make the country better. These programs included low-income housing, new educational standards, and better health care.

In addition to improvements in the United States, Americans wanted to stop the spread of communism in the rest of the world. Until the end of the 1980s, the Soviet Union was the most powerful communist country in the world. Much of the history of the United States from 1960 to the 1990s is closely linked to its relationship with the Soviet Union.

The United States in the 1960s

After World War II, the United States became a superpower, capable of influencing international events and the acts and policies of less powerful nations. The Soviet Union was also a superpower in the 1960s. The United States, a democracy, wanted to limit the power of the communist Soviet Union. The Soviet Union, on the other hand, did not want the United States to have too much power. The uneasy relationship between the Soviet Union (and other communist nations) and the United States (and the democratic countries of the Western world) was called the Cold War. It was fought mostly with words, threats, and money.

In 1960, John F. Kennedy was elected president of the United States. In 1961, Kennedy supported a revolt against Fidel Castro, the leader of Cuba (a communist country). About 1,500 Cuban exiles landed at the Bay of Pigs in Cuba. The exiles hoped others would join them and help overthrow the Soviet-backed communist government in Cuba. But the invasion failed.

Largely as a result of the Bay of Pigs invasion, the Soviet Union built missile bases in Cuba that could strike the United States. President Kennedy reacted by ordering that no offensive military equipment be delivered to Cuba. A war seemed inevitable, but was avoided when

Kennedy and the Soviet leader, Nikita Khrushchev, agreed that the Soviets would remove the missiles from Cuba.

The United States also fought the Cold War in Vietnam, a country in southeast Asia. For years, the U.S. government supplied weapons and military aid to democratic South Vietnam in its fight against communist North Vietnam. In 1965, President Lyndon B. Johnson increased U.S. involvement in the fight by sending troops to South Vietnam. Americans were divided over whether or not this was a good idea. Students across the United States joined in antiwar marches and demonstrations. But U.S. troops continued to fight in the Vietnam War for several years.

In the 1960s, another aspect of the conflict between the United States and the Soviet Union was the race into space. In 1961, the Soviets sent the first person to travel in space. In 1969, the U.S. astronaut Neil Armstrong stepped out of his spaceship, *Apollo 11*, and became the first person to walk on the moon.

Another major issue in the United States in the 1960s was the question of civil rights and the increased effort of African Americans to end discrimination against minorities. Martin Luther King, Jr., an African American minister, was a leader of the civil rights movement who led peaceful demonstrations to gain equal rights for all people. Another African American leader, Malcolm X, called for protests, revolts, and a separate nation for African Americans. In 1964, Congress passed the Civil Rights Act outlawing discrimination.

King and Kennedy were two popular, powerful leaders in the United States in the 1960s, but both died tragically. President Kennedy was assassinated while riding in an open car in Dallas, Texas, in 1963. In 1968, King was assassinated in Memphis, Tennessee. Malcolm X was also killed by a gunman in 1965, and Robert Kennedy, brother of John F. Kennedy and a senator, was assassinated in 1968.

These assassinations revealed the volatile, or unsettled, nature of the United States in the 1960s. The country was in conflict with outside forces, such as the Soviet Union, but it was also in conflict with itself. The war in Vietnam was supported by some and opposed by others. The civil rights movement met with great opposition, especially in the southern part of the United States. In the 1960s, almost all Americans were struggling to make the country a better place—but they did not always agree on how to do so.

The 1970s and 1980s

The Cold War continued between the United States and the Soviet Union. But in 1972, U.S. President Richard M. Nixon and Soviet leader Leonid Brezhnev signed the Strategic Arms Limitation Treaty (SALT I). This treaty placed limits on the number and types of nuclear arms in each country.

That same year, Nixon visited China. He worked with Chinese officials on improving communication and cooperation between the two countries. Nixon was the first U.S. president to visit the Soviet Union and China.

Nixon also ended U.S. involvement in the Vietnam War by gradually withdrawing troops. In that war, 50,000 Americans were killed or reported missing. A peace treaty was signed in 1973. This was the longest war the United States had ever fought. The cost was $120 billion.

In 1973, the Watergate scandal occurred. It began with a series of events. In 1972, President Nixon's officials broke into Democratic Party national headquarters, located in the Watergate building in Washington, D.C. They were looking for information that would help Nixon win his second term in office. The officials were caught, and a Senate investigation followed. The president faced impeachment by Congress. In 1974, Nixon became the first U.S. president to resign from office.

In 1979, the shah, or leader, of Iran fled his country and came to the United States. His government had been overtaken by revolutionaries. They demanded that the Shah be returned to their country for trial. U.S. President Jimmy Carter vowed to support the shah.

In response, the Iranians seized the American Embassy in Iran and took 63 American hostages. Carter stood firm and did not give in to the demands. Most of the hostages were not released until 1981.

During the Carter administration, inflation hurt the U.S. economy. Prices were rising, and the standard of living began to drop.

The Cold War was revived again at the end of the 1970s, when the Soviet Union invaded Afghanistan, a country in south central Asia. To protest the Soviet invasion, President Carter asked the U.S. team not to take part in the 1980 Moscow Summer Olympics.

In 1981, Ronald Reagan became president of the United States. Only half an hour after Reagan's inauguration, Iran released the American hostages. Under Reagan's administration, the largest peacetime military buildup in U.S. history occurred.

In 1987, however, Reagan and Soviet leader Mikhail Gorbachev agreed to limit the number of missiles in both countries. The Cold War was nearing an end.

Reagan's domestic policies centered on supply-side economics (a policy of huge tax cuts designed to bring new income and economic growth). The government had to borrow billions of dollars to carry out this plan.

The U.S. economy improved as a result of supply-side economics. Only seven percent of Americans were unemployed. However, while Reagan was in office, the national debt tripled.

When George H. W. Bush took office in 1989, the Cold War was almost over. A weak economy in the Soviet Union made it impossible for the Soviets to keep up with the United States in the building of nuclear weapons.

In 1989, the Berlin Wall was taken down. Soviet-backed East Berlin was no longer separated from free West Berlin. This marked the end of the Cold War.

■ OF NOTE

Space exploration continued in the 1970s and 1980s. In 1986, a tragic accident occurred. The U.S. space shuttle *Challenger* exploded soon after taking off. All six astronauts and Christa McAuliffe, a teacher from New Hampshire, were killed.

The 1990s

The Cold War was over. But a new conflict was on the horizon. In 1990, Iraqi troops invaded Kuwait, a small country in the northeast Arabian Peninsula. By taking over oil-rich Kuwait, Iraqi dictator Saddam Hussein believed he could control oil prices around the world. Troops from the

United States and its allies fought against Iraq in what is known as the Gulf War. After six weeks of military attack, Hussein admitted defeat.

In the early 1990s, the United States experienced an economic recession. Employment fell and prices rose. But, by the mid-1990s, the recession faded. After U.S. President Bill Clinton took office, the stock market rose, unemployment fell, and inflation was held in check.

In his first term, Clinton tried hard to get lesiglation passed that would provide universal health care. He was not able to get it through Congress. But he did push the North American Free Trade Agreement (NAFTA) through Congress. NAFTA lowered trade barriers among Canada, Mexico, and the United States. Clinton also supported the formation of the World Trade Organization (WTO) to help solve trade disagreements among its 117 member nations. In 1996, Clinton was elected to a second term.

During Clinton's second term, he was accused of improperly using money from a land deal before he was elected president. An investigation led to some of his friends being convicted of crimes. The president himself was not linked to these crimes. But during the investigation, Clinton lied about his relationship with a White House intern. Clinton became the third president in U.S. history to face an impeachment inquiry. In 1998, the House of Representatives formally accused him of lying under oath and other offenses. In 1999, the Senate said the president was innocent. Still, his presidency was harmed by the scandal.

A New Century Begins

The presidential election of 2000 was one of the closest in U.S. history. In fact, the U.S. Supreme Court played a major role in deciding the election. On election night, the votes in some states were too close to call. By the end of the night, neither candidate had enough electoral votes to become president.

One state in which the race was very close was Florida. Florida had 25 electoral votes. The candidate who won that state would win the presidency. The final tally said that the Republican candidate, George W. Bush, won in Florida—by about 500 votes, out of six million votes cast. Many Democrats wanted the votes in some counties to be recounted.

They argued that some ballots were not taken into account in the vote tally when they should have been. They also felt as though some voters in certain voting districts had been wrongfully turned away. They hoped that a recount would give the Democratic candidate, Al Gore, enough votes to win Florida. In the end, the Supreme Court said that there would be no recount. George W. Bush was named president.

President Bush faced great challenges. On September 11, 2001, the United States came under attack. Two hijacked airplanes crashed into the twin towers of the World Trade Center in New York City. At about the same time, another plane hit the Pentagon (U.S. military headquarters) in Washington, D.C. A fourth hijacked plane, which was also heading for Washington, crashed in Pennsylvania after the plane's passengers subdued the hijackers on board. Nearly 3,000 people died in the September 11 attacks.

No groups or individuals claimed responsibility for the attacks. But government officials immediately started to investigate. They said that the attacks were carried out by a terrorist group called al-Qaeda. Some of those involved in the attacks had been trained in camps in Afghanistan. The camps were run by a rich Saudi businessman named Osama bin Laden. Bin Laden himself was believed to be in Afghanistan. The Taliban, the group that ruled Afghanistan, refused to hand over bin Laden. With support from Great Britain, the United States started bombing Afghanistan and destroying the training camps. U.S. Troops and Afghan allies captured many suspected anti-U.S. terrorists. However, Osama bin Laden remained free.

To fight terrorism in the United States, the Bush administration created a new government department, the Department of Homeland Security. This department works to prevent terrorist attacks in the United States. It also aims to make sure individuals know what to do in the event of an attack.

President Bush also looked for other threats from abroad. He called North Korea, Iran, and Iraq "an axis of evil." The president thought that Saddam Hussein, the president of Iraq, had developed weapons that could quickly kill great numbers of people. President Bush urged the United Nations to act against Iraq. He argued that an attack on Iraq would really be self-defense. Bush suspected that Iraq had weapons that could kill many people—weapons of mass destruction. In that case, if Iraq attacked the United States, it could cause great damage. President Bush wanted to make a preemptive strike on Iraq.

In March 2003, President Bush acted on his proposal. With support from the United Kingdom, the United States attacked Iraq. Saddam Hussein's government soon collapsed. By May, the United States declared that the Iraq War was over. A temporary Iraqi government was set up. But Iraqi resistance to the U.S. occupation continued. U.S. soldiers were killed by suicide bombers. Foreign civilian workers were kidnapped, and many were executed.

Both in the United States and elsewhere, many people opposed the war in Iraq. The war was a major issue in the 2004 presidential election. Still, Bush was reelected. A majority of voters felt that Bush was more decisive than his opponent, John Kerry.

In his second term, the president still faced many problems. U.S. troops were still in Iraq and Afghanistan. At home, the economy was weaker. People were also divided about social issues, such as gay rights, stem-cell research, and social security. The first decade of the twenty-first century proved to be filled with challenges.

In 2008, the United States elected its first African-American president, Barack Obama. Faced with a difficult economic climate, he has worked to pass several reforms to stimulate the economy and provide jobs. He has called for the withdrawal of troops in Iraq by the end of 2011, and increased troop presence in Afghanistan.

In 2010, many landmark pieces of legislation were passed. The gay rights movement claimed a victory with the repeal of the military's "Don't Ask, Don't Tell" policy, which had prohibited openly gay people from serving in the U.S. Armed Forces. That same year, a health-care reform law was passed, signalling the first steps toward universal health care. The law has been strongly opposed by many congressional Republicans, and public opinion remains torn.

Canada from the 1960s to the Present

Canada is the northern neighbor of the United States. Like the United States, Canada grew economically after World War II. Much of Canada's land lies in the far northern part of the North American continent, where few people can live. Consequently, most Canadians live within 200 miles of the U.S. border. Canada and the United States agree on most international issues. However, U.S. involvement in Canadian companies has occasionally strained the relationship between the two countries.

Since the 1960s, Canada has become more and more regionalized. The Liberal Party is based in the east. The New Democratic Party dominates most of the country west of Ontario. The third leading party, the Conservatives, are spread throughout Canada.

The province of Quebec posed a problem for all the political parties. Quebec has the largest group of citizens with French heritage in Canada. French Canadians have always lived somewhat apart from the country's English majority because of differences in language, religion, and tradition.

During the 1960s, French Canadians in Quebec formed a separatist movement. The Quebec separatists wanted a stronger role in government, an end to discrimination, and recognition of their language and heritage. In 1969, the Canadian government passed laws that made French one of Canada's official languages, and created bilingual districts in most provinces. But separatists wanted more.

From 1968 until 1984 (with the exception of nine months), Canada was governed by the Liberal Party of Pierre Trudeau. Trudeau promoted the growth of French culture and a strong central government. Inflation and an eventual economic recession in the early 1980s led to the conservative government of Brian Mulroney.

Mulroney's government planned to privatize business. Mulroney also wanted to continue Canada's economic and political relationship with the United States. In 1992, the Free Trade Agreement was signed by Canada and the United States. This agreement expanded business opportunities and loosened restrictions on trade between the two neighbors. However, many Canadians complained that this would increase American pressure on the Canadians to make decisions favoring American business.

Mulroney tried to settle the separatist issue with the Meech Lake Accord of 1987. This was a constitutional provision that would recognize Quebec's status as a "distinct society" within Canada. But voters did not pass the Meech Lake Accord. Another effort in 1992, known as the Charlottetown Accord, was also defeated.

In 1993, Kim Campbell became Canada's first female prime minister. Lacking government support, Campbell was replaced five months later by the Liberal Party's Jean Chrétien. His government raised taxes, cut health-care spending, and reduced the rising budget deficit.

The issue of Quebec separatism had still not been solved. In 1995, voters in Quebec were asked if they wanted to secede, or become independent, from the rest of Canada. By a small majority, voters said "no." By the early years of the twenty-first century, support for separatism was weakening.

In the early 1990s, another group in Canada called attention to their claims for self-government. These were the native peoples of Canada, whose ancestors lived on the land before Europeans arrived. Different groups, such as Mohawks and Peigans, blocked roads, rail lines, and bridges. In 1999, the government agreed that Indians and Inuit had the right to govern themselves. With the support of people in the region, the Northwest Territories were separated in two. About 17,500 Inuit lived in the eastern part of the region. This part became a self-governing homeland for the Inuit. It is called Nunavut. This means "our land" in Inuktitut, the language of the Inuit.

The September 11, 2001, attack on the United States also affected Canada. The border between the two countries is over 5,000 miles long. The Canadian and U.S. governments have worked together to find ways to keep the border safe. Canadian troops took part in the bombing campaign of Afghanistan to destroy terrorist training camps there. But in 2003, Canada decided not to join the United States-led attack on Iraq. This caused some resentment in the United States. However, despite their different foreign policies, the two nations still work together to solve shared problems.

In 2003, after 10 years in office, Jean Chrétien retired. Paul Martin, who was Canada's finance minister, became prime minister. He was succeeded by Stephen Harper in 2006.

Like the United States, Canada suffered from a poor economy in the first few years of the new century. Unemployment went up. Fewer jobs were available in manufacturing. Also, Canada's health-care system is paid for by the government. As health-care costs rise, the government must find ways to keep the system going. However, Canada has rich natural resources and a skilled workforce. Because of them, Canada's economic future is sound.

Issues and Trends

From the 1960s to the 1990s, people in the United States and Canada were concerned with sexual equality, a safer environment, and the effects of science and technology. Women married later and had children later. More and more women entered the workplace.

But women weren't always treated fairly. As a result, they formed groups and started the women's liberation movement. This movement demanded that women be freed from sexual discrimination. It also called for women and men to earn equal pay for equal work.

The environment was another major issue. People saw pollution robbing them of clean air and safe water. They realized that forests and wildlife were disappearing. Citizens pressed for new laws to protect these natural resources. In the United States, Congress has passed laws to limit pollution. The United States and Canada have also pledged to work together to reduce water pollution in the Great Lakes. However, challenges remain. U.S. attempts to develop oil reserves in Alaska have caused disagreements in both the United States and Canada.

Developments in technology and science also raised a number of environmental issues. During World War II, the government supported scientists who developed more effective ways to fight the war. After the war, the government helped to adapt wartime discoveries to peaceful use.

However, North Americans had to cope with many resulting problems. Forests were destroyed to support industries such as mining and logging.

Scientists warned that too many fluorocarbons (chemicals used in refrigerators, air conditioners, and aerosol cans) were destroying Earth's ozone layer, exposing us to harmful ultraviolet radiation.

Technology allowed North America to remain a leader in the global economy. Better communication through cellular telephones and computers let nations conduct business quickly. The United States and Canada had the necessary technology and industry to move ahead.

■ OF NOTE

The women's liberation movement fought hard to get the Equal Rights Amendment (ERA) passed. It was first written in 1921 by Alice Paul, who worked for women's rights. The bill was introduced to Congress the same year but was defeated. It was reintroduced every year after that. The bill failed each time. The Equal Rights Amendment finally passed Congress in 1972. However, it had not been ratified by all the states by the 1982 cut-off date.

Chapter 18: Mexico and Central America

Mexico

In the 1960s, Mexico's economy was underdeveloped, and its government was unstable. Most of Mexico's people were poor and uneducated. In 1968, students in Mexico City protested against the government. The police opened fire and killed hundreds. This was known as the Tlatelolco Massacre. Mexicans were outraged and demanded reform.

In the 1970s, Mexican presidents Luis Echeverría Alvarez and Jose López Portillo made some popular changes. Imprisoned student protestors were released. The government gave millions of acres of land to the poor. Social security, housing, and transportation programs were developed and increased. Limited freedom of the press was granted. However, prices and unemployment rose.

During the 1970s, Mexico became a major oil-producing nation. Based on what it expected to earn in the future from oil, the government borrowed $80 billion from other nations. By the mid-1980s, oil prices fell, and Mexico could not repay its debts. To raise money, Mexico sold some of its state-owned businesses to private companies. However, Mexico's debt and unemployment grew larger.

In the 1980s, Mexicans were unhappy with United States-Mexican relations. America had tightened its borders against illegal immigrants and drug trafficking. Both countries felt the burden of enforcing this policy. In addition, many blamed the Mexican government for its inability to sufficiently help disaster victims in the Mexico City earthquake of 1985.

In the early 1990s, President Carlos Salinas de Gortari's government worked to stop corruption, drug trafficking, and human-rights abuses. But one important issue was about to explode. For centuries, the Maya and other native peoples of Mexico had been badly treated. In 1994, a group of peasants in southern Mexico rebelled against the government. They called themselves the Zapatistas. The Zapatistas demanded better living conditions and health care for Mexican Indians.

Ernesto Zedillo Ponce de León faced these issues when he became president in 1994. He attempted to improve the Mexican population's social conditions. He worked to ease the conflict with the United States over border problems. But his officials and family members were accused of helping the drug trade. His police were charged with violating human rights. By the end of the 1990s, Zedillo was rapidly losing popular support.

For 70 years, Mexico was run by the Institutional Revolutionary Party, known as the PRI. In 1997, candidates from other parties won Senate seats. In 2000, the PRI presidential candidate lost to Vicente Fox.

The Fox government faced serious problems. Crime rates in Mexico were very high. There was corruption in the government, the civil service, and the police. Income in the country was unevenly distributed. Some people were very rich, and many were very, very poor. Fox committed his government to wide-ranging reforms. In 2006, he was succeeded by Felipe Calderón, in the closest election the country has ever seen. Calderón's presidency has been defined by a crackdown on drug trafficking and improved access to health care.

President Fox has also worked to address the problem of illegal immigration from Mexico to the United States. Thousands of Mexicans cross the border into the United States every year, looking for work. Many of them do not have the papers they need to enter the United States, so they cross the border illegally. Many of them die of thirst or exhaustion in the harsh land they are trying to cross. Many more are stopped by border patrols and sent back to Mexico. Illegal immigration and border control continue to be issues today.

Central America

Central America is made up of seven countries: Nicaragua, Panama, El Salvador, Costa Rica, Honduras, Guatemala, and Belize. The Cold War was also fought in this part of the world. For example, U.S. President John Kennedy offered aid to Central America. He did this to help ease the economic and social problems there. The United States hoped that, as a result, more democratic and socially responsible governments would develop. However, U.S. financial aid was too little to help Central America's huge financial problems.

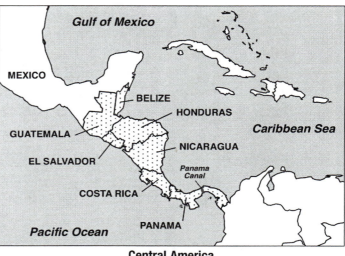

Central America

From the 1960s to the 1980s, much of Central America was caught up in years of bloody civil wars. The rich and powerful dominated the poor lower classes. Governments abused basic human rights.

In the 1970s, Central American states borrowed from bankers. At that time, banks were strong. But, by the 1980s, high interest rates put Central America in a state of financial crisis.

Nicaragua

The United States set up military bases in Nicaragua in 1912. Many Nicaraguans did not like the U.S. military presence. Guerrillas, led by Augusto Sandino, tried to force the United States out. To help the American soldiers, the U.S. government trained a Nicaraguan army called the National Guard. Their commander was General Anastasio Somoza. When the United States left Nicaragua in 1932, the National Guard was well trained.

In 1934, General Somoza had Sandino assassinated. Soon after, Somoza seized power. He became dictator. For the next 44 years, the Somoza family—father and sons—ruled Nicaragua. By 1967, the Somoza family owned one fourth of the land in Nicaragua. They also owned most of the country's businesses. In the 1970s, the United States stopped supporting the Somoza regime.

Most Nicaraguans were poor and illiterate. They had suffered under the Somoza government. For years, different groups had tried to overthrow the dictator. In the late 1970s, a number of different groups joined together. They included peasants, priests, Marxists, and members of Nicaragua's middle class. This anti-Somoza alliance was led by a group called the Sandinista National Liberation Front (FSLN), or Sandinistas. They took their name from assassinated rebel Augusto Sandino.

In 1979, the Sandinistas overthrew the Somoza government. The new government set about reorganizing Nicaragua's economy. It nationalized industries, such as banking and mining. The government set up programs to teach peasants to read and write. They improved health care in rural areas.

At first, the United States offered help. But many FSLN leaders were Marxists. Fearing a communist regime in Nicaragua, the United States cut off aid.

At the same time, the Sandinistas were losing support in Nicaragua. Their economic reforms included taking private property away from landowners and giving it to other people. An anti-Sandinista group called the Contras soon arose. The United States gave the Contras arms and military training. A new civil war began, between the Sandinistas and the Contras.

In the 1980s, presidents from Latin and Central America worked on peace negotiations. The plans called for democratic reforms, the ending of foreign support for rebels, and cease-fires in all guerrilla wars. In 1987, when Daniel Ortega was president, Nicaragua was among five states that signed a peace plan.

In Nicaragua's general elections of 1990, the Sandinistas lost. Violeta Barrios de Chamorro, of the United Nicaragua Opposition, claimed victory. Her government reversed many Sandinista policies. For example, her reforms favored education, trade, and private business. Seeking peace with the rebels, the Chamorro government reduced the Nicaraguan military. In return, the Contras agreed to break up their army. However, the conflict between Contra and Sandinista leaders continued into the 1990s. In 1996, voters elected Arnoldo Alemán, who called for more unity among all Nicaraguans.

After Alemán's term ended, officials found that he had stolen from the state. While many Nicaraguans live on less than a dollar a day, Alemán stole millions of dollars from the state. The new president, Enrique Bolaños, promised to reform the government and stop corruption. In 2004, the World Bank agreed to cancel most of Nicaragua's debt to the Bank. In 2007, Daniel Ortega, a Sandinista, again took office as the president of Nicaragua.

Panama

Panama was much like other Central American countries in the 1960s. Military governments ruled the country. Unemployment soared. Public protests and mob violence occurred regularly.

Panama had one big difference from its neighbors—the Panama Canal. Since 1903, the United States had owned and operated the Canal. The canal treaty gave the United States complete control over the Panama Canal and the land around it. It also gave the U.S. government broad rights to act in Panamanian affairs. This meant that the United States influenced Panama's politics and economics. The United States supported Panama's corrupt government in order to keep other foreign influence out of the area.

However, feelings of nationalism in Panama grew in the 1960s. Riots were common by the middle of the decade. In 1968, the wealthy landowners lost government control to the National Guard. General Omar Torrijos, an authoritarian leader, promised to help the poor. Torrijos negotiated a new canal treaty with the United States. The new treaty said that the United States would hand over control of the Canal to Panama by the end of 1999.

Torrijos died in a plane crash in 1981. The next year, General Manuel Noriega became head of the National Guard. Noriega had once worked for the U.S. Central Intelligence Agency, or CIA. He increased the Guard's power over Panama's political life. Noriega soon took over as president.

In 1988, the U.S. government accused Noriega of drug smuggling and other crimes. The next year, in Panama's presidential election, Noriega used violence and fraud to defeat his rival. U.S. President George H. W. Bush called for worldwide pressure to make Noriega step down. Then, in December, President Bush ordered an invasion of Panama. Noriega was arrested and taken to the United States to stand trial. He was found guilty and sentenced to 40 years in prison.

To keep the military from gaining power again, Panama broke up the army. A constitutional amendment bans forming a permanent army in Panama.

The United States handed over control of the Canal to Panama in December, 1999. Since then, Panama's rulers have worked to improve the economy. Today, almost two thirds of Panama's population work in service industries, such as banking, shipping, and tourism. To make sure the larger ships being built today can use the Canal, a canal widening project has been proposed.

In 2009, Ricardo Martinelli became president of Panama, winning by the second-largest majority of votes in Panama's history. Five years earlier, he had received little more than 5% of the vote. Since coming into office, he has worked to reduce poverty and increase the minimum wage.

El Salvador

El Salvador, the smallest nation in Central America, has a long history of peasant uprisings and protests. A small group of wealthy land and business owners governed the country with the support of the military for a long time. After World War II, the United States feared communism would spread to El Salvador. So, the United States made an alliance, or agreement of support, with the oligarchy and military.

By the early 1970s, El Salvador was one of the most industrialized countries in Latin America. However, most businesses belonged to a few very wealthy families. Most El Salvadorans were poor. People started to demand changes.

The government and rich landowners were very conservative and unwilling to change. They were afraid there would be a revolution. To prevent this, they hired death squads. These groups killed rebels and leaders who called for change.

One leader who was killed was Oscar Romero, a popular Roman Catholic bishop who worked for human rights in El Salvador. Romero was killed while he was saying Mass. In response, the rebels increased their attacks on the government. A bloody civil war broke out. Fighting continued for 12 years. Finally, in 1992, the government and the rebels agreed to a peace treaty.

Then, as the country began to recover from the years of war, a series of natural disasters hit. A 1998 hurricane left thousands homeless. Crops, roads, and industries were destroyed. In 2001, two major earthquakes struck El Salvador a month apart. Again, many people lost their homes.

The years of poverty, civil war, and natural disasters have left El Salvadoran society in disorder. The rate of violent crime in El Salvador is very high.

In 2009, Mauricio Funes was elected president of El Salvador. His administration has passed many social reforms to alleviate poverty, but criminal activity remains a serious threat in the country.

Chapter 19: The Caribbean

The Caribbean is a region of islands located south of Florida and north of South America in the Caribbean Sea. Foreign control has greatly influenced the Caribbean nations. Some of the islands are independent. Others are tied to mother countries. In this chapter, we will discuss four Caribbean states: Cuba, Jamaica, Haiti, and Puerto Rico.

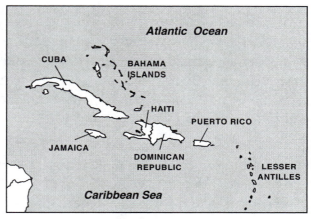

The Caribbean

Because of the Caribbean's location, the United States recognized these islands as a potential threat. After World War II, the worry was the spread of communism.

The United States knew that many of the Caribbean islands were ruled by dictators. Often, these dictators denied civil and human rights to their people.

However, the Cold War was in effect. Even though it knew about the dictators' abuses, the United States invested in plantations and factories on the Caribbean islands. The United States provided other forms of financial and military aid, too. As a result, most of the Caribbean nations remained free of communist control.

One example of Cold War conflict occurred on a Caribbean island during the 1980s. U.S. marines invaded Grenada, in the Lesser Antilles, after a communist group overtook the government. The invasion successfully drove the communists out of power. By the end of the Cold War, tension in the Caribbean had lessened.

Cuba

In the late twentieth century, Cuba was known to the world mainly for its leader, Fidel Castro. In 1959, Castro and his guerrillas overthrew Cuba's dictator, Fulgencio Batista y Zaldívar. Castro executed his opponents and legalized the Cuban Communist party. As a result, Cuba's relationship with the world changed. The United States and other democratic countries lost Cuba as an ally.

Castro was a dynamic leader, whom the majority of the people supported. Fulfilling his promises to the poor, Castro took over large estates and factories. Landowners were forced to give up their property to the government, and major businesses were nationalized. This included foreign holdings, such as U.S. telephone companies and sugar fields. Most United States-Cuban diplomatic and economic ties were broken in the early 1960s.

Castro's new government policies were welcomed by Cuba's workers and peasants. Prior to Castro's rule, unemployment had been as high as 20 percent. The new government created jobs. And new laws prohibited racial and sexual inequality. Castro's programs nearly wiped out illiteracy. Castro instituted free health and educational services. Moreover, all Cuban citizens were guaranteed employment.

However, this government approach angered the upper and middle classes. The wealthy lost their property and their civil rights. Their political influence disappeared. Batista supporters fled the country. A great number came to the United States. Those without money climbed on run-down, dangerous boats headed for U.S. shores. These exiles formed large Cuban communities within the United States.

In another Cold War action, the United States placed an embargo on one of Cuba's leading exports, sugar. The United States did not want to help support a communist nation. This was one reason the U.S. government helped pay for the Bay of Pigs invasion. But, America decided against sending its own troops to take Castro out of power. Instead, it organized other Latin American countries to boycott, or cease normal trade with, Cuba. However, this boycott did not weaken Cuba. Instead, Castro asked the Soviet Union for assistance. This strengthened Cuba's ties to communism.

From the mid-1970s to 1989, Cuban troops fought as proxies for Soviet troops in wars in Angola, Ethiopia, and Nicaragua. By the late 1980s, the Soviet Union was undertaking some democratic reforms. But Castro stayed with communism.

The fall of communism in the Soviet Union and in the Eastern European countries meant Cuba lost the financial support of those nations, too. The international boycott continued. The Cuban economy suffered. Yet, Castro stayed in control until illness forced him to resign in February 2008. Today, Cuba is ruled by Fidel Castro's brother, Raúl Castro.

Jamaica

Jamaica is a small island south of Cuba. In 1962, Jamaica declared its independence from Great Britain. It is still considered part of the Commonwealth of Nations, however.

Jamaica has full dominion status, which means that the nation is self-governing but united with other nations in the Commonwealth. Queen Elizabeth II of England is Queen of Jamaica.

In 1967, Jamaicans held their first general election as an independent country. In 1972, Michael Manley became prime minister of Jamaica. Under his government, censorship of information, such as literature, news, and motion pictures was eliminated. He also lifted the ban on civil liberties, or the freedom of speech and the right to public assembly.

However, Jamaica's poverty was too great to support Manley's programs. The economy almost collapsed. In addition, elections in Jamaica were often accompanied by violence. In an attempt to fix the country's financial problems, Manley strengthened ties with Cuba.

In 1980, Edward Seaga was elected prime minister. Seaga had to face the problems of overpopulation and unemployment. He privatized state enterprises and cut off official relations with Cuba. The United States responded by sending economic aid. But Jamaica's economy worsened.

In October 2011, Andrew Holness, who worked with Edward Seaga in the 1990s, became prime minister. However, Jamaica's economy still faces challenges.

Haiti

Haiti lies east of Cuba and northeast of Jamaica in the Caribbean. In the late 1950s, Haiti elected a former medical doctor as president. This president, François Duvalier, was called "Papa Doc." Duvalier took power from the minority group, the mulattoes (or people of mixed black and white heritage), and gave it to the majority black population. The wealthy and influential mulattoes criticized Duvalier for his actions.

To strengthen his position, Duvalier reduced the armed forces. He created the Tontons Macoutes, a force of secret police. Haitians called these violent police "bogeymen." They controlled Duvalier's opponents through terror and assassination. Duvalier survived more than one assassination attempt on his own life. Duvalier had amazing power in Haiti. In 1964, he even elected himself president for life. By the end of Duvalier's political career, Haiti was still coping with a poor economy. The United States withdrew most of its economic aid. Due to the nation's violence, tourism decreased dramatically. Before dying in 1971, Duvalier handed the government over to his 19-year-old son, Jean-Claude Duvalier.

The young Duvalier, known as "Baby Doc," was also named president for life. He became the youngest president in the world. Duvalier wanted to win the world's respect. He increased tourism and received more U.S. aid. But Haiti still had high unemployment. Political rights were limited. The Tontons Macoutes continued to terrorize the people. In 1985 and 1986, Haitians demonstrated against the poor living conditions, high unemployment, and limited political freedom. Most of the country's wealthy and educated citizens left Haiti during Duvalier's presidency. As a result, Haiti became the poorest nation in the West. Unable to hold onto his power, Duvalier and his wife escaped to France in 1986. A series of presidents followed, but all lost power quickly.

In December 1990, Haiti held its first presidential election free of political corruption. A Roman Catholic priest, Jean-Bertrand Aristide, won by a landslide. Aristide received support from the government's parliament, or law-making body. But the military removed him from power. Aristide was exiled from the country. The United States protested by stopping its trade with Haiti. Like the Cubans, tens of thousands of Haitians tried to emigrate to the United States by boat. But this time the

United States refused to take most of them. Instead, the United States and the United Nations tried to convince Haiti to return Aristide to office.

In 1993, the Haitian government agreed to allow Aristide's return. But Aristide was delayed by Haiti's political trouble and by military violence. His return did not bring peace. In 2004, after a violent uprising, Aristide was again forced into exile.

In January 2010, a 7.0-magnitude earthquake struck Haiti, causing massive damage to its capital, Port-au-Prince. Homes, schools, and government buildings were destroyed, and water contamination led to widespread illness. The country continues to rebuild, though recovery has taken years.

Puerto Rico

By the 1960s, Puerto Rico was considered a commonwealth under the U.S. government. This meant that Puerto Rico was a self-governing territory associated with the United States. Puerto Rico is governed by a governor.

In 1967, Puerto Ricans voted against becoming America's fifty-first state. Many Puerto Ricans argued that either statehood or independence would destroy the Puerto Rican economy. As a commonwealth, Puerto Ricans enjoyed U.S. citizenship and social benefits. As a result, the economy grew quickly.

Luis Ferrer was elected governor of Puerto Rico in 1968. He increased wages and created housing programs. New roads, copper mines, and an airport contributed to the commonwealth's progress. The agriculture industry was also upgraded.

Elected in 1973, Governor Rafael Hernandez Colon developed health programs and supported education. He openly criticized Cuba for interfering in Puerto Rican affairs. Colon agreed that Puerto Rico should remain a commonwealth. But he also saw room for greater autonomy. He asked for greater control of immigration, communications, and transportation.

Colon said that Puerto Rico should stop relying on the United States for economic aid. He wanted Puerto Ricans to remain U.S. citizens. And, he didn't want to upset military agreements with the United States.

Colon's ideas received mixed reactions in the United States. President Gerald Ford believed that Puerto Rico should become the fifty-first state. Colon strongly disagreed. But Ford's successor, Jimmy Carter, agreed that Puerto Rico needed to be more independent.

Puerto Ricans were split on the idea, too. Some wanted greater autonomy, and some wanted statehood. Still others wanted independence. Some members of the independence movement were linked to terrorist acts, such as bombings in the city of San Juan during the 1970s.

In both 1993 and 1998, voters in Puerto Rico were again asked to vote on the question of statehood. Both times, voters turned down statehood.

Chapter 20: South America

During the second half of the twentieth century, countries in South America played a major role in global conflicts. This was because of the Cold War. Democratic nations feared a communist revolution in South America through the end of the 1980s. The 1970s and the early 1980s witnessed the height of human-rights abuses in South America. Political powers tortured and killed their opponents in untold numbers. Today, political killings in South America are fewer, but still occurring.

With the end of the Cold War in 1989, world attention focused less on communism and more on another kind of war in South America. This was the war on drugs. The coca leaf, from which the drug cocaine is made, became a staple crop for many South American farmers. Drug barons who ran illegal refineries in Colombia made that nation the drug center of South America. Peru and Bolivia are also large producers of coca crops.

South America

The environment became another issue of global concern in the 1980s. In Brazil, vast stretches of rain forest continued to be destroyed. Scientists predict that the imbalance created by the rain forest's destruction will ultimately affect all life on Earth.

Brazil

In the 1960s, the Brazilian military overthrew the presidency. Until 1985, the country was run by a series of generals and their officers. The government controlled wages and helped businesses with low-cost loans.

At the time, the military's economic policies were called the "Brazilian miracle." Businesses made more money. There were more jobs. But, Brazil's miracle had a price. The great economic growth helped the rich. But, the poor worked longer hours for less pay. By the end of the 1980s, inflation was extremely high. Brazil's foreign debt grew to $100 billion, the highest in the world. Brazil was a major industrial nation. But the majority of Brazilians still lived in poverty.

By the mid-1980s, the military was ready to return the government to the people. In 1985, José Sarney, Brazil's first civilian (nonmilitary) president, took office. Sarney's political and economic policies looked hopeful. His new programs guaranteed work for all people. Wage and price freezes slowed inflation for a brief time. Brazilians were given greater freedom to speak out. But inflation soon rose again, and the economy was not greatly improved.

In 1990, Fernando Collor de Mello was elected president. He promised to reduce inflation and to halt government corruption. He did neither. Instead, unemployment rose. And his government was involved in a scandal. Collor de Mello was accused of stashing millions of dollars in secret bank accounts. He was charged with corruption and forced to resign.

In 2002, Luiz Inacio Lula da Silva was elected president. A former shoeshine boy, Lula is seen by some as a working-class hero. As president, Lula worked to improve the economy. He reduced the amount the government owes and raised the minimum wage. He served two terms, and in 2010, Lula's former chief of staff, Dilma Rousseff, was elected president. She is the first woman to hold Brazil's highest office.

Argentina

As you have learned, Juan Perón ruled Argentina from 1946 to 1955. The series of governments that followed failed to improve the economy or ease the poverty of most of the people. Perón's loyal followers pressed for his return to power from exile.

In 1972, the military leaders allowed Perón to come back. The next year he was elected president. Isabel Perón, his third wife, was elected vice president. When Perón died a year later, she became the first female president in South America. But political terror and economic decline came with her government. A military junta, or group of leaders, overthrew her government in 1976.

The new dictatorship did no better for Argentina. Police used torture and murder against their opponents. As many as 36,000 people died under this government. This was the bloodiest reign in Argentina's history. In 1982, the junta made a surprise invasion of the Falkland Islands. Known as las Islas Malvinas in Spanish, they were located off the southern tip of Argentina. The Falklands were under British rule. In response to the attack to take control of the islands, Great Britain crushed Argentina's military forces. Angry and embarrassed, Argentines demanded a new government. Slowly, democracy returned to Argentina.

Elections in 1989 brought Carlos Saul Menem to office. He was able to boost Argentina's poor economy. But his reforms did not benefit the poor. However, public support won him the presidency again in 1995.

In 2001, the economy fell apart. Argentina could not pay its debts to other countries. The banking industry fell into crisis. Middle-class people lost much of their savings. Soon, more than half the population was living in poverty.

In 2003, Nestor Kirchner became president. He worked to manage Argentina's foreign debt. In 2007, his wife, Cristina Fernández de Kirchner, ran for office and won. She advocates for human rights and continues to work toward poverty awareness.

There is also still much concern about the "disappeared"—people who disagreed with the junta and were never seen again. Laws had been passed to protect former military officers from being tried for human rights abuses. These laws were overturned in 2003. Still, many Argentines may never know what happened to family members who "disappeared."

Colombia

Technically, Colombia has long been a democracy. However, plantation owners and other wealthy business people had the real political power for years. In the 1960s, guerrillas organized the poor to fight the government. But the government responded with violence. By the mid-1960s, over 200,000 of the landless poor were dead.

The 1960s were a period of economic hardship in Colombia. Inflation was uncontrollable. The unemployment rate climbed above ten percent. In 1966, Carlos Lleras Restrepo was elected president, and the situation improved.

Under Restrepo, the economy became more stable. The government worked more democratically. More people moved to the cities for jobs and a better life. But the wealth was spread unevenly.

In addition, the world's illegal drug market opened up. Rich soil made Colombia a major grower of marijuana and coca plants. Coca leaves supplied the world's cocaine market. Through the 1970s, Colombia's crime rate increased, and the drug problem grew worse.

President Virgilio Barco Vargas began his presidency in 1986. He promised to return political, economic, and social order to Colombia. In the 1990s, later presidents offered to do the same. But the drug trade remained an unsolvable problem. During the 1990 presidential elections, drug traffickers murdered three presidential candidates. The drug lords were fighting against tougher drug-crime programs.

Cesar Gaviria Trujillo, a man noted for his tough antidrug stand, became president in 1990. Under Trujillo's government, the leading drug cartel lost power. But other cartels took its place. The situation had not improved by the beginning of the twenty-first century.

OF NOTE

Coffee is Colombia's major export. It makes up 25 percent of all products the nation exports each year. Much of the coffee consumed by people all over the world comes from Colombia. Other Colombian exports include rice, bananas, and sugar.

Peru

Before the 1960s, Peru was ruled by members of the wealthy class. They supported those in the military and in business. The workers and the poor were neglected. Peru's economy was poor. The country depended on sales from exports such as sugar, meat, and copper. When these products didn't sell, workers lost jobs, and prices went up.

In 1968, the military took control of the government and placed Juan Velasco Alvarado in power. To secure his control, Alvarado arrested his opponents. He took away many civil rights, such as free speech. However, he helped the poor. His government seized the land of nearly 75 percent of the wealthy landowners. Alvarado gave much of this land to poor Peruvians. The poor formed small cooperatives to run the farms. Alvarado also seized foreign-owned companies and gave them to Peruvians. He created jobs and built schools.

In 1975, the military replaced Alvarado with General Francisco Morales Bermúdez. The Bermúdez government failed to change Peru for the better. The military decided to return the government to the people. In the 1980 free presidential elections, the people chose Fernando Belaúnde Terry as their leader.

Terry encouraged foreign investment, and imports increased. But Peruvian workers lost jobs because their sales decreased. Interest rates on the foreign debt rose. Peru had difficulty paying. And conditions worsened for the poor. Radical guerrilla movements sprang up.

One guerilla group, the Shining Path, fought for communism. The Shining Path paid for its operation with money from Peruvian drug traffickers. This increased the government's fight against the rebels.

In 1985, a new president, Alan Garcia Perez, was elected. He lowered Peru's payment on the foreign debt, which had neared $14 million. He tried to stop human rights abuses and the sale of drugs. However, he couldn't end inflation, guerrilla wars, or drug crime.

Perez lost his office to Alberto Fujimori in the 1990 elections. Fujimori said his reforms would solve Peru's problems. Instead, he created a dictatorship by suspending the constitution and the congress. Fujimori also tried to make the economic and social decisions that would improve

Peru's living conditions. He was not successful. In 2001, Alejandro Toledo Manrique was elected president. Peru's economy finally began to expand, and it was one of the fastest growing in Latin America. However, charges of political corruption and turmoil continued to plague the nation. In 2011, Ollanta Humala was elected president of Peru.

Issues and Trends

Latin America includes the vast lands of Mexico, Central America, the Caribbean, and South America. While each country has a unique history, certain issues and trends have marked all of the Latin American nations in the late twentieth century. For example, living standards have changed as people have flocked to the cities. Women have taken on new roles. And industry and technology have tried to keep up with the changes.

Latin America's population soared after the 1960s. By the 1990s, the number of people was near 400 million. This was a particular hardship for the poor. Some owned family plots of land that were divided among many family members. This meant that each generation owned smaller parcels of land. Wealthy farm owners held the best land. And most of the people worked for them. Many barely made a living. They were forced to borrow money from the large landowners just to get by.

Urban areas attracted people hoping to make a better living. By the late 1990s, 70 percent of the Latin American population lived in urban areas. They worked in factories, stores, and small businesses. Most worked under poor conditions. They were paid low wages for long hours. Unemployment ran high. Many could not afford proper housing and lived in poverty. Many turned to rebel groups for help.

The Zapatistas in Mexico and the Sandinistas in Nicaragua claimed to represent these people against corrupt governments. Still other people entered the illegal drug trade. Peru and Colombia were among the countries with the highest drug crime. Even with all of these problems, urban areas did provide some benefits for Latin Americans. Children received a better education. And people were closer to government health care.

The 1960s also saw change within the family. All of the Latin American countries gave females the right to vote by 1961. Like women in North

America, Latin American women were moving into the workforce. But they were usually still expected to play the traditional role of wife and mother. Women organized and became a political force. They protested for gender equality in the workplace. In Argentina, women demonstrated for human rights. In Nicaragua and Cuba, they joined guerrilla movements. The liberation of women was slow in Latin America. But by the late 1990s, women were making important gains in areas such as education and health care.

To meet the needs of their people, Latin American nations tried to modernize their industries. Most countries invested in farming to reduce their food imports. They asked other nations, such as the United States and the Soviet Union, to supply them with new technology. And they traded in the global economy. But most Latin American nations could not supply their businesses with the latest computers. Their communications systems were outdated. And the more advanced countries took advantage of the workers.

Foreign companies set up factories in Latin America and hired cheap labor. The money these companies earned went to their foreign owners. And, there were environmental dangers, too. Countries lost rain forests as they were cut down to build farms and roads. Large tracts of land became infertile because of overplanting and overgrazing. In the 1990s, the nations of Latin America tried to solve these problems themselves. But they also sought support from the international community.

Topic 6

Europe and the Former Soviet Union

Chapter 21: Western Europe

Nations of Western Europe

The region known as Western Europe includes Ireland, the United Kingdom, and 11 countries on the western side of the continent of Europe. The 11 countries are France, Spain, Portugal, Italy, Switzerland, Germany, Belgium, the Netherlands, Austria, Denmark, and Luxembourg. Western Europe is not physically divided from other parts of Europe.

Here, we will look closely at the United Kingdom, France, and Germany. The histories of these three Western European countries illustrate the issues faced by many countries in this region in the late twentieth century and into the twenty-first century.

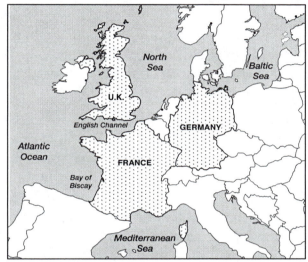

Western Europe

The United Kingdom

The United Kingdom, or Great Britain, consists of England, Wales, Scotland, and Northern Ireland.

The United Kingdom faced many economic problems starting in the 1960s. Its economy was weaker than those of other parts of Western Europe. British goods did not compete well with those of other nations. Unemployment was high. Labor unrest continued, because wages were poor. Its factories were old and unable to produce goods cheaply.

Great Britain's two major political parties, Conservative and Labour, have taken turns leading the country since 1960. Each party has a different approach to the country's economy. In the early 1960s, most of Great Britain's industries were nationalized, or turned over to government ownership. The government supplied health care and other services to workers.

From 1964 to 1968, Harold Wilson served as Britain's prime minister. Wilson was a member of the Labour Party. He dealt with trade-union unrest and low labor productivity. He also dealt with problems between Roman Catholics and Protestants in Northern Ireland. Protestants wanted to remain part of the United Kingdom, while the Irish Roman Catholics wanted to be part of the nation of Ireland. One Roman Catholic group, the Irish Republican Army (IRA), set off bombs and fought with British forces in Northern Ireland and in other parts of the United Kingdom. Tension between the two groups continued to be a major problem in the United Kingdom through the late 1990s.

In 1979, Margaret Thatcher, a Conservative, became Great Britain's first female prime minister. While she was leader, Thatcher led Great Britain in a war with Argentina over ownership of the Falkland Islands. She privatized some British industries. In the 1980s, she took away the civil liberties of suspected IRA terrorists. Thatcher also took a very strong stand against communism. Her strong, confident approach to issues earned her the nickname "The Iron Lady." Thatcher served until 1990.

John Major, another member of the Conservative Party, replaced Thatcher as prime minister in 1990. He was immediately faced with a recession, or period of declining economic activity. Major also faced continued problems in Northern Ireland. In 1995, he helped bring about a cease-fire between the two sides, but it lasted only a brief time.

In 1997, Tony Blair became prime minister. Blair belonged to the Labour Party. His victory showed the growing dissatisfaction of the British with the way the Conservatives were running the economy. Blair's government was committed to moving power away from the central government in London to local government.

Blair became very involved in finding solutions for the problems in Northern Ireland. In 1998, after 21 months of negotiation, a peace accord (agreement) was signed. Shortly after the peace accord was signed, a new

Northern Ireland Assembly was created. This Assembly had the power to pass laws on many topics that relate to Northern Ireland. Since then, events in Northern Ireland have led to suspending the Assembly and restoring direct rule from London.

In 1999, two other parts of the United Kingdom also gained some say in their own government. In Scotland, the Scottish Parliament had been closed in 1707. A new Scottish Parliament was elected in 1999. This Parliament can pass laws on a variety of topics, including health, education, housing, economic development, and some aspects of transport. Scotland has its own government, the Scottish Executive.

The first elections for the National Assembly for Wales also took place in 1999. The Assembly does not have the power to pass laws, or to overturn laws passed by Parliament. However, it is able to amend, or change, laws. The Assembly develops policies for issues, such as economic development, transport, housing, the environment, and the Welsh language.

Since the 1990s, Britain has also played a role in other parts of the world. In 1999, British troops were part of the multinational forces in Kosovo, a province in Serbia and Montenegro. In 2000, British forces stepped in to help foreign citizens caught up in the civil war in Sierra Leone. After the September 11, 2001, attacks in the United States, Tony Blair was a strong supporter of the U.S. campaign against terrorism. British forces took part in air strikes on targets in Afghanistan. In 2003, Blair also supported the U.S. government in the war on Iraq.

In 2007, Tony Blair resigned amid low approval ratings and accusations of misleading Parliament. Gordon Brown then became prime minister until 2010, when David Cameron took over.

France

During World War II, France was occupied (invaded and held) by Germany. France, like other nations in Western Europe, recovered slowly from the social and economic upsets caused by the war. The French people saw their prosperity slowly increase in the late twentieth century.

France is ruled by a president and a national assembly. In 1958, Charles de Gaulle, a World War II hero, became president. He held that office until 1969. In 1960, after many years of fighting, de Gaulle met with leaders from the French colony of Algeria. As a result of those meetings, Algeria became an independent nation. De Gaulle brought stability and international power to France in the 1960s.

In 1968, France refused to sign the Nuclear Nonproliferation Treaty, a treaty designed to limit the number of nations that could test and possess nuclear weapons. In the 1980s and 1990s, France tested nuclear weapons in the Pacific Ocean. This testing was strongly criticized by many nations.

Georges Pompidou became president after de Gaulle. Pompidou changed the focus of government. He was more supportive of business and less involved in international affairs. Pompidou died from an illness in 1974.

President Valéry Giscard d'Estaing maintained Pompidou's conservative focus from 1974 to 1981. Giscard's government dealt with growing unemployment and inflation (a sharp and continuing rise in prices). Trade declined and people wanted change.

As a result of this desire for change, François Mitterrand was elected president in 1981. His goal was to turn France into a social democratic state. He nationalized banks and industries. He increased taxes on the wealthy and froze prices and wages.

In 1995, Jacques Chirac took over the presidency. He brought a conservative approach to France's problems. Under Chirac's leadership, some parts of the French economy flourished. At the same time, however, the country experienced high unemployment and frequent strikes by workers. In 2007, Jacques Chirac was succeeded by Nicolas Sarkozy.

■ OF NOTE

In the 1990s, there were many student strikes in France. Students protested poor facilities at the nation's universities and demanded reforms to the educational system. In 1995, students in Toulouse sat on train tracks in protest. Near Paris, other students blocked the entrance to a theme park. As a result of these protests, some reforms were made.

Germany

After World War II, Germany became a divided country and remained so until its reunification in 1990. The two parts were the Federal Republic of Germany (West Germany) and the German Democratic Republic (East Germany). East Germany was closely allied to the Soviet Union.

In 1961, East Germany built a wall in Berlin to keep its people from leaving. By the time the wall was completed, nearly three million people had fled East Germany. The Berlin Wall was a constant reminder that the two Germanies were separated. In 1989, when the the wall came down, reunification looked possible.

Because of its role in World War II, Germany had to prove to other nations that it could be trusted. Germany was not allowed to maintain an army. Because it could not have an army, Germany was able to put more money into developing the country and taking care of its citizens. Aid from the United States helped it build modern factories. When Germany began to increase its economic and political power, other countries became nervous. Nevertheless, West Germany had developed a very strong economy by the early 1960s.

The leader of the West German government was called the chancellor. In 1969, Willy Brandt became chancellor. He started a policy known as Ostpolitik. This policy encouraged openness toward East Germany and the Soviet Union.

As a result of Ostpolitik, the Basic Treaty was signed by East and West Germany in 1972. This treaty gave East Germans greater access to West Germany. Both countries were then taken into the United Nations.

Brandt resigned in 1974, when one of his aides was revealed to be an East German spy. Helmut Schmidt became chancellor after Brandt.

In 1982, Helmut Kohl succeeded Schmidt as chancellor. In the early years of Kohl's leadership, the West German economy continued to grow steadily. Kohl worked with East Germany and the Soviet Union on the terms of German reunification. In 1990, Kohl was elected as the first chancellor of the reunified Germany. After 16 years in office, Kohl was defeated in the 1998 election by Gerhard Schröder.

Erich Honecker was the leader of East Germany from 1971 until reunification in 1990. Honecker slowly granted more freedom for visits from West Germans. Later, he allowed East Germans to visit West Germany. However, East Germany did not greatly improve its economy or living conditions under Honecker.

After reunification, Germany spent large amounts of money on the eastern part of the country. Roads were improved, buildings were fixed, and industries were modernized. Hundreds of thousands of refugees came to Germany from other parts of the world. Money had to be spent to meet the needs of these refugees.

In 2005, Angela Merkel became Germany's first female chancellor. She was re-elected in 2009.

The European Union

Six European nations created a common trade market in the 1950s. Other countries in Europe saw how successful this common market was. They, too, wanted to join and many did. In the 1980s and 1990s, the group combined more activities and became the European Union, or EU. The table below shows the current members of the EU. The date each country joined is in parentheses.

Austria (1995)	Germany (1951)	Netherlands (1951)
Belgium (1951)	Greece (1981)	Poland (2004)
Bulgaria (2007)	Hungary (2004)	Portugal (1986)
Cyprus (2004)	Ireland (1973)	Romania (2007)
Czech Republic (2004)	Italy (1951)	Slovakia (2004)
Denmark (1973)	Latvia (2004)	Slovenia (2004)
Estonia (2004)	Lithuania (2004)	Spain (1986)
Finland (1995)	Luxembourg (1951)	Sweden (1995)
France (1951)	Malta (2004)	United Kingdom (1973)

As more links were formed among the nations, the EU needed more policies. The European Union now has its own lawmaking body, the European Parliament. EU countries no longer have individual passports. They have EU passports. A citizen of one EU nation can freely travel to any other EU nation.

The biggest change came in 2002. The European Union introduced a new currency, the euro. The euro replaced the currencies of most EU members. (The United Kingdom still uses its own currency.) This has made trade among countries even easier. There is no need to convert money from one currency to another in order to do business.

In 2011, the EU became mired in the worldwide financial crisis. A number of countries appeared to be hopelessly endebted, and more stable countries (led by Germany and France) were helping to determine how to "bail" them, and their creditors, out.

Issues and Trends

One problem faced by many of the countries of Western Europe from 1960 to the present was the role of the government in managing the economy. In the United Kingdom, industries, banks, and services, such as railroads and electricity, were nationalized by the 1960s. In France and West Germany, this was not as common. East Germany's services, industries, and agriculture were under government control. As it came closer to unification with West Germany, East Germany changed its approach. It adopted the West German system of private ownership of industries and services.

When she assumed leadership in 1979, Margaret Thatcher began to privatize industries, banks, and services in the United Kingdom. In 1981, François Mitterrand started to nationalize key industries and banks in France. Neither leader succeeded in making major changes to their countries' original policies, however.

The nations of Western Europe also had to decide what kind of stand to take toward the Soviet Union and communism. The Western European nations you have learned about were opposed to communism and Soviet influence and control. Margaret Thatcher was a vocal opponent of communism. France was less vocal and even had a strong communist party whose members ran for public office. West Germany was particularly critical of Soviet policies in East Germany. Willy Brandt, however, wanted trade and communication with the Soviet Union.

Because of their improved economies, all Western European countries attracted many people from all over the world. But there were strong anti-immigration feelings in Western Europe. The United Kingdom and France sought to limit the number of people who entered those countries. West Germany received millions of refugees from East Germany and other nations. It also tightened its immigration policies.

The problem of unemployment is often linked to the problem of immigration, since citizens think immigrants take away jobs. From the 1960s to the late 1990s, Great Britain, France, and West Germany had large numbers of unemployed people. All three countries had strong social welfare programs aimed at helping the unemployed.

Finally, most nations of Western Europe were faced with issues of intolerance and social unrest. Germany and other nations continued to deal with the problem of neo-Nazi hate groups. In Northern Ireland, Protestant and Roman Catholic violence continued to flare up. In France, tensions about immigration ran high. Unrest and occasional violence resulted.

In 2003, the United States and the United Kingdom urged European nations to join them in attacking Iraq. However, most European nations did not agree with the idea of attacking Iraq. Leaders in France and Germany spoke out strongly against the war. This led to tension between them and the United States.

Chapter 22: Eastern and Central Europe

Nations of Eastern and Central Europe

Eastern Europe is the name given to the region of European nations allied with the Soviet Union from the late 1940s to the late 1980s. These nations belonged to the Soviet bloc. Many Soviet bloc nations shared a border with the Soviet Union. Yugoslavia, though led by a communist government, was not allied with the Soviet Union. Other European countries with a ruling communist party were Albania, Bulgaria, Czechoslovakia, East Germany, Hungary, Poland, and Romania.

The democratic nations of the world (including the nations of Western Europe, the United States, and Canada) were hostile toward the Soviet Union and the spread of communism. They formed NATO, the North Atlantic Treaty Organization, to defend against possible attack from the Soviet Union. The Soviet Union and many Soviet bloc countries belonged to a defense group formed under the Warsaw Pact. Under the terms of the pact, the Soviet Union could keep military forces in each member nation.

The communists lost power in many countries in 1989, and the Soviet bloc ceased to exist. In 1991, the Soviet Union broke up. From then on, the countries of both the former Soviet Union and the Soviet bloc created new relationships with one another. Many former Soviet bloc countries began referring to themselves as Eastern European or Central European countries.

In this chapter, we will review two important nations in Eastern and Central Europe: Poland and Czechoslovakia (which, since 1993, has been divided into two nations—the Czech Republic and Slovakia).

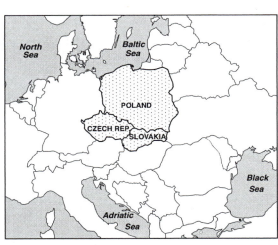

Eastern and Central Europe

Poland

Poland is in Eastern Europe. Its eastern border touches Belarus and Ukraine, both parts of the former Soviet Union. Poland was occupied by Germany during World War II.

After World War II, Poland was ruled by the Polish Communist Party. Until the early 1970s, the Polish Communist Party had strong connections to the Soviet Union. The Soviet Union considered Poland vital to its security.

During the 1970s, Soviet influence in Poland decreased. Two major events challenged the alliance between Poland and the Soviet Union in the late twentieth century: the selection of a Polish Roman Catholic as pope in 1978, and the emergence of the Solidarity labor union in 1980.

Wladyslaw Gomulka was first secretary of the Polish Communist Party. He served from 1956 to 1970. He had a great deal of control. During this time, low wages for workers created great hardship. Toward the end of his term, Gomulka increased prices on many items. Strikes and riots occurred in 1970. In trying to stop the riots, soldiers killed many people.

Edward Gierek became first secretary after Gomulka resigned in 1970. Gierek tried to get foreign loans to remodel Poland's aging factories. He tried to improve farming. Shortages of oil in 1973 and 1974 stopped these efforts. Prices increased, and workers went on strike again.

In 1978, Polish Roman Catholics were overjoyed when their own archbishop of Kraków, Karol Wojtyla, was elected pope. He took the name of Pope John Paul II.

Roman Catholics had worked hard to remain a strong force during the communist years. Wojtyla's election as pope proved that their struggle was recognized beyond Poland.

By 1980, higher prices and poor living conditions had caused much hardship in Poland. In the city of Gdansk, the entire workforce of 17,000 shipyard workers stopped working. Gierek negotiated a settlement with the workers.

One of the leaders of the Gdansk strike was Lech Walesa, an electrician. Strikes spread to other industries. Solidarity, an independent trade union, was cofounded by Walesa. The union was recognized by the government. Soon, it had 10 million members.

Solidarity sought to bring rapid changes in the government. It proposed a nationwide vote for establishing a noncommunist government. This vote was rejected by Wojciech Jaruzelski, who became first secretary in 1981. In December 1981, Jaruzelski declared martial law. Solidarity leaders were arrested and jailed.

In October 1982, the government outlawed Solidarity. For the next six years, Jaruzelski kept strong control. But in 1988, he negotiated with Solidarity. Poland did not use violence to get rid of the Polish Communist Party. Instead, Jaruzelski gradually shared leadership. In 1989, Solidarity was restored to legal status to stop labor unrest. The senate was reinstituted (started again). Solidarity ran candidates for all legislative offices. Many won.

Jaruzelski became Poland's first elected president since 1952. Later, there was strong dissatisfaction with Jaruzelski's lack of control of the economy. He resigned, and Lech Walesa was elected president in 1990.

Living conditions were difficult during this period. Wages were low, and people lived in cramped conditions. On occasion, there were food shortages. Prices increased, but wages did not.

Even after the Polish Communist Party no longer controlled Poland's economy, things were bad. Rapid changes in economic policy brought unemployment. Most Polish people struggled to make a living. When Poland joined the EU in 2004, hopes for economic improvement rose.

The Czech Republic and Slovakia

Until 1993, the Czech Republic and Slovakia were one country: Czechoslovakia. Czechoslovakia was in Central Europe. Czechoslovakia was occupied by Germany during World War II. The Soviet Union helped drive the Germans from this country.

Czechoslovakia had a democratic government for three years following the war. Then Czechoslovak Communists took control.

The Czechoslovak Communist system was modeled on the economic practices and political institutions of the Soviet Union. Private ownership was eliminated. Agriculture was collectivized (changed to a system of many people working together). Planning for the economy was done centrally. Leisure time, education, and the arts were all used for instruction about communism. Opposition from dissidents was dealt with immediately and harshly.

In 1968, Alexander Dubcek was leader of the Czechoslovak Communist Party. He wanted to create "socialism with a human face." Human rights movements grew. Newspapers became more open in what they printed.

The spring of 1968 was called the Prague Spring. Prague was the capital of Czechoslovakia. The events of this time briefly brought new hope. Many intellectuals and communist leaders started new policies. Their goal was to bring back democracy.

Many leaders within the Czechoslovak Communist Party were opposed to these changes. So were leaders in other Soviet bloc countries and, most importantly, in the Soviet Union. On August 20, 1968, Warsaw Pact aircraft, tanks, and troops invaded Czechoslovakia.

Dubcek and other leaders were supported by the people for a short time. Nevertheless, Dubcek soon lost power. By 1969, all the reforms were canceled, and Dubcek was forced from office.

Gustáv Husák, the deputy premier, became first secretary after Dubcek was removed. He reversed many of Dubcek's reforms and got rid of the leaders who had made them.

Husák's policies, however, did not improve the economy. Husák became president in 1975. In 1977, Václav Havel, a playwright, signed a petition against Husak's leadership. This petition became known as Charter 77.

The collapse of communism in Czechoslovakia came quickly. Late in 1989, police beat students who were peacefully demonstrating in Prague. Huge numbers of people protested in the streets. Groups of activists called on the leadership to honor human rights and allow more freedom.

Václav Havel spoke for Civic Forum, a group protesting the brutal treatment of students. He and Alexander Dubcek emerged as leaders.

Crowds as large as 500,000 gathered in Prague. The response from the people was so overwhelming that Husák and the communist government resigned. Havel was immediately elected president. Dubcek became speaker of the new parliament. This swift, peaceful change was called the Velvet Revolution.

After Havel became president, in December 1989, a new constitution and a new economic plan were needed. People in the Czech and Slovak regions held widely different views. Despite working for over two years, no agreement was reached between the two regions.

Havel resigned as president in 1992, and the two regions created separate countries. In January 1993, the Czech Republic and Slovakia were formed. The split was a peaceful one. Both countries joined the United Nations. Both countries also joined the European Union in 2004.

Havel was elected president of the Czech Republic. Mihal Kovác was elected president of Slovakia. Kovác had served as finance minister in the Czechoslovak government after the overthrow of the communists in 1989. He guided the new country through major economic difficulties.

In the 1960s and 1970s, living conditions in Czechoslovakia were difficult. In the 1980s, the standard of living declined even more. After the communist government left, however, conditions improved. Businesses and farms became privately owned. Income increased, and more products became available. People enjoyed greater freedom of speech.

Issues and Trends

In both Czechoslovakia and Poland, the Communist Party leadership had to decide how to handle people who disagreed with their policy. Newspapers, radio, and television were controlled. People who did not obey the Party's rules often lost their jobs.

In Poland, the militia stopped the workers' strikes. Later, martial law was declared and people were arrested and jailed. In Czechoslovakia, Warsaw Pact troops were used. People who dissented were arrested. Police used force to break up a student protest in 1989.

As Soviet bloc members, both countries were subject to Soviet Union direction. In Czechoslovakia, Husák received strong Soviet support to stop the 1968 Prague Spring changes. Pressure from the Soviet Union convinced the Polish communist leadership to use force against Solidarity in 1980. Soviet influence greatly decreased in the late 1980s.

In the early 1990s, Poland and Czechoslovakia tried to change to a free market economy. It required strong foreign investment and foreign aid. New money was needed to replace worn-out factories and outdated technology. Poland, the Czech Republic, and Slovakia all worked to attract foreign investors.

When positive changes were slow to come, some leaders wanted to return to an earlier economic policy. Many people benefited from the economic changes. Many did not. Debate continued about how to best manage the economies of these countries.

Chapter 23: The Balkans

Countries of the Balkan Peninsula

In 1960, the Balkan countries were Albania, Bulgaria, Greece, Romania, and Yugoslavia. They occupied the Balkan Peninsula in southeastern Europe. All but Greece were governed by a national communist party in 1960. Except for Romania, the Balkans do not border the former Soviet Union. By the 2000s, Serbia, Montenegro, Bosnia-Herzegovina, Croatia, Macedonia, and Slovenia were new Balkan countries. They were formed by the collapse of Yugoslavia.

The Balkan countries have a history of conflict between one ethnic group and another. In some countries, the conflicts led to fighting and wars. Often these conflicts involved one nation fighting with another nation.

In this chapter, we will discuss Romania and Yugoslavia, two important Balkan nations.

The Balkans Today

Romania

A century-long tradition of democratic rule in Romania came to an end after World War II. By 1948, the Communist Party was in control of Romania. A Soviet-style constitution was adopted. The Securitate (security network) was set up to manage dissent. Agriculture was collectivized. Industry was controlled through central planning. At first, Soviet successes were praised and imitated.

Many people resisted the coming of communism. Determined leaders kept Romania firmly on a communist path for over 40 years. Later,

Romania began to criticize the Soviet policies. Romania became more independent and isolated.

Gheorghe Gheorghiu-Dej helped establish the Communist Party in Romania after World War II. He was head of that party for 20 years. In the early 1960s, he sharply disagreed with the Soviet leaders. Gheorghiu-Dej then developed a nationalistic form of communism for Romania. Housing improved, and consumer goods increased. Scholars had more contact with Western countries. In 1965, Gheorghiu-Dej died.

Nicolae Ceausescu became leader of the Romanian Communist Party in 1965. In 1968, Ceausescu showed his independence from Soviet control by refusing to send troops into Czechoslovakia as required by the Warsaw Pact.

In 1971, Ceausescu decided to follow the policies of an early Soviet leader, Joseph Stalin. In 1974, Ceausescu became president of Romania.

Ceausescu's power grew until he had absolute control and authority. He ruled in very harsh ways. He constantly moved leaders in and out of office. He put members of his family in important government positions. His wife, Elena Ceausescu, held several powerful posts. Any opposition was dealt with by the Securitate.

Ceausescu increased his control in the 1970s and 1980s by using the Securitate. The Securitate had the power to arrest and detain (keep) people who criticized the party. It got rid of party members who opposed the leader. By the late 1980s, Ceausescu had formed a police state.

Ceausescu misused power and wasted money on huge buildings to glorify himself. He exported natural resources to pay the huge debts he created. This led to great hardship for the people. Food and fuel were in very short supply. Despair was a daily reality. As other Soviet bloc countries got rid of communist control, his control seemed unchanged.

Nevertheless, Ceausescu was overthrown in a single week in late 1989. Demonstrations in the city of Timisoara turned violent. The violence spread to other cities. Soon, the army joined the protesters against the secret police and Ceausescu. The ruler was unable to control the demonstrations. He fled but was captured. At a special military trial, he was accused of mass murder and other crimes. Ceausescu and his wife were shot by a firing squad. His policies had almost totally destroyed the country's economic well-being.

Ion Iliescu became president of Romania in 1990. The new government had to deal with the collapse of the economy. Another problem was hostility between the Romanians and the Hungarians who lived in Transylvania, the northwest part of Romania.

The land settlements after World War II returned northern Transylvania to Romania from Hungary. Romania tried to reduce the power of the people of Hungarian background living in Transylvania. After 1990, there was an increase in hostility against them. Some Romanians wanted to force them out of Romania.

In the 1960s, Romania traded with other Soviet bloc countries. Living conditions were good. The economy did well, and individuals had many consumer goods and benefits. This changed for the worse in the 1970s and 1980s. Fewer consumer goods were available. Factory goods were of poor quality. Housing got worse. People were unable to express their opinions for fear of arrest. Aid from the West stopped.

In the 1990s, there was some improvement. A law was passed in 2001 aimed at returning property to its original owners. Yet economic reforms have been very slow to happen.

In 2004, Romania joined NATO and signed an agreement with the EU. More reforms were carried out, and Romania finally joined the EU in 2007.

The Former Yugoslavia

After World War II, several republics on the Balkan Peninsula were combined into one country: Yugoslavia. They included the republics of Bosnia, Croatia, Macedonia, Montenegro, Serbia, and Slovenia.

Unlike other countries with communist leadership, Yugoslavia did not have a strong relationship with the Soviet Union. The Soviet Union did not trade with Yugoslavia. Yugoslavia declared itself a nonaligned nation. It was not allied with either the Soviet bloc or the Western bloc.

Marshal Tito was prime minister and later president of Yugoslavia from 1945 until his death in 1980. Tito's disagreements with Joseph

Stalin caused the Soviet Union to stop trade and diplomatic relations with Yugoslavia. Without this contact, Yugoslavia developed its own style of communism. Workers self-managed their own industry. They had control of economic decisions. There were few price controls. Products competed on the open market. This approach to economic management was called market socialism. Self-management extended to political administration and social-services workers. This approach brought prosperity and kept the six republics together.

Yugoslavia's economic success in the 1970s brought a desire for more growth. Yugoslavia and the individual republics borrowed to finance new industries. Interest on the debts became a major burden. This weakened the economy, and people questioned Yugoslavia's economic health. Economic difficulties affected all the republics, some more than others. More prosperous republics did not help less prosperous ones. This weakened the support of the central government.

The leadership of Yugoslavia was shared by all six republics. After the death of Tito, no strong leader appealed to all six. Loyalty to Yugoslavia declined. Mistrust grew as republics talked of independence. Minority ethnic groups feared what would happen to them in an independent republic. Reform movements in Eastern and Central Europe, the Soviet Union, and other Balkan countries created pressure for a new form of government.

In the late 1980s, relations between the republics grew worse. Yugoslavia was falling apart. In 1991, Slovenia and Croatia declared their independence. Macedonia and Bosnia soon followed. By 1994, only Serbia and Montenegro remained in Yugoslavia.

Slobodan Milosevic became the leader of the League of Communists of Serbia. Milosevic wanted to keep a united Yugoslavia. At the same time, he thought the Serbian people should have more power. He tried to keep other republics from leaving the Yugoslav Federation.

Milosevic sent troops to Slovenia to prevent Slovenia's withdrawal. He supported minority Serb groups in Croatia who took territory by armed force. He also supported Serb resisters in Bosnia and Herzegovina.

Some of the worst violence was in Bosnia. Bosnia included groups with different ethnic and religious backgrounds. Some were Serbs. Some were

Croats. Many Bosnians were Muslims, followers of Islam. Muslims and Croats had voted for an independent Bosnia. Many Serbs wanted Bosnia to stay part of Yugoslavia. They tried to force out Muslims and Croats. Many were killed. Many more were forced to leave their homes and land.

Other European nations were slow to respond to the fighting. This was also true of the United Nations. By the time other nations intervened, much bloodshed had already occurred. This increased the hatred of one group for the other.

Franjo Tudjman became president of Croatia in 1990. He was the leader when United Nations troops occupied Croatia. Alija Izetbegovic was a leader of the Bosnian Muslim group during the fighting with Bosnian Serbs. He later became president of Bosnia and Herzegovina.

In November 1995, prime ministers from Bosnia and Herzegovina, Croatia, and Yugoslavia met to end the hostilities in Bosnia and Herzegovina. This meeting was held in Dayton, Ohio. The plan they agreed to became known as the Dayton Peace Accord. This plan was signed by Milosevic and the presidents of Bosnia-Herzegovina and Croatia. An international tribunal, or court, has been set up. It works to bring to justice people accused of war crimes in the former Yugoslavia. In 2001, Slobodan Milosevic was charged with war crimes at the tribunal.

In 2003, the country of Yugoslavia was restructured. It became a loose federation of two republics, and was renamed Serbia and Montenegro. In 2006, the two republics declared independence from each other and became separate nations, effectively dissolving what had once been Yugoslavia.

Under Tudjman, people in Croatia suffered. The economy was poor. There was a great deal of corruption in the government. The government took away citizens' civil rights and political rights.

Tudjman died in 1999. Since then, Croatia has made progress. The constitution has been changed so that the president has less power. Croatia is trying to develop a more open economy.

The United Nations peacekeeping forces were replaced by NATO forces. Their job was to guarantee that all groups in Bosnia-Herzegovina followed the agreement. In 2004, a European Union peacekeeping force took over.

The years of fighting hurt all the republics. Roads, bridges, and industries were destroyed. Many people were forced to move away from their homes. Since the fighting ended, these nations have worked to rebuild. Slovenia joined the European Union in 2004, and Croatia is poised to join in 2013. Serbia, Montenegro, and Macedonia have started the process to join.

Continued unrest in Bosnia has slowed progress there. However, Bosnia also hopes to join the EU some day.

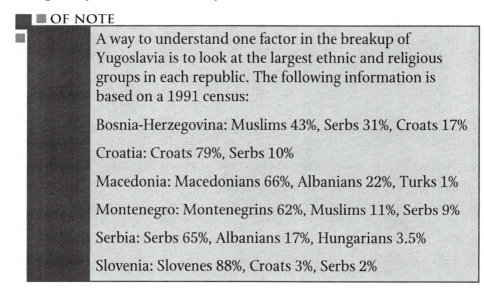

■ OF NOTE

A way to understand one factor in the breakup of Yugoslavia is to look at the largest ethnic and religious groups in each republic. The following information is based on a 1991 census:

Bosnia-Herzegovina: Muslims 43%, Serbs 31%, Croats 17%

Croatia: Croats 79%, Serbs 10%

Macedonia: Macedonians 66%, Albanians 22%, Turks 1%

Montenegro: Montenegrins 62%, Muslims 11%, Serbs 9%

Serbia: Serbs 65%, Albanians 17%, Hungarians 3.5%

Slovenia: Slovenes 88%, Croats 3%, Serbs 2%

Issues and Trends

Both Romania and Yugoslavia rejected the leadership of the Soviet Union. Romania chose an even stricter form of communism than was being practiced in the Soviet Union or other Soviet bloc countries. Yugoslavia's nonaligned status led to greater economic gains and personal freedoms than in the Soviet Union. Clearly, communism was not the same everywhere.

Both countries had one leader for a long period of time. Marshal Tito was the leader of Yugoslavia for about 35 years. Nicolae Ceausescu led Romania for 24 years. Leadership of so many years produced very stable governments.

After each leader died, his country had difficulty making decisions supported by a majority of people. Many voices emerged, each with a solution to the issues.

In Yugoslavia, this eventually led to its breakup. For Romania, political parties developed, each with a different solution. Keeping a successful government was difficult for Romania.

Ethnic identity continued to influence political decisions in Yugoslavia and its former republics. Actions taken by different ethnic groups during the war in Bosnia and in Croatia created deep anger.

Ethnic groups within Serbia also experienced difficulties. Romania had to find ways to deal with ethnic hostility between Romanians and Hungarians.

Romania also had difficulty deciding on a workable economic and political plan. No one political party emerged that represented the majority of Romania's citizens. Yugoslavia and the independent republics continued to look for ways of developing stable governments to keep the region at peace and promote its economy.

Chapter 24: The Former Soviet Union

From Union to Breakup

The full name of the former Soviet Union was the Union of Soviet Socialist Republics (USSR). The USSR included 15 republics. The Soviet Union stretched from Europe to the Pacific Ocean. The national government was in Moscow. Moscow was the largest city in Russia, the most powerful republic. More than 240 million people lived in the Soviet Union. They represented 92 nationalities and 112 different languages. Both its size and power made the Soviet Union a major world force.

In 1991, the Soviet Union ceased to exist. All its republics became independent. Many republics joined a new organization called the Commonwealth of Independent States (CIS).

The Soviet Union before 1991

The Soviet Union

After World War II, the Soviet Union supported communist parties in Europe. Often it sent troops or political advisers to other countries to help local communists. Sometimes they were welcomed, sometimes not. Nevertheless, the Soviet Union had an impact on all nations in Europe.

By the 1960s, the Soviet Union was one of the world's superpowers. Countries allied to the Soviet Union were part of the Soviet bloc. Many countries throughout the world created policies to deal with the actions of the Soviet Union.

Leonid Brezhnev was the Soviet Communist Party leader from 1964 until his death in 1982. Though often challenged for leadership, he kept control. The Soviet Union opposed the Prague Spring reforms in Czechoslovakia in 1968. Brezhnev sent Warsaw Pact troops there to stop the reforms. This action resulted from a policy that became known as the Brezhnev Doctrine. This doctrine said the Soviet Union could get involved in other communist countries. They could even send troops to invade.

With nations outside the Soviet bloc, Brezhnev acted differently. He improved relations with Western nations, such as the United States. This approach was called détente. Through détente, Brezhnev and U.S. President Richard Nixon signed a treaty to limit nuclear arms. It was called SALT I. Tensions eased between the Soviet Union and West Germany. Trade and cultural exchanges increased.

People who criticized the government were still punished. Andrey Sakharov, a Russian physicist, was put under house arrest for his outspoken comments. Many dissidents were put in prison. Others self-published articles and books criticizing the state. These publications became known as samizdat. They kept up pressure for change.

Serious economic mistakes led to a major crisis in the mid-1970s. Agricultural workers did not produce enough food because of several years of bad weather. The Soviet Union imported wheat from Western countries. This increased Soviet debt. People lost confidence in Brezhnev's leadership.

In 1979, Soviet troops helped Afghanistan communists fight Muslim fundamentalists. This war eventually involved 100,000 Soviet troops. Soviet prestige suffered. The Afghan war was impossible to win.

After Brezhnev's death, two new leaders maintained his general direction. Nevertheless, the Soviet Union faced difficulties. New approaches were needed. They were brought by the next leader, Mikhail Gorbachev.

Mikhail Gorbachev became general secretary in 1985. He was elected as president of the Soviet Union in 1990. For his efforts to improve relations with other countries, he received the Nobel Peace Prize.

Gorbachev believed there had to be major changes. He called the changes perestroika (restructuring). Under perestroika, citizens could again criticize the state. This new openness (glasnost) helped change old policies. The dissident Andrey Sakharov was released. Newspapers published critical articles.

People also received the right to elect representatives in a multiparty election. In 1989, a Congress of People's Deputies was elected.

The Soviet Union worked with other nations to bring greater arms control. It withdrew from Afghanistan. It eliminated control over countries in the Soviet bloc. There was an increase in the number of privately owned businesses and private properties.

All the changes brought by perestroika were not enough to keep the Soviet Union together. Gorbachev's reforms took on a life of their own. He tried to keep the reforms within the communist organization. But that did not work. People's living conditions became worse. Many people had difficulty getting food and heat.

When glasnost allowed criticism, some ethnic groups wanted more power. They talked about freedom from the Soviet Union. Some republics demanded independence.

The new political structures allowed people opposed to Gorbachev to gain political power. Boris Yeltsin became a strong opponent of Gorbachev and other Soviet Communist party leaders.

In an attempt to stop reform, a group of antireformers arrested Gorbachev. They tried to seize power. People in Moscow successfully resisted their attempt. Russian Federation President Boris Yeltsin was one of these people. The antireformers were arrested, and Gorbachev was released.

Boris Yeltsin declared the Russian Federation independent. It became clear that Gorbachev and the Soviet Communist Party no longer had support. When Gorbachev resigned in December 1991, the Soviet Union collapsed.

The Russian Federation

The Russian Federation consisted of 21 republics, a wide array of territories and provinces, and two federal states—Moscow and St. Petersburg. A new constitution was adopted in 1993. Citizens received the right to housing, free medical care, and free education. The president and federal assembly members were elected by popular vote.

The Russian Federation was the largest of the independent countries to emerge from the U.S.S.R. It was the leading power in the Commonwealth of Independent States.

Boris Yeltsin became president of the Russian Federation in 1991. He was reelected to a four-year term in 1996.

Early in Yeltsin's presidency, the Russian Federation became independent. Soon after that, the Soviet Union ended. The Russian Federation joined with Ukraine and Belarus to form the Commonwealth of Independent States. Later, most of the other former Soviet Union republics joined. They had to decide how to share the weapons of the former Soviet Union.

Yeltsin's immediate focus was the failing economy. He decided on a quick shift to a free-market economy. His plan was called "shock therapy." Yeltsin wanted more private ownership of small and medium-sized businesses. Many state and town businesses were sold to local and foreign investors. This practice continued in the late 1990s.

The Russian Federation received promises for billions of dollars of foreign aid. These promises allowed Yeltsin to continue his reforms. But problems remained. Beginning in 1990, production fell. Prices soared. For several years basic foods were in short supply. Many workers went without pay for months. Factories closed, and workers lost their jobs. Yeltsin appealed to the international community for help in continuing the reforms.

Organized crime rapidly grew in the Russian Federation. Black market activities added to the instability of the country.

Yeltsin also sent Russian Federation troops to the Republic of Chechnya. This republic had threatened to withdraw from the Russian Federation. Years of fighting there with no victory increased dissatisfaction with Yeltsin's leadership.

Yeltsin kept the Russian Federation connected to the international community. He received aid from the International Monetary Fund. He participated in major European economic summits.

By the late 1990s, Russia's economy was failing. The ruble—Russia's currency—fell in value. Russia's government said it could not pay its foreign loans.

At the same time, the violence in Chechyna grew worse. Chechen guerrillas invaded another Russian republic. Chechyna was also blamed for a series of bombings in Russia.

The new prime minister, Vladimir Putin, sent troops to Chechyna. His tough line made him popular with Russians. In 2000, Putin became president of Russia.

Putin's election brought some stability to Russia. The economy improved, as did relations with other parts of the world. However, Putin also increased government control in Russia, and cut back on democracy by ending the election of regional governors. Putin remains the prime minister of Russia, but was succeeded by Dmitry Medvedev as president in 2008.

The Republic of Chechyna remained unsettled into the early years of the twenty-first century. There were violent incidents in Russia and attacks from suicide bombers. In 2004, a group with Chechen ties attacked a school in Russia. They took 1,000 people hostages, many of them children. After three days, Russian forces stormed the building. In all, 360 people died in the attack, including 172 children. The tragedy caused both grief and anger in Russia. In 2009, Russia announced the end of its occupation of Chechnya and withdrew much of its army, giving hope for peaceful resolution to the years of violence.

Topic 7

The Middle East and Africa

Chapter 25: The Middle East

Saudi Arabia

Saudi Arabia is a monarchy based on religious law. There are no political parties. Islam is the religion of Saudi Arabia. It is also the religion of most of the neighboring countries. There was tension among some of these countries during the 1960s, as well as tension within Saudi Arabia itself.

King Saud became the Saudi ruler in 1953. The leader in Egypt was Gamal Abdel Nasser. Nasser wanted other Arab countries to follow his lead. King Saud, however, was not willing to support all of Egypt's actions in the region. He also had differences with people in his own country.

Petroleum is Saudi Arabia's major resource. In fact, Saudi Arabia has one third of the world's known oil reserves. However, Saud was not using the country's income (money) from selling oil to modernize Saudi Arabia. Many government leaders wanted to replace him with his younger brother Prince Faisal.

In 1964, King Saud was in poor health. He was deposed and replaced by Faisal. King Faisal began to modernize Saudi Arabia. He constructed new roads, schools, and oil plants. He built modern airports.

As in other parts of the world, the Middle East felt the effects of the Cold War. This was because of the tremendous oil reserves in the Middle East. Saudi Arabia aligned itself with the United States. Yet, the United States backed Israel,

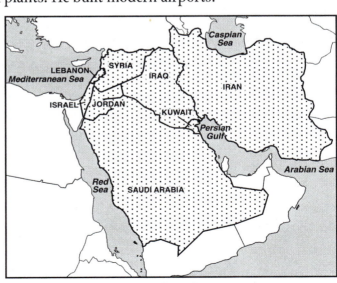

The Middle East

which was at war with some Arab countries. Saudi Arabia and Israel were on opposite sides. In the 1967 war, for example, Saudi Arabia backed Egypt. However, it did not give Egypt any military help.

Many of the oil companies in Saudi Arabia were owned by foreigners. King Faisal gained ownership of over half of those companies. He increased oil production, and Saudi Arabia grew very rich. Then, in 1975, Faisal was assassinated by one of his nephews. His brother Khalid succeeded him.

King Khalid continued his brother's modernization. He encouraged the growth of cities and industry. He established a system of mass education. In addition, Khalid invited foreign workers in to help further develop the Saudi oil industry. The workers brought with them new technology to make the industry more efficient. However, Khalid was careful that the country did not get too westernized. Saudi Arabia is a very traditional country. It tries to protect its culture and customs, in some cases through censorship of Western elements.

King Khalid's foreign policy was also cautious. He supported Arab states but kept a friendly relationship with the United States. OPEC is a good example of Khalid's caution. In 1960, a group of major oil-exporting nations joined to form the Organization of Petroleum Exporting Countries. This eventually included the eight largest oil producers of the region. It also included countries from South America, Africa, and Asia. Within OPEC, Saudi Arabia played a major role in urging a moderate policy.

King Fahd became the Saudi ruler in 1982. Fahd was pro-Western. He moved ahead with modernizing the country. He also made changes in the country's foreign policy. For example, between 1980 and 1988, Iran and Iraq were at war. Saudi Arabia backed Iraq. Iran was led at the time by the Ayatollah Khomeini. The Saudis feared the spread of Islamic fundamentalism if Iran won the war.

In 1990, though, Iraq invaded neighboring Kuwait. This time the Saudis took a stand against Iraq. The United States organized other countries to drive the Iraqis out of Kuwait. The allies also sent troops to Saudi Arabia to help it defend itself. They used military bases there from which they could attack Iraq.

King Fahd intended to pay for the costs of the war by producing and selling more oil. Unfortunately, a number of other countries began increasing their oil production at the same time. (This included some OPEC countries, which had previously agreed not to do such a thing.) This made the price of oil go down. Saudi Arabia made much less oil revenue than expected.

This was bad news for the country's modernization plans. Government leaders feared it would lead to social unrest. It also reduced the country's influence in the Middle East.

After the war, Fahd regained public support by announcing some changes. Leaders outside the royal family finally got a limited say in government decisions. The king granted the right of privacy to citizens. Also, he prohibited human rights abuses. Though Fahd was still king in the 1990s, most power was in the hands of his half-brother Abdullah.

Iraq

Iraq became a kingdom in 1922. The monarchy lasted until 1958. That year, Iraqi military officers overthrew the government. For the next 21 years, there was a series of harsh military regimes. In 1979, Saddam Hussein took power. He maintained a strongly secular and modern state. He also used his secret police to silence his opponents. He put his family and friends in powerful government positions. However, even those people were not safe. At one time, he had his own sons-in-law executed.

Hussein thought he could become the leader of the Arab world by increasing Iraq's power, land, and wealth. He spent millions on the military. Iraq soon had one of the most powerful armies in the region. By the 1990s, Iraq had taken part in a series of wars. Its army fought in the 1967 war against Israel. Then, in 1980, Hussein invaded Iran. This war went on for eight years. Ayatollah Khomeini, the leader of Iran, was a religious fundamentalist. He believed in a strict understanding of Islamic law. Most Arab states supported Iraq. They feared that Islamic fundamentalism would spread to their countries, undermining the status quo.

The United States and other nations placed warships in the gulf to protect the flow of oil from the Middle East. In the late 1980s, Iraq even used poison gas against Iranian troops. Finally, in 1988, the two exhausted nations agreed to a cease-fire. A million people may have died during the war. The economies of both countries were badly damaged.

There were also ongoing battles with the Kurds. These upland shepherds live in northern Iraq. They did not want to be under Iraqi rule. After the Iran-Iraq War, Hussein tried to crush the Kurdish rebels once and for all. He dropped poison gas on their villages. Thousands of Kurdish refugees fled to Turkey.

In 1990, Iraq became involved in yet another war. This time it invaded Kuwait. Iraq still had a powerful army, but it needed money. Hussein wanted the rich oil fields of Kuwait. U.S. President George H. W. Bush organized an alliance to drive Iraq out of Kuwait. The Gulf War lasted less than a week. Before Hussein's troops withdrew from Kuwait, they set fire to some of Kuwait's oil fields, causing severe environmental damage.

The United Nations then imposed sanctions on Iraq. The sanctions put Iraq's economy under even more strain. Iraq could sell only a limited amount of oil. The sanctions were to stay in effect until Iraq complied with the rules laid down by the United Nations. This included destroying all chemical weapons. Despite this, Hussein kept an iron grip on the country. When the Kurds rebelled again in the 1990s, Iraq swiftly put them down.

In the late 1990s, Hussein refused to follow the cease-fire terms that had ended the Gulf War. Iraq was supposed to let an international team of experts inspect its military sites. The experts wanted to make sure Iraq had destroyed its missiles and chemical weapons. But Hussein kept dodging their requests. In 1998, President Bill Clinton warned Iraq to open the sites to inspection. If they did not, they risked another military attack. Hussein finally agreed to allow the inspections to continue. Then, soon after, he again put a halt to inspections.

The United Nations report on weapons inspections was critical of Iraq. Still, the inspectors had not found any weapons of mass destruction.

After terrorist attacks in the United States, U.S. President George W. Bush began to call for change in Iraq. He urged the United Nations to act. Most Arab countries disapproved of Bush's position. Many European countries also disapproved.

In March 2003, with support from the United Kingdom, the United States attacked Iraq. Within a few weeks, Baghdad fell to U.S. troops. Saddam Hussein went into hiding.

A few months later, Hussein was captured. He was charged with a number of crimes. A special Iraqi tribunal was set up to hear the case against Hussein and members of his government. Hussein was found guilty of crimes against humanity, and was hanged in 2006.

By May of 2003, the United States declared the war in Iraq was over. However, fighting continued. Many Iraqis resisted the U.S. occupation, killing U.S. troops, foreign workers, and fellow Iraqis. Basic services, such as electricity and water, were thrown into disorder. And months of searching gave no evidence that Iraq had weapons of mass destruction—the reason given for attacking Iraq. The release of graphic photographs showing U.S. soldiers abusing Iraqi prisoners fed the people's anger.

In 2004, a temporary Iraqi government was set up. In early 2005, elections were held to choose an Iraqi National Assembly. U.S.-led military forces continued fighting insurgents on the ground and using air strikes. One of these air strikes killed the leader of al-Qaeda in Iraq, Abu Musab al-Zarqawi, in 2006. The "troop surge" raised the number of American soldiers in Iraq to 170,000. Eventually, there were fewer insurgent attacks, and the United States opened an embassy in Baghdad in 2009. The active combat mission in Iraq ended in August 2010, and all U.S. soldiers were scheduled to withdraw from the country by the end of 2011.

Iran

In 1960, Mohammad Reza Pahlavi was the shah, or ruler, of oil-rich Iran. He had made some moves to modernize the country. For example, the government sold its industries to private businesses. It gave women the right to vote. In the early 1970s, oil sales increased, bringing the government vast wealth. But, most of the money went to government and businesspeople. The poor were left out.

Certain religious leaders opposed the shah. They thought he would westernize the country—partly because the shah accepted U.S. military aid. His opponents believed the government should strictly enforce Islamic law. In response, the shah told the army and SAVAK to put down the opposition. (SAVAK was the country's secret police.)

By 1977, people were demonstrating in the streets, demanding an Islamic state. When the police tried to put down the demonstrations, the crowds rioted. The police opened fire, and thousands of protesters were wounded or killed.

In 1978, the shah placed Iran under martial law. But the opposition gained strength. Even some of the military began to rebel. Finally, the shah and his family fled the country.

The people of Iran turned to Ayatollah Ruhollah Khomeini to lead them. The ayatollah (a religious leader) had been exiled for criticizing the shah. When Khomeini returned from exile in France in February 1979, Iran proclaimed itself an Islamic republic. There was still opposition to Khomeini. However, he had enough power to carry out his plans.

The Khomeini government arrested hundreds of the shah's supporters. Islamic courts tried and executed SAVAK members. Women were ordered to wear the traditional chador, an outer garment that covers almost all of a woman's body when out in public. Khomeini banned alcohol and bathing at beaches with members of the opposite sex. He even prohibited music from radio and television. Often, people who broke these laws were publicly beaten.

Khomeini tried to spread economic wealth more evenly among the upper, middle, and lower classes. He gave land to the people. This made him popular with workers and farmers. To further strengthen his power, Khomeini struck out against foreigners.

In 1979, Khomeini supported Muslim militants who seized the U.S. embassy in Tehran, Iran's capital. The militants took the embassy staff hostage and demanded the shah's return. The shah had gone to the United States for medical treatment. The militants wanted to punish him. After the shah died in exile in 1980, Iran agreed to set the remaining 52 hostages free.

The unrest in Iran may be why Iraq invaded its old rival in 1980. Both countries wanted to be the strongest country in the area. The conflict between Iran and Iraq heavily damaged Iran's oil production and its economy. Yet, when Iraq was ready to end the war, Khomeini refused to negotiate. In 1988, however, the Iranian military was losing ground. Only then did Khomeini agree to a cease-fire. The next year, he died.

After Khomeini's death, the government placed more stress on economic development than religious reform. Iran also made small moves to broaden relations with non-Muslim countries, such as the United States.

Iran was trying to regain international influence. However, Iran now had a reputation for providing support for acts of terrorism all over the world. These included bombings, kidnappings, and hijackings of planes.

In its 1997 election, Iran chose Mohammad Khatami for president. Khatami held wide public appeal. Young voters liked him because his religious ideas were less strict. Women hoped he would bring them greater freedom. Some of his reforms protected labor and civil rights.

However, other government leaders thought Khatami was making too many changes. They accused him of being pro-Western. This opposition suggested that Khatami would not be able to change Iran's direction very quickly. However, the country did become more open to the West, even welcoming U.S. tourists.

In 2005, Mahmoud Ahmadinejad was elected president, and re-elected in 2009 amidst accusations of election fraud, sparking numerous protests in Tehran. Many people were arrested, including reformist politicians and foreign news correspondents, and authorities took action to block Internet access and censor media coverage of the protests.

Israel

The history of Israel has often been one of conflict. Its conflicts with the Arabs began when Israel first became a nation in 1948. The land that Israel occupied used to be called Palestine. There were Arabs living in Palestine at the time. Many Palestinian Arabs fled or were driven off their land when Israel became a country. This was deeply resented by many Arabs in the region.

As the 1960s opened, Israel was building a modern democratic nation. The economy was growing stronger. The United States and other Western countries loaned Israel money and supplied military weapons.

Israel's last clash with its Arab neighbors had been in 1956, after Egypt took over the Suez Canal. Yet, nearby Arab countries still refused to recognize Israel's right to exist. Now tension was building again.

In 1967, Israel warned Syria to stop raiding its border. Instead, Syria asked for aid from Egypt. The two countries gathered their troops. However, it was Israel that struck the first blows. Its air force made simultaneous raids on Syrian, Egyptian, and Jordanian air bases.

The Israeli army drove back the Arab armies. As it moved, it took possession of new territory. The Six-Day War, as it is called, resulted in Israel's tripling its size. The Israelis were determined to occupy this land until the Arab countries officially recognized Israel as a legal country.

Following the Six-Day War, Israel's Labor Party chose Golda Meir to lead the country. As prime minister, Meir saw her country expand economically. Industry and trade climbed. Unfortunately, friction with Arab neighbors rose, too.

In 1973, Egypt led a surprise attack against Israel. This was called the Yom Kippur War, or the Ramadan War. The Arabs attacked on Yom Kippur, the holiest day on the Jewish calendar, during the Muslim holy month of Ramadan. This time it was the Arabs who moved fast across the borders. But, Israel fought back, again beating the Egyptian and Syrian troops. Israelis were angry, though, that they had been surprised by the Yom Kippur War. The suddenness of the attack resulted in many Israeli casualties.

An election in 1977 led to the rise of a more conservative political party. However, it was Menachem Begin, the prime minister, who took a historic step toward peace. Anwar el-Sadat had been president of Egypt since 1970. In 1977, he declared that he was willing to go anywhere to talk peace.

U.S. President Jimmy Carter worked for about a year with Sadat and Begin to develop a peace treaty. In 1979, the two former enemies signed a treaty. Israel gave up some land, and Egypt recognized Israel's right to exist. Together, Sadat and Begin won the 1978 Nobel Peace Prize.

However, most other Arab countries did not follow Egypt's example. In fact, they treated Egypt coldly and refused to give it aid. In 1981, Sadat was assassinated by a Muslim extremist. The issue of the Palestinians had not been solved. In 1978, a number of them were still living in refugee camps just over the border from Israel. And, there were now many other Palestinian Arabs living under Israeli control. They lived in the territories Israel had captured in the Six-Day War.

The Palestinians wanted to form their own country and have their own government. Israelis resisted this idea. They did not think they would be safe with such a country on their border. Even within Israel, there were terrorist attacks. And a violent Arab uprising called the intifada took place in the occupied territories.

In 1992, Yitzhak Rabin became prime minister. In 1993, he made an agreement with PLO leader Yasser Arafat to establish peace. The agreement gave Palestinians more territory and the right to some self-rule.

Then, in 1995, Rabin was assassinated by a Jewish extremist. In 1996, a more conservative government took over. For a long time, peace talks were stalled.

Ariel Sharon became prime minister in 2001. Sharon used the army to stop Palestinian fighters. Israeli soldiers stormed the buildings where Arafat lived and worked. They surrounded the buildings and refused to let Arafat leave. He remained there for the next three years.

In 2003, Mahmoud Abbas became the Palestinians' first prime minister. He promised to work with Sharon to find a peaceful solution.

In late 2004, Arafat became very ill. He was flown to Paris to receive medical treatment. He died there in November 2004.

Yasser Arafat's death marked the end of an era. Mahmoud Abbas was elected president. In early 2005, he and Ariel Sharon announced a cease-fire agreement. Later that year, Sharon ordered the removal of Israeli soldiers from the Gaza Strip. A series of strokes forced him to leave office, and in 2009 Benjamin Netanyahu assumed office.

Another problem that remained to be solved was Israel's occupation of part of Lebanon. Israel had attacked that country in 1982 to destroy terrorist bases. In the late 1990s, Israelis still occupied an area near the border of the two countries called the Golan Heights. Israel had fought many wars to defend itself. The war with Lebanon was the only one that did not have the full support of the public. Many Israeli citizens called for Israel's withdrawal.

Israel had the huge expense of keeping a strong military and staying alert. Another enormous expense involved the absorption of Jews from all over the world. These people usually came to Israel needing homes and jobs. The immigrants spoke many different languages. So, the first thing they needed to do was learn Hebrew, the official language of Israel. Israel received help from other countries, especially the United States.

Jordan

Hussein Ibn Talal, king of Jordan, took the throne when he was only 17. Hussein set a course for gradual, steady improvement in the country's economy. His projects reduced Jordan's illiteracy rate and increased housing. He built roads and encouraged modernization. Hussein asked for, and got, loans and advisers from other nations. In the early 1960s, the United States sent Jordan around $100 billion a year.

Hussein had to walk a careful road between different dangers. On one border, he had Israel and its powerful army. On the other borders were Arab countries, with their strong feelings of nationalism. Another factor was inside his own country. A large population of Palestinian Arabs lived in Jordan. This drew Hussein into the conflict between Israel and the Palestinians.

In the late 1960s, the Palestine Liberation Organization (PLO) was based in Jordan. It staged terrorist attacks on Israel. To keep peace, Hussein began to shut down the guerrilla operations. This made other Arab countries angry, because they backed the guerrillas.

Hussein feared that Syria and other countries would support a Palestinian uprising against Jordan. So, in 1967, Jordan sided with Syria and Egypt in the Arab-Israeli Six-Day War. As a result, Jordan lost its West Bank—the territory to the west of the Jordan River—to Israel. About 200,000 Palestinian refugees flooded from there into Jordan. Jordan's economy suffered from this additional burden.

Hostility (bitterness) between the PLO and Hussein grew. In 1970, a ten-day civil war broke out. Syrian tanks rolled into Jordan to support the guerrilla movement. However, Hussein's well-trained army defeated the invaders. By mid-1971, Hussein had forced the Palestinian rebels out of Jordan. Most of the guerrilla fighters fled to Lebanon.

However, other Arab countries put pressure on Hussein for the Palestinian cause. They persuaded him to give up the West Bank officially in 1974 so that the Palestinians could negotiate with Israel for the territory. They hoped to build a Palestinian state or homeland there. When Sadat and Begin signed a peace treaty, Hussein sided with the countries that boycotted Egypt.

In the following years, Hussein tried to stay neutral in Middle Eastern conflicts. He worked with Saudi Arabia and the United States, both of which gave him financial aid. When Iraq invaded Kuwait, leading to the Gulf War, Hussein officially sided with no one. However, he did make statements suggesting that he understood Iraq's position. This made him unpopular with the United States.

In 1991, Hussein joined the Middle East peace talks. This helped his position with the United States. When the PLO and Israel reached their 1993 agreement, Hussein gave his support.

On October 26, 1994, Jordan and Israel signed a formal peace treaty. It ended a 46-year state of war. This improved Jordan's relations with the United States and the more moderate Arab states, including Saudi Arabia.

King Hussein ruled Jordan for 46 years. When he died in 1999, his son, King Abdullah, took the throne.

Lebanon and Syria

Lebanon

The story of Lebanon is one of internal conflicts. Different factions have fought frequent civil wars there. The various factions include Maronite Christians, Sunni Muslims, Shiite Muslims, and the Druse. Many of these groups have had their own private militias.

Outside pressures have also added to Lebanon's problems. Syria often intervened in Lebanon's civil wars. Syrian troops stationed themselves in Lebanon so that Palestinian guerrillas could attack Israel more easily. The Israelis attacked Lebanon in 1982 and occupied territory there until 2000.

In 1991, Lebanon's government, backed by Syria, regained control of much of the country by disarming militias. Still, the divisions within the country made it hard to govern.

Syrian troops remained in Lebanon into the twenty-first century. In February 2005, Lebanon's popular former prime minister Rafik Hariri, was assassinated. This triggered massive protests against Syria, which the Lebanese people blamed for the killing. Syria responded by withdrawing some troops and promising to withdraw the rest.

Syria

Thanks to a settlement worked out by the United States, Syria recovered much of the territory it had lost in its wars with Israel. At times, it seemed there was the possibility of a formal peace settlement between the two countries. However, Israel held on to Syrian land it felt was important for Israel's security, or safety. Tension between the two countries continued.

During the Gulf War in 1990, Syria was the first Arab country to condemn Iraq's invasion of Kuwait. It also sent troops to Saudi Arabia to help defend that country from an attack by Iraq. In the late 1990s, the leader of Syria was still Hafez al-Assad. Assad had been in power since 1971. No opposition parties were allowed in Syria, so Assad won every election. Meanwhile, Syria continued to be an important force in Lebanon. It controlled much of the country, both militarily and politically.

Assad died in 2000. He was succeeded by his son, Bashar al-Assad. One of Bashar's first acts was to order the release of 600 political prisoners. However, civil rights campaigners said hundreds of political prisoners remained in Syrian jails. President Assad has worked to improve relations with other nations. However, Syria is suspected of supporting ongoing violence in Iraq. Syria only pulled its troops out of Lebanon because the UN Security Council demanded it.

Issues and Trends

The major issues in the Middle East are oil, religion, war, the division between rich and poor, and human rights. Wealth, in the form of petroleum reserves, is not divided equally among the nations of the Middle East. Those countries with oil have a lot of influence in the area—and in the world.

Many countries around the globe depend on oil imported from the Middle East. Anything that interferes with the flow of oil is dangerous to the world economy. That is why many countries came to the aid of oil-rich Kuwait when it was attacked by Iraq.

Sometimes just a small number of people receive high incomes in an oil-rich country. The rest of the people remain poor. Countries such as Saudi Arabia have some very wealthy families. Rulers from some of these families have used oil income to modernize and to improve schools, roads, and hospitals. However, if oil revenues fall, programs of economic and social reform may be cut. Also, the gap between the rich and the poor has widened in some countries. These conditions can cause unrest.

A country can be divided by religious beliefs. Groups of people in one country may have conflicts based mainly on the fact that they follow different religions. Lebanon is one example of this.

People may share the same religion and still be in conflict. Some people prefer a strict interpretation of religious law. Others have a more moderate point of view. This is true of any of the major religions of the area—Judaism, Islam, or Christianity. It was extremists of different religions who assassinated the peacemakers Anwar el-Sadat and Yitzhak Rabin.

For Israel and the Palestinians in the 1990s and into the 2000s, making peace was an ongoing process. Many nations, including the United States, were involved in that process. Yet, the only ones who can really make peace are the people involved in the conflict. That is why there was international pressure on the leaders of Israel and the Palestinians. They were the ones who had to negotiate a lasting peace that would be fair to both peoples.

Human rights is a major issue in the area. Israel is a democracy. Yet, Palestinians have complained that their human rights have often been ignored under Israeli control. Saddam Hussein and other authoritarian rulers in the area brutally silenced their opponents. Another human rights issue is the status of women in the Middle East. In countries such as Iran, women have had their freedoms restricted. In Saudi Arabia, women were not even allowed to drive cars.

Arab Spring

All these problems—poverty, joblessness, discrimination, oppression, violence—boiled over in December 2010. In the African country of Tunisia, a young man named Mohamed Bouazizi sold fruit from a cart to support his mother, uncle, and sisters. Police harassed him and demanded bribes. When Bouazizi couldn't pay, the police took his cart. Bouazizi went to the mayor of the town for help, but the mayor refused to see him. Frustrated by years of poverty and police harassment, Bouazizi set fire to himself in the middle of the street. He suffered burns over 90 percent of his body, but didn't die until 18 days later. Word spread quickly about Bouazizi, and thousands of young people who shared his frustration and anger over the lack of jobs and a corrupt government began to riot. Violent clashes between protesters and police spread across the country. On January 14, 2011, the president of Tunisia fled to Saudi Arabia, and a new government was formed.

The protests in Tunisia started a chain reaction throughout the Middle East. Demonstrators flooded the streets of Libya, Yemen, Egypt, Syria, and other countries with oppressive regimes. People wanted freedom and opportunity. They demanded human rights and new governments. They wanted the dictators who had abused them to be brought to justice. Citizens used social media tools like Facebook and Twitter to organize. They were also able to share photos and videos of violence against the protesters, which brought international support. Dictators like Hosni Mubarak of Egypt were forced out of office. Muammar al-Qaddafi, who had ruled Libya for more than 40 years, refused to step down. Civil war broke out. Qaddafi was captured and killed in October 2011.

The Arab Spring protests continued through the end of 2011, and would continue to affect Middle Eastern politics indefinitely. The protests had worldwide repercussions.

Protests Around the World

People around the world marched in support of the Arab Spring movement. In the United States, demonstrators against financial corruption marched in New York. The Occupy Wall Street movement was inspired by the Arab Spring. "Occupy" demonstrations sprung up across the U.S. and in other countries as well. The Occupy protestors wanted many things, but mostly for the financial system to be more fair. They said that the wealthiest Americans, who made up only one percent of the population, had more money than all the rest, and used that money to control society. The Occupy movement showed that many people in America were dissatisfied, and wanted change. The long-term effect of the Occupy protests remains to be seen.

Chapter 26: Africa I: Egypt, Libya, Ghana, Ethiopia

Africa is a large, diverse continent. To illustrate the diversity, the following sections look in detail at four different African nations.

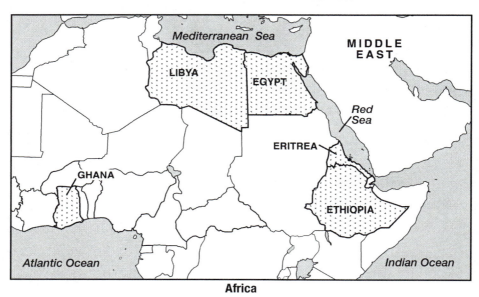

Africa

Egypt

Though located in North Africa, Egypt has been heavily involved in the affairs of the Middle East. Gamal Abdel Nasser led Egypt from the late 1950s until his death in 1970. During that time, he tried to improve Egypt's standing with other nations. He also wanted to be the leader of the Arab world. During the Cold War, Nasser took aid from the Soviet Union. Nasser accepted arms and aid from the West as well. He wanted to supply Egypt's military with new weapons and technology.

In his effort to gain respect, Nasser kept Egypt in a state of war nearly all the time. After losing territory in the 1967 war with Israel, Nasser began a war of attrition against Israel in 1968.

Israel was already under pressure from Palestinian guerrilla raids. Egyptian forces also attacked off and on. This kept Israel in a continual state of alert.

In 1970, the United Nations arranged a cease-fire. That cease-fire seemed to hold a promise for future peace. One hope was that Egypt would accept Israel's existence if it could reclaim its land. The other hope was that Israel had agreed in principle to consider withdrawing from territory it occupied.

Nasser died a month after the cease-fire was arranged. The new president was Anwar el-Sadat. Though the United States tried to bring Egypt and Israel together again, it failed.

In October 1973, Egypt and Syria attacked Israel on Yom Kippur, the Jewish Day of Atonement. The surprise attack resulted in many Israeli casualties. Soviet-supplied missiles brought down many Israeli fighter planes. However, the United States quickly sent replacement fighters, as well as other military equipment.

To show their support of Egypt and Syria, the Arab oil states imposed an embargo. They would not export oil to any country that did not support the Arab cause. While the embargo lasted, Western Europe and other countries had oil shortages and large price increases.

The United Nations again arranged a cease-fire. It had the backing of both the United States and the Soviet Union. One good thing came out of the Yom Kippur War: Each side now recognized it could not use military might to overthrow the other. When Sadat announced he was ready to talk peace, Israel accepted the idea.

President Jimmy Carter invited Sadat and Israeli Prime Minister Menachem Begin to the United States. The three men spent 13 days together in 1978 at a place called Camp David. The agreements they finally produced were called the Camp David Accords.

The new peace between the old enemies did not please everyone. Of all the Arab countries, only Morocco, Tunisia, Sudan, and Oman approved of the treaty. There was also unhappiness within Egypt.

By 1980, Israel had returned most of the Sinai (the Egyptian land it had occupied). In 1981, Sadat was assassinated by Islamic extremists unhappy about the peace with Israel.

Vice President Hosni Mubarak succeeded Sadat. Mubarak honored the Camp David Accords. However, he also promised to help Palestinians build a homeland. This improved Egypt's relations with other Arab nations.

Within Egypt, however, there was continued unrest. Muslim extremists even tried to assassinate Mubarak. They also conducted a terrorist campaign, aimed mostly at foreign tourists. Much of Egypt's economy depended on income from tourism. The extremists also targeted Egyptian Christians. Mubarak used strong measures to control the terrorists, but some attacks continued.

After more than two weeks of demonstrations by protestors, Mubarak resigned in early 2011. The country has since been under military rule.

Libya

Until the 1960s, Libya was a poor desert country in North Africa. Then oil was discovered. Libya went from being one of the poorest countries to being one of the richest.

In 1969, the king was overthrown by the army. The government that emerged was a military dictatorship. At its head was Muammar al-Qaddafi. He was still in power until the end of 2011. Qaddafi made his presence felt all over the world.

Within his own country, Qaddafi applied a mix of socialist and Islamic values. For example, he used Libya's oil riches to improve the economic life of the people. He built schools, health clinics, and highways. However, when oil prices fell, as they did in the 1980s, Qaddafi had to cut back on many programs.

Qaddafi also nationalized many businesses. In addition, he imposed Islamic laws on society. Alcohol was banned. Women were encouraged to wear traditional Muslim clothing.

Qaddafi tried to make himself the leader of the Arab world. However, his attempts to form alliances with other Arab countries always failed. Many Arab nations were suspicious of Qaddafi's actions. He built his army into a major military power in North Africa. He interfered in the business of other countries.

In the late 1970s, Qaddafi sent Libyan troops into Chad to support antigovernment rebels. His troops occupied part of northern Chad for a time. Qaddafi even proposed merging Chad with Libya. Eventually, he had to withdraw his troops, when the French came to the aid of the government of Chad.

What made Qaddafi notorious, though, was his support of terrorists anywhere in the world. Some of this terrorism was directed against Israel.

According to the United States, Qaddafi actually sponsored terrorist training camps. "Graduates" of the camps carried out guerrilla attacks in Western Europe. To punish Libya, the United States boycotted its oil.

Qaddafi did not stop his support of terrorists. So, in April 1986, U.S. forces tried to kill him by bombing his home. The raid killed some civilians but did not harm Qaddafi. However, after that, Qaddafi tried to keep his continued support of terrorists secret.

The United States, though, was sure that Qaddafi had a part in a terrorist bombing in 1988. A Pan Am 747 jet exploded over Scotland. All 259 passengers on board were killed, along with 11 people on the ground. Evidence pointed to two Libyan terrorists. In 2003, Libya formally took responsibility for the bombing.

In 1992, the entire United Nations agreed that Libya supported international terrorism. It called for Libya to surrender the two suspected Pan Am terrorists. When Libya refused, the United Nations approved trade and air traffic embargoes. This seriously affected the Libyan economy. In 1995, the United States failed to get a worldwide embargo on Libyan oil. But, in 1996, it placed sanctions on businesses that invested in Libya.

In the early twenty-first century, Qaddafi tried to improve his worldwide image. After the September 11, 2001, terrorist attacks on the United States, he was one of the first Muslim leaders to condemn al-Qaeda. In 2002, he apologized for the 1988 Lockerbie, Scotland bombing and offered compensation to the victims' families.

Anti-Qaddafi protests in early 2011 as part of the Arab Spring were met with violent government resistance. A civil war broke out and several government officials resigned. Later that year, Qaddafi was captured and killed. A governing body called the National Transitional Council was set up as the interim government.

Ghana

Ghana, formerly the Gold Coast, became a republic in 1960. Its first president was Kwame Nkrumah. He had been a leader in the West African country's fight for independence. Nkrumah's aim was to throw off Western influence. He believed in pan-Africanism, the belief that all Africans could unite, no matter what country they came from. Nkrumah hoped to be the leader of the pan-African movement. For Ghana, he promised a kind of African socialism. Instead, Nkrumah showed that he was strongly influenced by the Soviet Union and China.

By 1966, it was clear that Nkrumah's plans were not working. Nkrumah had abolished political freedom and become an authoritarian ruler. The people complained about the corrupt and inefficient government. Ghana's standard of living had actually fallen since independence. The country was harmed by a drop in the price of cocoa, Ghana's most important export.

While Nkrumah was visiting China in 1966, the military in Ghana took over. There was a series of military coups over the next 13 years. Each regime failed to improve Ghana's political, economic, or social position.

Ghana became a civilian government in 1969. But, by 1972, it had returned to military rule. None of the governments could overcome low incomes, high prices, and poverty. Widespread corruption and political repression were common. Leading politicians were arrested. People were forbidden to hold public meetings.

In 1979, Jerry Rawlings, an air force flight lieutenant, led another military coup. Many former government leaders were executed. After this bloody beginning, Rawlings allowed the transfer of rule to a civilian government.

By the end of 1981, though, Rawlings decided the civilian government was not making necessary reforms. He took over again. Rawlings's economic programs began to work. He lowered inflation. He sold state-owned businesses to private individuals.

By the early 1990s, Ghana's had the fastest growing economy in Africa. However, there had not been much progress in political freedoms. Many people were demanding a democratic government.

In 1991, Rawlings called for a new constitution. Under that constitution, Ghana held a free election in 1992. Rawlings ran for president and won by a landslide.

After that, Ghana's economy continued to improve. By the mid-1990s, gold production was at record highs. Women were encouraged to own and operate businesses. Schools and hospitals sprang up with local support. Rawlings was reelected in 1996, though by a smaller majority. Rawlings' vice president during this second term, John Atta Mills, was later elected president and assumed office in 2009.

Ethiopia

Ethiopia is an ancient country in what is called the Horn of Africa, the part of East Africa that juts into the Indian Ocean. In the 1960s, Ethiopia was ruled by Emperor Haile Selassie. He had been on the throne since 1930. As emperor, Haile Selassie tried to modernize his country.

Many different groups of people live in Ethiopia. Over 70 languages are spoken there. Haile Selassie tried to bring the different groups together. He made progress in education and began industrializing the country. He also made some reforms in the government. These included permitting a constitution, parliament, and court system. However, he was careful to hold on to his own power.

Despite these changes, Ethiopia remained a very poor country. The United States sent aid. This aid included equipping and training the army. It was the army, though, that deposed (overthrew) Haile Selassie in 1974.

Conditions in Ethiopia were very bad. Oil prices were high, and there was a terrible drought (long dry spell). Famine was killing people, especially in the Tigre province.

Then there was the rebellion in Eritrea. During World War II, Ethiopia had been taken over by fascist Italy. The Italians annexed Ethiopia to two of its colonies, Eritrea and Italian Somaliland. Now Eritrea wanted its independence.

A group of army officers mutinied, or rebelled. They were joined by students and others in the capital, Addis Ababa. However, what started as a revolt against terrible conditions soon became more extreme. The military took over the government. It dissolved parliament and suspended the constitution. Ethiopia was declared a socialist state.

Mengistu Haile Mariam became head of the government. He used brutal techniques to make a communist state. Under Mengistu, the military grew more powerful. Anyone declared an enemy of the state was rounded up and immediately executed. That included the emperor and his family. The government also nationalized businesses, banks, and farms.

The new Ethiopian government depended on the Soviet Union for weapons and military training. The army was now fighting Eritrean rebels in the north and Somalis in the southeast. Living conditions in the country were worse than ever. Fighting, famines, and a corrupt government cost many lives.

In 1984 and 1985, the famine drew international attention. Television programs showed starving people. Aid flowed in from around the world.

However, that aid was only a temporary help. It did not solve Ethiopia's real problems. In 1991, Mengistu declared that the country would no longer be communist. It was too late, though. By then, the Soviet Union was collapsing. It stopped all aid to Ethiopia. Rebel forces in Ethiopia were able to overcome a huge army equipped with modern weapons. Mengistu fled, and new leaders took over the shattered country.

In 1993, Eritrea peacefully won its independence. In both countries, new governments tried to put the pieces together. However, economic problems and another famine in 1994 showed how hard that was to do. The Horn of Africa was not stable, either. Both the Sudan and Somalia were torn with violence. That sent thousands of refugees over the border. It seemed, though, that between Ethiopia and Eritrea, at least, there was no longer danger of war. They had, after all, fought together to get rid of a dictator. Also, both countries were again allied with the United States.

However, in 1998, Ethiopia and Eritrea began to quarrel over a disputed border. Each country claimed parts of the province of Tigre.

The United States rushed advisers to both countries to prevent the fighting. But the quarreling turned to violence, with heavy fighting all along the border. Working with the United Nations, the United States helped arrange a cease-fire. Businesspeople on both sides hoped the two countries would come to a peaceful agreement. They knew that the economies of both countries would not survive another war. Also, the fighting came after poor harvests in both countries. War would increase the danger of another famine.

In 2000, Eritrea and Ethiopia signed a peace agreement. Then an independent commission was set up to decide where the border should lie. When the new border was presented, both countries agreed to it—with one exception. Both claimed the town of Badme. Only in 2004 were these disagreements settled.

At the same time, the government began a huge resettlement program. They are trying to move more than two million people away from the dry eastern highlands. The government says this is the only way to solve food shortages. Today, most Ethiopians continue to rely on food aid from abroad.

■ OF NOTE

Some of Africa's 53 countries are incredibly rich. Others, however, are incredibly poor. The difference is due to unequal resources, such as petroleum. Another resource is rainfall. Depending on the region, there is either too much or too little rain. The west coast gets more than 100 inches a year. The desert regions usually get fewer than 10 inches. There are three great desert regions in Africa. The Sahara, in the north, is the largest hot desert in the world. The Namib is along the west coast. The Kalahari is in the south. These deserts are spreading. For some time, farmers have been cutting down trees near the deserts to create more farmland. Without these plants to hold the soil in place, the topsoil has scattered, and the deserts have been allowed to spread. The constant expansion of the deserts is especially hard on the poor countries along the fringes. Environmentalists are encouraging all African countries to cooperate in stopping the spread of the deserts.

Chapter 27: Africa II: Nigeria, Democratic Republic of the Congo, Zimbabwe, South Africa

Many nations of Africa live within borders that were drawn by Europeans. These invaders claimed the land, but they could not claim the loyalty of the people. The following sections look in detail at four different African nations.

Africa

Nigeria

Nigeria won its independence in 1960. Almost immediately, the country seemed to pull apart. Within Nigeria's borders lived 250 different ethnic groups. The government was a federation of three regions: north, east, and west. The Ibo dominated the eastern part. The Yoruba were in the western region. The north was mostly Muslim Hausa-Fulani. Each group wanted to protect its own interests. The Hausa-Fulani had the largest population and, therefore, more political power.

In 1966, Ibo officers of the federal army led a mutiny. They were trying to overthrow the north's political power. An army general regained control and took over the government. He set about unifying Nigeria. He wanted to abolish the loose federation that had led to such conflict. However, he favored the Ibos. The northerners interpreted this as an Ibo plot to take over the country. This rumor led to mass killings of Ibos who had moved to the north. Revenge killings of Hausas followed. Panicked refugees moved across the country, looking for safety. Nigeria seemed to be in complete disorder.

The biggest tragedy was still to come: a disastrous civil war. In May 1967, Odumegwu Ojukwu, the military commander of the eastern

Ibo region, declared his region's independence. The new country, he announced, was called Biafra. But Colonel Yakuba Gowon, the military ruler of Nigeria, was determined to hold the country together. The fighting lasted nearly three years. Gowon had the larger army, and he used it to set up a blockade. The blockade kept food supplies from reaching the people of Biafra. The famine that followed killed hundreds of thousands of people. Pictures of starving people reached the West. However, no country wanted to get involved in the civil war. The Ibo were defeated, and Biafra was reunited with Nigeria. In 1970, Biafra ceased to exist.

Following the war, Gowon announced a period of rebuilding. He wanted to modernize the nation and unite the people. Nigeria is a country rich in resources, including petroleum. It is the seventh largest oil producer in the world. The oil boom of the 1970s helped, but it was not enough. The standard of living of the majority of the people did not improve. Only a small group of businesspeople made money. At the same time, agriculture could not keep up with the rapidly growing population. Nigeria actually had to import food.

In 1975, Gowon was overthrown by another military coup. A series of governments followed. The political instability (unrest) made economic development difficult. Nigeria's resources were being mismanaged. The oil boom ended, and the price of petroleum went down. Oil sales were still good, but the country imported more goods than it sold. From 1979 to 1983, a civilian government ran the country. Then the military took over again. This time, it promised to return the government to civilian control. First, the authorities said they had to make sure corrupt officials would not return to power. The government also made an effort to cut imports and increase food production.

In 1993, the country held free elections. However, the government refused to honor the results. Another military ruler rose to power. He was General Sani Abacha. Abacha had been in power five years when he died suddenly of a heart attack. During those five years, he brutally put down opposition. Those who spoke up against the government had to flee the country or be imprisoned or executed. With Abacha's death, there was new hope that Nigeria would have another chance at democracy. Elections were held and in May 1999, Olusegun Obasanjo became the president. He ruled until 2007, when Umaru Musa Yar'Adua was declared the winner of

203

Chapter 27: Africa II: Nigeria, Democratic Republic of the Congo, Zimbabwe, South Africa • Simply History: 1900 to Present

a controversial election. Following his death in 2010, he was succeeded by the vice president, Goodluck Jonathan.

Democratic Republic of the Congo

In 1960, Congo was a Belgian colony. In 1959, Belgium began to lose control. It could no longer run the government. However, it wanted to keep control of many of the Congo's rich natural resources. There were also power struggles along ethnic, regional, and political lines. The Soviet Union saw this unrest as an excuse to intervene (step in). It supported one of the most extreme groups.

The first step in the civil war was the attempt by the Katanga region to secede. This part of the country was rich in minerals. Kasai, another mineral-rich region, also tried to secede. Without these two regions, the Congo would have become one of the poorest states in Africa. Finally, the United Nations sent a peacekeeping force to restore order and end the bloodshed.

Eventually, General Mobutu Sese Seko, army chief of staff, emerged as the major power. He took over in 1965 and forced order on the country. He used European aid to put down rebellions. At the same time, he encouraged African people to reject foreign influence. They were urged to wear traditional clothing instead of Western dress and to adopt African names. The Congo was renamed the Republic of Zaire to erase any reminder of the past Belgian rule. (Another country, the Republic of the Congo, is a separate nation.)

Mobutu nationalized Zaire's key industries, such as copper mining. He also tried to boost food production. Under his harsh dictatorship, though, Zaire lost ground economically and politically. There was more order. However, it was at the expense of freedom. Mobutu did not allow any political opposition. Also, the government had many corrupt officials. Mobutu and his friends mismanaged government funds or used them to make themselves rich.

As Mobutu's rule went on, Zaire lost financial aid from the United States and other Western countries. Many protested Mobutu's abuse of human rights. Within Zaire, riots broke out to protest poverty and the lack of civil rights.

In 1994, ethnic civil war in neighboring Rwanda spilled over into Zaire. Hutu refugees fleeing Tutsi soldiers entered Zaire in large numbers. Fighting broke out between Hutus and Tutsis living in Zaire. Mobutu ordered the Tutsis out of the country. Instead of going, they organized under rebel leader Laurent Kabila.

By this time, the regular army was discouraged. It was not willing to fight hard for Mobutu. Kabila and his army had little resistance as they moved toward Kinshasa, the capital. After a seven-month rebellion, Mobutu was defeated. He fled the country and died a short time later.

In 1997, Kabila was welcomed as a liberator, someone who would free the country. When he first came to power, Kabila promised democracy and better living standards. A year after the revolution, though, people were still waiting to see that happen. In fact, they were wondering if things were going to be any different. Kabila had declared himself president and renamed the country the Democratic Republic of the Congo. There was a new government and a new flag, but all political activity was banned.

Also, the country's economy was in a poor state. Prices for basic foods were high. Nor was the Congo getting help from other countries. Kabila was accused of having allowed massacres of Rwandan Hutu refugees during the civil war. Other countries were unwilling to send financial aid until these charges were investigated. This was something Kabila refused to allow.

In 2001, Kabila was shot dead by one of his bodyguards. His son, Joseph Kabila, succeeded him as president. In 2002, a peace deal was signed by the government and the rebels. However, fighting still continues.

Zimbabwe

Zimbabwe's road to independence was long and difficult. By the 1960s, other African nations were getting their freedom fairly easily. What made Zimbabwe's independence movement different was the makeup of its population.

Zimbabwe was formerly called Rhodesia, the name given to this region by British colonizers. White settlers in Rhodesia were a minority. Despite their

205

Chapter 27: Africa II: Nigeria, Democratic Republic of the Congo, Zimbabwe, South Africa • Simply History: 1900 to Present

numbers, they owned the most land—and the best. They also controlled the government. They had set in place a social system that severely restricted blacks' rights. Great Britain was ready to grant independence if it could protect the majority blacks. But white Rhodesians were unwilling to change their way of life. They were led by Ian Smith of the Front party.

Black Rhodesians also rallied behind forceful leaders. They formed the National Democratic Party. It was led by Joshua Nkomo and Robert Mugabe, among others. Of the two men, Mugabe was the more radical leader.

In 1965, the white minority government unilaterally declared its independence from Britain. Great Britain did not accept the declaration. In 1967, the United Nations imposed sanctions against Rhodesia. For more than ten years, the country had to endure British pressure, economic sanctions, and guerrilla warfare.

The government had a strong army. Smith could count on help from at least two countries: South Africa and Portugal. The African nationalists had split into two parties. One was the Zimbabwe African People's Union (ZAPU). The other was the more radical Zimbabwe African National Union (ZANU). They formed a loose alliance called the Patriotic Front. Both groups set up guerrilla bases in nearby countries. ZAPU got aid from the Soviet Union. ZANU received training and arms from China. This allowed Smith to accuse the rebels of being communists.

The civil war lasted through most of the 1970s. Despite its military strength, the government could not completely put down the rebellion. The war and economic sanctions damaged the economy. Many whites were leaving the country. In addition, Portugal and South Africa were no longer able to offer aid. By the mid-1970s, the government was more willing to negotiate with the nationalists.

Finally, in 1979, British Prime Minister Margaret Thatcher's government brought white and nationalist leaders together. Great Britain and other countries tried to work out an agreement acceptable to both sides. Mugabe was the least willing to accept any compromises. Finally, all parties agreed on a settlement. A cease-fire ended the fighting. In April 1980, the world recognized Zimbabwe as an independent country.

After an election, Mugabe emerged as the leader. During the civil war, he had made it clear that he wanted a one-party, Marxist-socialist state. However, as the country's leader, he was more realistic. He did not try to drive out the white settlers and businesspeople. Mugabe knew that the economy depended on them.

Unrest in Zimbabwe from ethnic and political rivalries continued through the 1980s. There was the question of how to distribute land so that blacks would hold a fair share. The other part of that issue was how to compensate white settlers for that land.

Mugabe was reelected president in 1987 with an even larger majority than before. In the 1990s, however, drought and poor harvests made life more difficult. Yet, there was no civil war in Zimbabwe. The situation was better than anyone might have expected during the violent years of the 1970s.

More recently, Mugabe seized white-owned land. Some of the land was given to black Zimbabweans. But a great deal of this land was given to members of the government. These landowners often did not know farming methods. As a result, the country saw a drop in food production. This has led to serious food shortages in some areas.

South Africa

The winds of change were blowing through Africa in the 1960s. That is how the British prime minister, Harold Macmillan, described the end of colonialism. However, that was not true of South Africa. Apartheid was still in force there. White South Africans were the minority, but they were a large minority. They owned the best land, received better educations, and got better jobs. They held political and economic power.

Black South Africans, however, had begun to organize. Two organizations they formed were the African National Congress (ANC) and the Pan-Africanist Congress (PAC). Both groups led public demonstrations against the hated pass law. This law required all nonwhites to carry a pass that showed their race and where they had permission to live and work. The white government controlled both the military and the police. Through them, the government used force to put down strikes and protests. Each such incident, though, only increased black militancy.

207

Chapter 27: Africa II: Nigeria, Democratic Republic of the Congo, Zimbabwe, South Africa • Simply History: 1900 to Present

In the early months of 1960, the ANC and the PAC began a campaign against the pass laws. A peaceful protest in the small town of Sharpeville turned into a massacre, as police opened fire. They killed 69 people.

All over the country, blacks stayed away from work in protest. The government's reaction was to declare both ANC and PAC illegal. Many blacks were arrested.

In 1961, South Africa declared itself an independent republic. It had been a member of the Commonwealth of Nations. The Commonwealth was made up of Great Britain and its former colonies. Therefore, it included people of all races. South Africa dropped out before it was asked to leave because of its racist laws. As an independent republic, South Africa no longer had other countries telling it what to do.

The following years saw the tightening of controls. Nelson Mandela, a young black lawyer, organized a military wing of the ANC. Its purpose was to blow up places without injuring anyone. However, in 1962, Mandela was captured. At his trial, Mandela spoke of a "democratic and free society in which all persons live in harmony and with equal opportunities." He received a life sentence and was shut away. Yet, his story continued to inspire black Africans.

The cycle of demonstrations and government crackdowns continued. South Africa became more and more isolated. International sanctions and embargoes put economic pressure on the country. Investors were not willing to put money into the economy. South African athletes were not allowed to take part in international competitions. Meanwhile, guerrilla warfare continued. Mass protests often ended in bloodshed. A peaceful student demonstration in Soweto, in 1976, left 600 students dead and led to even more protests.

The isolation and economic pressures began to have an effect. The government began to tinker with its racist laws. Many of the changes just made matters worse. The laws were still based on keeping whites in a dominant position. Finally, white South Africans began to realize that they had to work out a way to live peacefully with their black fellow citizens.

In 1989, white South Africans elected a moderate, F. W. de Klerk, as president. The new president began a series of real reforms and negotiations. In 1990, de Klerk lifted the bans on the ANC and the PAC. He released Nelson Mandela after 27 years in prison. Mandela became the chief negotiator for South African blacks.

Within the next few years, the whole government changed. Finally, in 1994, a national election led to a majority government, with Nelson Mandela as its president.

Not all of South Africa's problems were solved. There was black-on-black violence. Much of it was the result of disagreements between the ANC and Zulu chief Mangosuthu Buthelezi of the Inkatha Freedom party. There were still whites who were not happy with the new political system. And, though apartheid ended, its effects did not. Most of South Africa's wealth was still in the hands of whites. There was still a great deal of poverty among blacks. South Africa still had work to do to make a better future for all its people.

Issues and Trends

Several serious and difficult-to-solve problems have plagued Africa in recent years. Chief among these are violence, in the form of civil wars and ethnic conflicts, and the AIDS epidemic.

Three long-lasting areas of violence were in Sudan, Somalia, and Rwanda. In Sudan, the Muslim Arab north region controlled the government. It clashed with the black African animists and Christians in the south region. A seemingly endless civil war dragged on, starting in the 1980s. A peace agreement was reached in 2004. Yet, in that year, government-backed Arab militias began and continued killing—in large numbers—black Muslim farming peoples in the northwestern Darfur region.

In Somalia, groups of opposing clans took control of different areas of the country in the 1990s. No central government has ruled the nation since then, in spite of years of peace talks.

In Rwanda, the two main ethnic groups—the Hutu and Tutsi—exploded into crushing violence in the 1990s. Ruling Hutu forces killed hundreds of thousands of Tutsis. Then Tutsi rebel forces killed many Hutu

209

Chapter 27: Africa II: Nigeria, Democratic Republic of the Congo, Zimbabwe, South Africa • Simply History: 1900 to Present

and drove many more out of the country. In 2003, most voters in Rwanda approved a legal mandate of shared power between the Hutu and Tutsi.

A second major crisis in Africa is the AIDS epidemic. Millions of people around the world are infected with AIDS. By far the greatest number of these people live in sub-Saharan Africa. As of the end of 2003, as many as 28 million people in this region were infected with HIV/AIDS. Expected length of life for these people dropped from 67 without HIV/AIDS to 47 with HIV/AIDS. Also, hundreds of thousands of babies in this region have been and continue to be born with HIV/AIDS. They were infected before birth by their infected mothers. Millions of African children have lost one or both of their parents to the disease.

The AIDS epidemic has been stripping Africa of its current and future people. Yet medicines to control (but not cure) AIDS are expensive and not affordable in much of Africa. Also, African society has often resisted recognizing AIDS as an African—not just a Western—problem. Dealing with and controlling the AIDS epidemic continues as a critical problem for Africa as the twenty-first century unfolds.

Topic 8

Asia and Australasia

Chapter 28: The Indian Subcontinent and Southeast Asia

Colonialism in most parts of Asia ended after World War II. For all the now-independent nations, it was like a new beginning. But the new governments soon found that the problems of the past still remained to be solved.

The Indian Subcontinent

Two major countries on the Indian Subcontinent are India and Pakistan. The stories of India and Pakistan are very closely tied. The two nations have often been in conflict, but at one time they were one country under one colonial ruler, Great Britain.

The borders for the two countries were based mainly on religion. Pakistan was formed from a region in the northwest and Bengal in the east. This new country was made up mainly of Muslims. But the two parts—East and West Pakistan—were separated by 1,000 miles.

India itself was mainly Hindu. At the time of independence, in the 1930s and 1940s, fighting

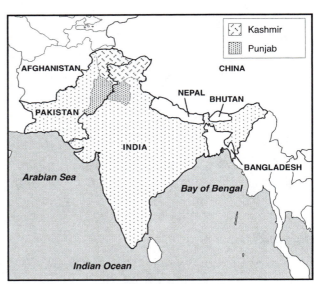

The Indian Subcontinent

between the Hindus and Muslims had already cost many lives. Millions of people moved from one part of the subcontinent to the other. To many of them, it seemed safer to live with people of their own religion, even if it meant moving many, many miles to do so.

OF NOTE

> When you see the terms *Islam, Muslim,* or *Moslem,* you should recognize that they all refer to one religion. Islam is the religion. Its founder, in the year 622, was Mohammed. A follower of Islam is a Muslim (or Moslem).

India

India is a diverse country. Its wide variety of peoples, cultures, and languages makes it difficult to govern. Sometimes, a large minority demands autonomy, or even complete independence. The central government of India rejects such demands. If one state pulls out of the republic, other states may want to do the same thing. Then the whole union would fall apart.

These quarrels have turned deadly at times. The border state of Punjab is an example. In 1984, Indira Gandhi was prime minister. There had been protests and armed conflicts between government forces and Sikhs wanting autonomy. (Sikhs are members of a religion that has a strong military tradition.) Gandhi ordered army troops to go after a band of rebel fighters hiding in a Sikh temple. The fighters had been using the temple as a base for terrorist attacks.

Sikhs were shocked by this attack on their holiest site. Even more violence followed. Four months later, Indira Gandhi was assassinated. Police identified two Sikh members of her bodyguard as the murderers.

Pakistan

East and West Pakistan had little in common except for the Islamic religion. The two regions had different cultures, languages, histories, ethnic backgrounds, and geography. Even their economies were different. East Pakistan had less land but a larger population. Yet, West Pakistan tried to control the whole country. East Pakistan rebelled in December 1971. Army troops tried to put down the independence movement. The war drove about ten million refugees across the border into India. This created many economic, social, and health problems there. Finally, India attacked the Pakistani army in support of East Pakistan. In two weeks, the

Pakistani army surrendered. East Pakistan then became an independent country called Bangladesh.

Different Kinds of Leaders

Great Britain was an imperialist country, with colonies in different parts of the world. Yet, it also had a tradition of parliamentary democracy. The Republic of India followed in that tradition. Its first prime minister was Jawaharlal Nehru. He was a strong believer in democracy and set the country on that course.

Pakistan, however, did not follow Great Britain's model. It has been ruled mostly by authoritarian military rulers. Nehru, on the other hand, made sure that India's army was under civilian control. Another thing Nehru wanted was for India to be a secular state, treating all religions with equal importance and respect.

Relations Between Countries

By the 1990s, India and Pakistan had fought three wars in 50 years. They quarreled for years over Kashmir, a province that borders both India and Pakistan. When India was divided in 1947, Kashmir became part of India. Pakistan also claimed the region. The next year, war broke out over Kashmir. The United Nations arranged a cease-fire in 1949. War broke out again in 1965. The United States and the Soviet Union helped bring the war to an end within three weeks. As you have read, India and Pakistan also fought in 1971, when East Pakistan rebelled. In 1976, India and Pakistan resumed normal relations.

In the 1990s, the two countries were still watchful of each other. In 1998, India announced it was a nuclear power—and proceeded to perform test explosions, despite world protest. Pakistan followed with its own announcement and testing—also despite protests from other world powers.

Fighting in Kashmir resumed in 1999. War—possibly with nuclear weapons—loomed in 2002. Other nations, including the United States, the United Kingdom, Russia, and China, worked to restore calm. In 2003, India and Pakistan agreed to a cease-fire, and tensions eased.

Afghanistan

Afghanistan is another country in this region, to the northwest of Pakistan. During the Cold War, Afghanistan was closely allied with the Soviet Union. The nation went through a series of regime changes in the 1970s. In 1979, the U.S.S.R. invaded Afghanistan and set up a Soviet-controlled regime. Muslim resistance fighters called *mujahideen* waged an intense guerrilla war against the occupying Soviet troops. As part of Cold War strategy, the United States supported the Afghan resistance and supplied it with weapons. Hopelessly bogged down in a no-win situation, the U.S.S.R. withdrew from Afghanistan in 1989.

Warring factions now vied for control. A radical Islamic group called the Taliban took the capital, Kabul, in 1996. They controlled almost all of Afghanistan by 1998. The Taliban ruled according to a very strict version of Islamic law. Women were especially affected. They could no longer hold jobs. They could not leave their homes unless a male relative came with them. Women and girls were barred from schools.

The Taliban also provided a safe haven for Osama bin Laden. He was a wealthy Saudi linked to the anti-United States, anti-Western al-Qaeda terrorist network. Bin Laden and al-Qaeda operated terrorist training camps in Afghanistan. The United States attacked these camps with cruise missiles in 1998. Soon after the September 11, 2001, airline attacks in New York and Washington, D.C., the United States determined that bin Laden had planned them. The Taliban refused to hand over bin Laden. The United States and U.S. allies then bombed and invaded Afghanistan. They had driven the Taliban from power, and bin Laden into hiding, by the end of 2001.

Hamid Karzai became president of Afghanistan in 2002. He was elected to that position by popular vote in 2004. But Karzai struggled to maintain central government rule over areas of the nation controlled by powerful warlords. U.S. troops remained in the nation, battling—as Soviet forces had in the 1980s—fierce resistance by armed insurgents. By the end of 2011, the U.S. had lost 1,800 lives in Afghanistan and spent more than $400 billion on the effort.

Vietnam

Vietnam is larger than New Mexico but smaller than Montana. Yet, in the 1960s and 1970s, it was the bloody battlefield of the Cold War.

The United States supplied South Vietnam with weapons and military aid. The Soviet Union (as well as Communist China) helped North Vietnam.

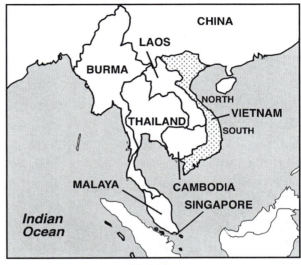

Vietnam

Vietnam had been a French colony. During World War II, it was occupied by the Japanese.

After the war, Ho Chi Minh led a communist government in North Vietnam. The United States backed the noncommunist South. Its leader, Ngo Dinh Diem, was an authoritarian who suppressed all opposition. But he still could not defeat the Viet Cong—the communist rebels fighting in the South. Their aim was to unite the whole country under Ho Chi Minh.

At first, the United States sent only materials and military advisers to Vietnam. As the war continued, however, more and more military personnel headed for Vietnam. Then American troops joined the battle. Instead of just a cold war, the United States was fighting a shooting war.

Ho Chi Minh died in 1969, at the age of 79. But that did not slow the war down. The United States began bombing Viet Cong bases in neighboring Cambodia. By then, the U.S. military was fighting mainly from the air. Troops of the South Vietnamese army were supposed to take over the ground fighting.

The End of the War

Americans were deeply divided about the war. Protests against the war often turned violent. Many people thought that the United States should never have become involved. Others felt that it was important to stop communism from spreading. Either way, the toll of the war was staggering: More than 58,000 Americans died, and the Vietnamese lost millions, including many civilians.

Though the United States and its allies had better weapons, they could not win the war. The Viet Cong were unlike other armies. They did not wear uniforms. There was no way to tell them apart from ordinary citizens. They were jungle fighters. They often built underground tunnels to go from place to place. These tunnels made good hiding places.

In 1973, the United States and Vietnam negotiated an end to the war. Vietnam was still divided. But by April 1975, Saigon—the capital of South Vietnam—had fallen to the army of North Vietnam. All of Vietnam was under communist rule. Twenty years later, the United States and Vietnam resumed normal relations.

Burma, Cambodia, Singapore, and Thailand

Burma, Cambodia, Singapore, and Thailand have also seen changes in recent years.

Burma

After independence, Burma was led by U Nu. He tried to keep Burma democratic. But, ethnic conflict and fighting with communist groups created great unrest. In 1962, the military overthrew U Nu's government. The military stayed in power for more than 20 years.

In the late 1980s, it looked as if the country might move toward democracy again. Unfortunately, an even harsher military government soon took over. In 1989, that government changed the name of the country to Myanmar. However, the United States refused to recognize this name or the illegally installed government.

Hope for democracy did not die in Burma. In 1991, Aung San Suu Kyi was awarded the Nobel Peace Prize. She had spoken out frequently against government repression. The government kept her under house arrest for periods of years, from 1989 to 2010. But she remained a symbol of hope for many people in Burma.

In 2007, Buddhist monks led protests against the government. The next year, with the approval of the military regime in power, a new constitution was drawn up. It called for the creation of a "discipline-flourishing democracy" and allowed the military to retain a great deal of political power. Elections were held in 2010; amid assertions of polling fraud, the military regime claimed to win 80% of votes. The former prime minister, Thein Sein, took office as president in early 2011.

In addition to its political problems, Burma has also dealt with severe environmental calamities. On May 2, 2008, Cyclone Nargis hit Burma. It is considered the country's worst natural disaster ever recorded, and resulted in 138,000 deaths.

Cambodia

Probably no country in this region suffered more than Cambodia. Its leader, Norodom Sihanouk, tried to keep the country independent and neutral. During the Vietnam War, however, he decided that North Vietnam was likely to win. So, Sihanouk turned from the West and sought the friendship of China. The North Vietnamese brought supplies south on the Ho Chi Minh Trail. Some of the trail went through Cambodia. Sihanouk was powerless to stop this activity.

Because of these factors, the United States helped overthrow Sihanouk in 1970. That ended any hope of Cambodian neutrality. Both United States and Vietnamese troops invaded Cambodia. They wanted to destroy Viet Cong bases and supply lines. When the war ended, the U.S.-backed government quickly fell to the Khmer Rouge. The Khmer Rouge was led by a fanatical communist named Pol Pot.

What followed next was genocide, the deliberate and systematic destruction of a group of people. Pol Pot directed a campaign of genocide against all educated Cambodians who might have resisted his control. He forced large numbers of people into labor camps, which have been called the "Killing Fields." There, conditions were so poor that many people died from the lack of food and from disease. Many others were executed. As many as two million people may have died.

In 1979, communist Vietnam stepped into the battle. That put an end to Pol Pot's bloody rule. But the fight for control of Cambodia went on for years. In 1990, the United Nations got all sides to agree on a peace plan. Free elections in 1993 brought some stability and peace. Pol Pot died in disgrace in 1998. Yet, the new government still battled with what was left of the Khmer Rouge until the late 1990s.

Following the discovery of oil and natural gas deposits off of Cambodia's coast in 2005, oil companies started taking an interest in the country. This new revenue source will likely boost the country's economy, but the long-term effects remain to be seen.

Singapore

Singapore stood out amidst the poverty, warfare, and authoritarian governments of the region. During the period of unrest, this tiny (246.7 square miles) island republic had a parliamentary system. A prime minister led the government. There was universal suffrage, meaning every adult could vote. The economy was one of the strongest in the area. Unemployment was low. There were a number of industries. They included petroleum refining, ship repair, electronics, and financial and business services. However, residents of Singapore were required to obey very strict laws of behavior.

Thailand

The kingdom of Thailand was the only country in the region to escape colonial control. It did not, however, escape Japanese occupation. In the 1960s, Thailand's major problem was putting down guerrilla action by communist invaders in the north. Guerrillas are fighters who do not engage in standard warfare. They may slip into a country or an area to attack people and destroy buildings. Then they slip away, only to come back again and again.

Thailand's location put it in a difficult position after the Vietnam War. Refugees from Laos, Cambodia, and Vietnam flooded into the country. Unrest led to a series of military governments. Free elections were held again in the 1990s. Although Thailand was rich in resources, such as tin, rubber, and rice, its economy collapsed in 1997 because of foreign debt. Since then, reforms have brought some recovery. Islamic militants plagued Thailand's southern provinces with attacks beginning in 2004.

In 2006, a military coup occurred. A new constitution was drawn up and democratic elections were held in late 2007. However, the years that followed were turbulent and the political situation remains unstable.

The Global Economy

The economies of Southeast Asia changed in several important ways in the years after 1960. One change was the green revolution. Famine and undernourishment were common in the area. The high birthrate made it even worse. But in 1960, new methods of cultivation (raising crops) were introduced. Farmers produced bigger and better crops. This "green (crop) revolution" helped feed many more people. However, famine was still a concern.

In the later years of the twentieth century, multinational corporations provided growing numbers of jobs in Southeast Asia. These companies wanted to sell more of their products all over the world. They tried to keep their prices competitive. So, they started up factories in places such as Vietnam or Indonesia. Workers in those countries got paid a lot less than U.S. workers.

U.S. labor leaders worried that Americans were not getting those jobs. Also, some of the Asian factories had very poor working conditions.

Environmentalists also had concerns. The West had controls to limit pollution and the destruction of resources. What happens, though, when people build factories in other parts of the world? Are they so eager to have the work that they allow harm to the environment? How much harm might be acceptable so that poor people can have jobs? What is the proper balance? These are ongoing concerns.

New industries and improving wages meant a growing middle class. For a smaller group of people, it meant great wealth. Unfortunately, that still left many millions in poverty. The division between the haves (those who have wealth) and the have-nots was still great. That division meant continued unrest for the countries of Southeast Asia, as well as many others.

Chapter 29: China

The communist revolution in China was to be an ongoing event. A series of steps was designed to bring the country closer to what its leaders considered "perfection."

In Charge of the Revolution

The man in charge of China's revolution was Mao Zedong (or Mao Tse-tung), who lived from 1893 to 1976. Mao wanted to use the revolution to modernize China. That would improve the life of its people. To keep everyone dedicated to this goal, he indoctrinated them. That is, Mao used his writings and speeches to teach the population to think a certain way. If people doubted him, he controlled them through terror.

Mao knew that nothing united a people like having an enemy to blame for whatever went wrong. Once Mao declared who the enemy was, he could punish that group. This also showed others what would happen to them if they opposed him. Mao was a ruthless dictator, a man without mercy.

The Great Leap Forward

China needed increased industrial productivity. It also needed greater yields from the land. Its farmers would need to produce more crops. There was a huge population to feed. A low yield could mean famine, with millions of people starving.

To encourage farmers to work even harder, Mao started the Great Leap Forward. There were actually two leaps. One was in 1958, and the other in 1959 to 1960. At the time, Chinese farmers were grouped in cooperatives. They shared work, animals, and whatever equipment they had. For the Great Leap Forward, farmers were forced into larger cooperatives called communes. The communes, though, were not just for farming. They also had to industrialize. That meant building small furnaces to make steel. These were not modern, efficient factories. And they were run by people who did not really know what they were doing.

The results were a disaster. The country showed industrial losses rather than gains. Agriculture suffered, too. Grain was in short supply. Yet, the population increased. Famine became widespread. Many millions of people died of starvation in China during this time.

The Cultural Revolution

Mao also kept very tight controls on the intellectuals—the scientists, teachers, artists, and other thinkers. The Communist Party did not allow freedom of thought. That would threaten the revolution. It would challenge the leaders who controlled the country.

So, Mao called intellectuals the enemies of the people. One of the worst examples of this was the Cultural Revolution. It began in 1966 and lasted until 1968. In that time, it wrecked millions of lives.

Mao urged people to denounce each other. In this case, the crimes were supposed to be against communist principles.

Many young people formed themselves into groups they called Red Guards. Most of them were students, along with some workers. They were to carry out Mao's wishes. Their weapons for doing so were terror and humiliation. Their target was anyone with any kind of authority, such as teachers or professionals.

The Red Guards were really just mobs. They burned, killed, and destroyed as they went. Finally, the People's Liberation Army had to restore order. Many of the Guards were executed.

Mao used this as an excuse to further intimidate intellectuals. He had about 20 million people rounded up. They were forced into the countryside to work as farm laborers. This was supposed to "reeducate" them. Schools and universities were closed. They were not opened again until the 1970s.

Millions saw their careers and education ended. Industrial production went down. It took ten years to make up the losses. At no time did Mao take any responsibility for what happened. Nor did anyone dare to blame him.

OF NOTE

Mao's *Little Red Book* was a collection of Mao's writings. It had many quotations from his writings and speeches. Everyone was encouraged to learn them. Many people carried the book with them. Crowds would wave the book in the air. They often recited parts of the book in unison. This had a powerful effect on the minds of the Chinese population.

An Opening to the West

For many years, China had the support of the Soviet Union. However, it was not always a peaceful relationship. Russia often tried to use its support to control Chinese policy. Then, in 1953, Soviet dictator Joseph Stalin died. Nikita Khrushchev took over. He began what was called de-Stalinization. That is, he criticized and changed many of the things Stalin had done.

This caused a break with Mao. Mao accused Khrushchev of going back to capitalism. In 1960, Khrushchev stopped all aid to China. He called back about 30,000 Soviet engineers and technicians. He had already stopped helping China develop an atomic bomb.

Mao now feared both the Soviet Union and the United States. They both had atomic bombs. So, China pushed ahead with its own program. In 1964, it exploded its first atomic bomb. About this time, Mao began to think about reaching out to the United States, hoping to achieve a good balance of power against the Soviet Union.

In 1971, Henry Kissinger went to Beijing, the capital of China, as President Richard Nixon's adviser. He prepared the way for a visit by the president himself in February 1972. By December 1978, Beijing and Washington had resumed normal relations. Mainland China had taken its place in the United Nations. Thousands of Chinese students were sent to the capitalist United States to study advanced technology and management. Once, these students would have gone only to the Soviet Union for their advanced education.

The Fall of the Four

After Mao died in 1976, China changed. A group of hard-liners were the first to fall from power. The hard-liners wanted to follow communist philosophy exactly. They were called the Gang of Four. One of them was Mao's widow, Jiang Qing. Jiang Qing was the only one who did not admit any guilt for the destructive Cultural Revolution. She was sentenced to death, but this was later changed to life in prison.

The leader who soon took power was Deng Xiaoping. Deng was more of a reformer. He wanted to make China a modern economy. He was not interested in a Western-style democracy. But he felt he could borrow ideas and technology from the West. Between 1979 and 1984, Deng replaced China's agricultural communes. The new arrangement was more like private ownership. And agricultural production increased.

Industry, too, was freed from much government control. And small, privately owned businesses were encouraged. Even the army ran a number of businesses. In most parts of the country, people were making money. They could build nice houses. They could buy luxuries like television sets. In other words, capitalism had come to China.

There were still problems, though. In some regions of the country, there were still not enough jobs. Not everyone shared in the wealth. Meanwhile, prices of many goods rose. Less government control made it easier to cheat and steal. Corrupt government officials did favors for people who paid them bribes. Finally, there was the problem of raised expectations. Given some freedom, many Chinese people expected and wanted more.

Tiananmen Square

China has a tradition of student protest. This was the case in the 1980s. Students had been closely controlled by their elders. In the 1980s, students wanted to be free of these restrictions. In the winter of 1986, they took to the streets. They gathered in Tiananmen Square in Beijing. This protest ended fairly peacefully. But 1989 was different.

For seven weeks, the students occupied the square. They said they wanted democracy. They even built a statue called the Goddess of

Democracy. It looked a lot like the U.S. Statue of Liberty. Then it seemed that a large number of workers would join the student protest. That ended Deng's patience. On Sunday, June 4, 1989, the army moved on the unarmed students. What followed was a massacre. Hundreds were killed.

Many students were arrested. Some had public trials that were televised. Everyone could watch the prisoners receive sentences of execution. Others were sent to prison for years. The universities were closed. Workers were forced to return to their jobs. And the army immediately suppressed all protests. Quiet returned to China. But it took many years to heal the wounds of 1989.

Deng died in 1997. He was succeeded by younger leaders. One of these was Communist Party leader Jiang Zemin. He served as China's president from 1993 to 2003. In 2003, Hu Jintao took over as president.

China continued to modernize its economy during this time. In 2001, it was admitted to the World Trade Organization. This gave China full trading rights with capitalist countries. By early in the twenty-first century, China's economy was a global powerhouse. China's demand for oil to fuel its growing industries kept worldwide oil prices high. Other countries watched this Asian giant's growth closely. They looked for chances to invest, and to sell their goods in China's huge market. Yet they also worried about the impact of Chinese imports and the demand for oil on their own economies.

China and Its Neighbors

India

India shares a long border with China. There have been some quarrels between the two nations. During the leadership of Jawaharlal Nehru, the two countries had good relations. But, in 1959, the Chinese put down a revolt in Tibet. India welcomed the Tibetan leader, the Dalai Lama, and many Tibetan refugees. The Chinese did not like that. In 1963, India and China fought an armed conflict over a border. China easily won. In 1998, new Indian leaders spoke of their fear of their giant neighbor. Shortly afterward, India set off a series of atomic explosions. India had become an atomic power. The government said this was necessary to protect India from an attack by China. In 2005, though, India and China agreed on a "roadmap" for resolving their border dispute.

Hong Kong

Hong Kong is an area of about 416 square miles. It is a highly developed area with many industries. These include textiles, toys, and electronic components. Hong Kong was for many years a colony of Great Britain. However, Great Britain only had a lease on Hong Kong. Great Britain had to return the territory to China in 1997. First, though, Great Britain negotiated an agreement with China. It said that China would not rush to change Hong Kong, a booming capitalist economy.

The arrangement was called "One Country, Two Systems." China promised that Hong Kong's freedoms would be guaranteed by law. But the chief executive would be appointed by Beijing. Many citizens of Hong Kong left before the takeover.

The takeover was peaceful. But those who stayed remained alert to any changes coming from Beijing. Changes soon came. In 2003, mass protests erupted against proposed curbs on civil rights. In response, China canceled and postponed elections. And although pro-democracy parties won in the 2003 and 2004 elections, the Chinese system limited the effect of this victory. Tensions continued to simmer.

Taiwan

In 1949, the Nationalist Government of the Chinese leader Chiang Kai-shek retreated to Taiwan. Taiwan is an island about 100 miles from mainland China. It has an area of nearly 14,000 square miles. (Mainland China has over three million square miles.) Native Taiwanese already lived on the island. But Chiang and his large army soon took control of the island. At the time, the United States recognized the nationalists as the legitimate government of China. It stationed a fleet in the Strait of Formosa to prevent an invasion from the mainland.

With U.S. help, Taiwan hung on to the "China seat" in the United Nations until 1971. Taiwan was ruled under martial law, with the army enforcing the law, until 1991. By then, Taiwan had a successful capitalist economy. Its new leaders vowed that they would stay independent from mainland China. These leaders were native Taiwanese, rather than mainland exiles.

This, however, was not the way Beijing saw the situation. China claimed Taiwan as part of its nation. And it expected to take over Taiwan. China's leaders saw the peaceful handover of Hong Kong as a step toward that goal. They thought Hong Kong would prove that capitalism and socialism can exist side by side. There were occasional shooting incidents. But China made no moves to take over Taiwan by force. However, tensions revived with the 2004 election of a pro-independence president of Taiwan. China responded by declaring that it would use military force to prevent Taiwan from becoming independent.

Chapter 30: Japan and Korea

Japanese Politics

The island nation of Japan is a democracy. But it is a democracy with a traditional Japanese style. One party has been in power in Japan ever since the end of World War II. Despite its name, the Liberal Democratic Party (LDP) is actually rather conservative, and does not change quickly.

Business and politics are very closely tied in Japan. Japan has a capitalist economy. But the government is very much involved in it. For one thing, it helps to make the business environment as profitable as possible. It offers incentives, information, and tax breaks. The government also imposes restrictions on imports. At the same time, Japan depends heavily on its exports.

Sometimes businesses give big donations to politicians. Those government officials then do special favors for those businesses. This has, at times, led to political scandals in Japan—as well as in other countries.

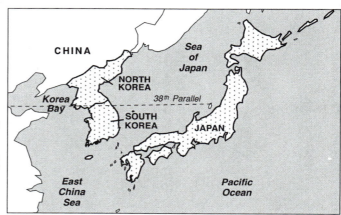

Japan and Korea

Taking to the Streets

Some groups in Japan do not feel they are represented by the government. They do not share the views of the LPD. Young people, for example, are less traditional. So, students and others have often made themselves heard through street protests. These protests sometimes get violent. However, they have never been so bad that they have endangered the government.

Protesters went into the streets in 1960. The cause was a Cold War defense agreement between the United States and Japan. Many Japanese feared that U.S. ships might carry atomic weapons. Japan was the only country to have experienced the horrors caused by atomic weapons. Demonstrations in 1968 demanded the return of Okinawa—taken by the United States during World War II—to Japan. In 1972, the United States did return Okinawa and other islands. But it retained some of its military bases. Later, protesters demanded the removal of those military bases.

The Japanese Military

Before and during World War II, Japan had a powerful military. After the war, Japan was forced to disarm. Its citizens liked it that way. During the Cold War, the United States wanted Japan to rearm. That was because the United States was looking for as many allies as it could get in its face-off with the Soviet Union. But the Japanese government refused. Instead, it said it would provide the United States with places for military bases. In exchange, the United States would help defend Japan. Eventually, Japan developed a small defense force.

None of Japan's neighbors wanted Japan to rearm, either. Japan had occupied many Asian countries during the war. Those nations had not forgotten the suffering of those years. Japan insisted that its forces were strictly for self-defense. And Japan claimed it would never develop a nuclear weapon.

Japan and the United States

Postwar Japan became an economic giant. Japanese industry boomed, as technology developed and efficiency improved. By the 1960s, a skilled, well-educated workforce was turning out high-quality goods. And Japan produced these goods at cheaper prices. Electronic devices and small Japanese cars were especially popular.

The United States became a huge market for Japanese goods. However, although it began to export huge amounts of goods, Japan itself was not open to most imports. Foreign companies could not easily sell their goods in Japan. As a result, the United States had a trade deficit with Japan.

Japanese businesspeople liked having their home-based industries protected. They used their influence to keep it that way. However, the

United States did work out agreements for Japan to increase some imports. Japanese firms also set up factories in the United States. By the 1990s, these plants were producing many Japanese-designed cars and electronic devices.

By the late 1990s, Japan was beginning to have problems. One issue was the environment. For a long time, industrial growth was seen as the most important thing. Only afterward did people begin to recognize the consequences, or effects, of that growth. Also, Japan was finding that some of its traditional ways of doing business did not work anymore. In 1998, the Japanese economy slipped into a recession.

Japan's conservative party ruled for much of the latter half of the twentieth century. In 2009, Japan's socially liberal party won a majority of the legislative seats and, in September 2011, Yoshihiko Noda became the prime minister.

2011 Earthquake and Tsunami

On March 11, 2011, a magnitude 9.0 earthquake struck off the coast of Japan. Though earthquakes are not unknown to Japan, this was the most powerful in the country's history. It generated tsunami waves of over 130 feet in parts of Japan and several feet high across the Pacific, including Russia, the Philippines, the western United States, Canada, and even Antarctica, where 31,000 acres of ice were broken away by tsunami waves.

Deaths and property damage were reported in many of these countries, but nowhere was hit as hard as Japan. Over 15,000 people were killed, with 10,000 more missing or injured. More than 125,000 buildings were either damaged or wiped out entirely. Several people were also evacuated from their homes as a result of the nuclear hazards the earthquake produced.

Nuclear meltdowns at three reactors in Fukushima, Japan, following the earthquake have resulted in widespread concern over the safety of nuclear energy. The severity of the accident is second only to the Chernobyl disaster. The radiation effects are yet unknown, but unsafe levels of radioactive particles were found in Japan's water and food supply, and trace amounts of radiation were detected around the world.

South Korea

South Korea was always a noncommunist country. However, it was not a democracy. Its leaders jailed political dissidents.

South Korea has had a lot of political unrest. In 1961, General Park Chung Hee took power. Park built up the country. It had suffered greatly from a civil war. Park used the army to put down violent protests. He imprisoned opposition leaders.

The United States sent South Korea military aid. It wanted to contain communist North Korea. So, antigovernment protests in South Korea were often also anti-American. The United States was embarrassed by South Korea's authoritarian government. But fighting communism was more important.

In 1979, Park was assassinated. In the years that followed, different men led the country. Yet, the military held the real power. The protests continued, and many people died. Meanwhile, South Korea's industry was developing fast. The country had to keep up a good image in the West. Therefore, the government occasionally eased up on the opposition. Then, when things got too disorderly, it cracked down again.

One opposition leader was Kim Dae-jung. In 1976, Kim Dae-jung was jailed as a dissident. Kim was released in 1980. In 1997, he became president in a free election. He began to clean up corruption and get rid of many military officers. Kim also promised to support human rights in South Korea. Koreans began to hope that their country might be able to have both economic prosperity and democracy.

Kim eased tensions with neighboring North Korea by meeting with its leader in 2000. This was the first-ever meeting of these nations' leaders. In 2000, Kim was awarded the Nobel Prize for his efforts. But North Korea's threats about nuclear weapons made it difficult for Kim's successor, Roh Moo Hyun, to continue Kim's "Sunshine Policy" toward North Korea.

In 2008, Lee Myung-bak took over the presidency. Through his term, tensions with North Korea have continued to run high, and in recent years the situation has escalated. In March 2010, the *Cheonan*, a South Korean warship, was sunk. South Korea blamed North Korea, but North Korea denied involvement. The United States placed further sanctions on North

Korea, and in the fall of that year North Korea attacked a South Korean island. Some thought this action would provoke a resumed war between the two Koreas. Though the situation remains unstable, neither country has made a move toward declaring war.

North Korea

North Korea has a harsher climate and fewer resources than does South Korea. It also has a harsher history. Its communist government came into power in 1948. Kim Il Sung ruled the country until his death in 1994. He was succeeded by his son, Kim Jong Il. During that time, North Korea was isolated from most of the world. In the 1990s, however, the two Koreas began to exchange visits. In 1991, they signed a nonaggression agreement. Neither country would attack the other, they promised.

In 1994, the North hinted that it would build an atomic bomb. The United States promised to supply the North with nuclear power for peaceful uses. However, the North would have to give up its plans for a bomb. Kim Jong Il agreed. In the late 1990s, rumors reported widespread starvation in his country. The North was finally forced to accept humanitarian aid from other countries.

There was talk of reuniting the two Koreas. But some South Koreans had doubts because North Korea's economic situation in the late 1990s was desperate. Yet, the benefits to South Korea would be having a smaller army and fewer weapons. A drawback might be a lower standard of living for the South. In 2000, the leaders of the two Koreas did sign a declaration paving the way for more peaceful relations.

In 2004, North Korea announced that it had been developing nuclear bombs. Kim threatened to build and use such bombs if the United States and other nations failed to deliver economic aid. Rounds of talks between North Korea and these nations struggled to resolve the issue. In late 2010, Kim Jong Il's youngest son, Kim Jong Un, was reported to be his eventual successor.

Chapter 31: Indonesia, the Philippines, and Australasia

Indonesia

Indonesia gained its independence in 1949. It started out with a constitutional government. By 1958, Achmed Sukarno, the first president, had put an end to that. Instead, he moved the country toward what he called a "guided democracy." In fact, however, he was an authoritarian ruler who put down all opposition.

Many of Indonesia's people are Muslims. There are also other ethnic minorities. Two groups were on opposite sides in the 1960s. They were the military and the communists. The military thought the communists were getting too strong. So, in 1965, the army acted. It killed many communist supporters. Then the army took over the government. Another strongman appeared. He was General Suharto. He pushed Sukarno out of office. Suharto stayed in power for more than 30 years.

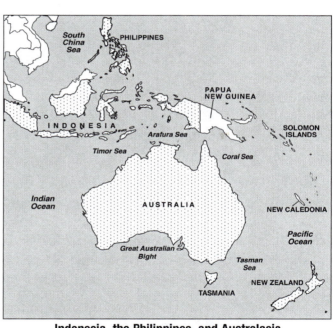

Indonesia, the Philippines, and Australasia

During his rule, Sukarno played the Cold War game. Sometimes he took aid from the West, sometimes from the Soviet Union. In his own region, he followed an expansionist policy, taking nearby territories by force. Suharto followed a similar policy. In 1976, the army brutally took over East Timor after the Portuguese left it. The army then brutally crushed a 1999 movement for an independent East Timor. As many as 700,000 people may have died. The United Nations then took over. In 2002, East Timor received its independence from Indonesia.

Suharto's tight control did give the country some stability. There was less unrest. This encouraged foreign investment and development. Multinational companies found their way to Indonesia. A small middle class developed. A few people got very rich. Some of those wealthy people were members of Suharto's own family. Others were cronies, or pals, of his. But that still left millions of Indonesians in poverty or near poverty.

In the late 1990s, an economic slump hit much of Asia. All levels of society suffered except the very wealthy. In 1998, there were student protests and riots. Mobs attacked businesses of prosperous ethnic Chinese. They also destroyed companies owned by Suharto's family. Many people died in the rioting. Some were shot by the army, which was trying to restore order.

Protesters demanded that Suharto resign. When the army no longer backed him, Suharto had to step down. Free elections began in 1999, but problems remain. Ethnic and religious violence erupted, with hundreds killed. Islamic terrorist groups with ties to al-Qaeda were active. New leaders of Indonesia in the early 2000s promised to suppress the violence and stabilize the economy.

But economic stability has not come easily. On December 26, 2004, an earthquake in the Indian Ocean caused a powerful tsunami. More than 225,000 people died. Fishing communities were particularly hard hit, as boats, gear, and skilled fisherman were all lost to the disaster. Tourism, another important piece of the economy, suffered as well. Billions of dollars of aid were pledged to the region.

The Philippines

One problem in the island nation of the Philippines in the 1960s was warfare with communists rebels. Another problem was Muslim separatists who wanted independence. (The majority of Filipinos are Roman Catholics.) There were also student demonstrations over various issues. The president in 1965 was Ferdinand Marcos. He used the unrest as an excuse to declare martial law and arrest thousands. Marcos did not end martial law until 1981.

Then one of Marcos's outspoken opponents, Benigno Aquino, was assassinated. Most Filipinos believe Marcos ordered the killing. Finally, in 1986, Marcos agreed to have an election. He ran against Corazon Aquino, the widow of the murdered man. Marcos claimed he won the election fairly. But few people believed him. Marcos fled the country when he realized that the military no longer supported him.

When Aquino took over as president, she found widespread corruption. Many people suffered from poverty. Political unrest continued. Aquino just managed to survive several coup attempts during her term of office.

During Aquino's term, the government ratified a new constitution (1987). The constitution limited the president to a single six-year term. This was to prevent another authoritarian leader like Marcos from taking over.

The Philippines had gained independence in 1946. The United States, however, had kept military bases on the islands. Some groups protested this. Finally, in 1992, the United States ended its long military presence in the Philippines.

In the early 2000s, Philippine democracy seemed to be working. The economic situation had improved somewhat. Conflicts with communists and Muslim separatists still remain a problem. But presidential candidates declared they wanted to show that democracy and economic development can go together. In 2010, Benigno Aquino III, the son of Corazon and Benigno Aquino, became president.

Australia

Australia is the largest country in Australasia. (That is the name sometimes given to Australia, New Zealand, and islands in the South Pacific.) For hundreds of years, Australia's history and economy were closely tied to the United Kingdom. Australia is a member of the Commonwealth of Nations. The Commonwealth of Nations is an association of former members of the British Empire. But, Australia has been moving closer to the United States in trade and defense.

Australia's economy has always depended on its exports. Up until the 1960s, the United Kingdom received most of those exports. However, this changed after 1967. That is when exports to the United States and Canada became larger than those to the United Kingdom. Australia also developed close ties in Asia. Its trading partners included Japan, China, and nations of Southeast Asia.

This was a dramatic change for a nation populated mainly by Europeans. For years, Australia felt threatened by Asian nations with large, poor populations. It feared communist influence from China. Indonesia's expansionist policy was also taken seriously. Therefore, Australia became a founding member of the South-East Asian Defense Treaty (SEATO). SEATO includes the United States, the United Kingdom, and France. Like NATO, its purpose was to stop the spread of communism.

For many years, Australia strictly limited the number of immigrants from any place other than northern Europe. It eased these policies in the 1960s and 1970s. The resulting intake of people from Asia and elsewhere created a more diverse Australian society.

Australia's politics are fairly conservative. However, the country is known for its liberal legislation. Its laws include protection for trade unions. One group that has not benefited as much as others is the Aborigines. They are the original native Australians. After World War II, the Aborigines began to organize to fight discrimination. However, they have remained disadvantaged.

New Zealand

Like Australia, New Zealand was settled by Europeans. They, too, found a native population living there—the Maoris. New Zealand is also a member of the Commonwealth of Nations and SEATO. New Zealand's economy is dependent on its exports. These have always been mainly agricultural. Meat, dairy products, and wool are still New Zealand's major exports. This means that the country has to import many of its manufactured goods.

Trade with the United Kingdom was important to New Zealand's economy. But in the mid-1970s, the United Kingdom joined the European Economic Community (EEC). It traded more with its European partners.

So, New Zealand had to expand its markets to other countries. Soon it was exporting as much to Japan as it did to the United Kingdom. However, it still had to import a lot. And imports were expensive—especially crude oil. New Zealand began to have economic problems.

New Zealanders have always been leaders in passing laws to improve social welfare. These included safeguards for the poor, child and retirement benefits, and medical insurance. Such programs, however, are costly. In the 1980s, the country realized that it had to be more competitive. It had to make it less expensive to do business in New Zealand. Therefore, deregulation became a big issue, and government ownership and control of industry was lessened. There were cuts in such areas as market protection. Farmers and industry were now open to competition. Also, many cuts were made in the welfare program. People had to pay more taxes.

By the 1990s, Australia, Japan, and the United States were New Zealand's largest trading powers. The country still had economic problems, including unemployment. Many of the unemployed were Maoris. Overall, though, New Zealand had one of the highest standards of living in Asia.

Appendix, Glossary, and Index

APPENDIX

Names to Know

Abacha, Sani—a Nigerian leader, 1993 to 1998

Abbas, Mahmoud—the first prime minister of the Palestinians, beginning in 2003

Abdullah—the half-brother of King Fahd of Saudi Arabia

Abdullah, King—the king of Jordan, beginning in 1999

Adenauer, Konrad—Germany's leader from 1949 to 1963

Ahmadinejad, Mahmoud—the president of Iran, elected in 2005

al-Assad, Bashar—the leader of Syria, beginning in 2000

al-Assad, Hafez—the leader of Syria, 1971 to 2000

Alemán, Arnoldo—a Nicaraguan leader elected in 1996

al-Qaddafi, Muammar—the leader of Libya, who ruled from 1969 to 2011

al-Zarqawi, Abu Musab—a leader of al-Qaeda in Iraq

Alvarado, Juan Velasco—the leader of Peru, who helped the poor

Alvarez, Luis Echeverría—the president of Mexico from 1970 to 1976, who made popular changes

Aquino, Benigno—an opponent of the Marcos government in the Philippines, who was assassinated

Aquino, Benigno III—the president of the Philippines elected in 2010 and son of Benigno and Corazon Aquino

Aquino, Corazon—the president of the Philippines from 1986 to 1992 and widow of Benigno Aquino

Arafat, Yasser—the leader of the Palestine Liberation Organization (PLO) for many years until his death in 2004

Aristide, Jean-Bertrand—a Catholic priest elected president of Haiti in 1990; served in 1991, 1994 to 1996, and 2001 to 2004

Atatürk, Mustafa Kemal—the leader of the Turkish revolution; founder and first president of the Republic of Turkey (1923 to 1938)

Attlee, Clement—the leader of Great Britain's Labour Party from 1935 to 1955

Aung San Suu Kyi—the 1991 Nobel Peace Prize winner and voice against government repression in Burma

Begin, Menachem—the prime minister of Israel, who was elected in 1977

Bell, Alexander Graham—a Scottish inventor who patented the telephone in 1876

bin Laden, Osama—a rich Saudi man closely linked to the al-Qaeda terrorist network

Blair, Tony—the prime minister of Great Britain, 1997 to 2007

Brandt, Willy—the West German chancellor, 1969 to 1974

Brezhnev, Leonid—the leader of the Soviet Union, 1964 to 1982

Brown, Gordon—the prime minister of Great Britain, 2007 to 2010

Bush, George H.W.—the U.S. president, 1989 to 1993

Bush, George W.—the U.S. president, 2001–(second term expires in 2009)

Buthelezi, Mangosuthu—a Zulu chief and leader of the Inkatha Freedom Party

Calderón, Felipe—the president of Mexico, elected in 2006

Cameron, David—the prime minister of Great Britain, elected in 2010

Campbell, Kim—Canada's first woman prime minister, 1993

Carter, Jimmy—the U.S. president, 1977 to 1981

Castro, Fidel—a Cuban leader who led rebels to overthrow Cuban dictator Fulgencio Batista in 1959; set up Latin America's only communist government

Castro, Raúl—the president of Cuba and brother of Fidel Castro

Ceausescu, Elena—a Romanian government official and wife of Nicolae Ceausescu

Ceausescu, Nicolae—the president of Romania, 1974 to 1989

Chamorro, Violeta Barrios de—the president of Nicaragua from 1990 to 1996 who reversed many policies of the Sandinista government

Chiang Kai-Shek—a Chinese general who became leader of the Nationalist Party and led many battles against the Chinese warlords

Chirac, Jacques—the president of France, elected in 1995

Chrétien, Jean—the Canadian prime minister, 1993 to 2003

Churchill, Winston—Britain's prime minister from 1940 to 1945 and 1951 to 1955

Clinton, Bill—the U.S. president, 1993 to 2001

Collor de Mello, Fernando—the Brazilian president who was charged with corruption and forced to resign

Colon, Rafael Hernandez—the governor of Puerto Rico, 1973 to 1977 and 1985 to 1993, who wanted Puerto Rico to remain a commonwealth but have more autonomy

Curie, Marie and Pierre—French scientists who explored radioactivity and discovered the radioactive elements polonium and radium

d'Estaing, Valéry Giscard—the president of France, 1974 to 1981

Dalai Lama—a Tibetan religious and political leader

Darwin, Charles—an English scientist who developed the theory of evolution in the mid-1800s

de Gaulle, Charles—the World War II hero and president of France, 1958 to 1969

de Klerk, F. W.—the president of South Africa, 1989 to 1994

Deng Xiaoping—the leader of China

Díaz, Porfirio—the Mexican dictator from 1876 to 1880, and from 1884 to 1911

Dubcek, Alexander—first secretary of the Czech Communist Party

Duvalier, François—the president for life of Haiti from 1957 to 1971; known as "Papa Doc"

Duvalier, Jean-Claude—president for life of Haiti from 1971 through 1986; known as "Baby Doc"

Eastman, George—an American who marketed a simple box camera using rolled film in 1888

Edison, Thomas—an American who designed the first electric power system in 1882, invented the phonograph in 1877, and developed motion picture technology in the 1890s

Einstein, Albert—a German scientist who developed the theory of relativity

Eisenhower, Dwight—a general of the United States army during World War II; later became the 34th president of the United States (1953 to 1961)

el-Sadat, Anwar—a president of Egypt, 1970 to 1981

Fahd, King—a Saudi Arabian ruler, who came to power in 1982

Faisal, King—a ruler of Saudi Arabia, 1964 to 1975, when he was assassinated

Farouk I, King—a king of Egypt from 1936 to 1952

Fernández de Kirchner, Cristina—the president of Brazil, elected in 2007, and widow of Nestor Kirchner

Ferrer, Luis—the governor of Puerto Rico from 1969 to 1973 who increased wages and created housing programs

Ford, Henry—an American who built one of the earliest American cars in 1896

Fox, Vicente—a president of Mexico, 2000 to 2006

Franco, Francisco—a general and leader of the Nationalist forces that overthrew the Spanish Democratic Republic in the Spanish Civil War (1936–1939)

Freud, Sigmund—an Austrian psychologist who studied the unconscious parts of the human mind

Funes, Mauricio—the president of El Salvador, elected in 2009

Gandhi, Indira—a prime minister of India, who was assassinated in 1984

Gandhi, Mohandas—the head of the Indian National Congress; developed a form of nonviolent protest called "passive resistance"

Gheorghiu-Dej, Gheorghe—a leader of Romania's Communist Party

Gierek, Edward—the first secretary of Poland's Communist Party, 1970 to 1980

Gomulka, Wladyslaw—the first secretary of Poland's Communist Party, 1956 to 1970

Gorbachev, Mikhail—a leader of the Soviet Union, 1985 to 1991

Gowon, Yukuba—a military leader of Nigeria, who was overthrown in 1975

Harper, Stephen—the prime minister of Canada, elected in 2006

Havel, Václav—the president of Czechoslovakia, 1989 to 1992, and of the Czech Republic, as of 1993

Hirohito—an emperor of Japan from 1926 to 1989

Hitler, Adolf—the leader of Germany's Nazi Party from 1920 to 1921; German premier from 1933 to 1945

Ho Chi Minh—a communist leader who organized the Viet Minh (League for the Independence of Vietnam)

Holness, Andrew—the prime minister of Jamaica, beginning in 2011

Honecker, Erich—an East German leader, 1971 to 1989

Hu Jintao—the president of China, beginning in 2003

Humala, Ollanta—the president of Peru, elected in 2011

Husák, Gustáv—the president of Czechoslovakia, 1975 to 1989

Hussein Ibn Talal—King Hussein of Jordan

Hussein, Saddam—the leader of Iraq, who ruled from 1979 to 2003

Iliescu, Ion—the president of Romania, 1989 to 1996 and 2000 to 2004

Izetbegovic, Alija—the president of Bosnia-Herzegovina from 1990 to 2000

Jaruzelski, Wojciech—the first secretary of Poland's Communist Party, 1981 to 1989

Jiang Qing—the widow of Mao Zedong, Gang of Four member

Jiang Zemin—the president of China from 1993 to 2003

John Paul II, Pope—Polish Roman Catholic Karol Wojtyla, pope from 1978 to 2005

Johnson, Lyndon B.—the U.S. president, 1963 to 1969

Jonathan, Goodluck—the president of Nigeria, beginning in 2010

Kabila, Joseph—the president of the Democratic Republic of the Congo, beginning in 2001

Kabila, Laurent—the president of the Democratic Republic of the Congo, 1997 to 2001

Karzai, Hamid—the president of Afghanistan, beginning in 2002

Kennedy, John F.—the U.S. president, elected in 1960 and assassinated in 1963

Kenyatta, Jomo—the first president of Kenya

Khalid, King—a ruler of Saudi Arabia, 1975 to 1982

Khatami, Mohammad—the president of Iran, who was elected in 1997

Khomeini, Ayatollah Ruhollah—the religious and political leader of Iran, 1979 to 1989

Khrushchev, Nikita—the premier of the Soviet government from 1958 to 1964

Kim Dae-jung—a dissident who became president of South Korea in 1997

Kim Il Sung—the communist leader of North Korea from 1948 to 1994

Kim Jong Il—the communist leader of North Korea, beginning in 1994

Kim Jong Un—the youngest son of Kim Jong Il and his presumed successor

King, Martin Luther, Jr.—an African American minister who became a leader of the civil rights movement; assassinated in 1968

Kohl, Helmut—the German chancellor, 1982 to 1998

Kovác, Michal—the president of Slovakia, as of 1993

Lee Myung-bak—president of South Korea, beginning in 2008

Lenin, V. I.—the leader of Russia's Bolshevik Party and leader of the USSR from 1922 to 1924

Lula da Silva, Luiz Inacio—the president of Brazil, 2003 to 2010

MacArthur, Douglas—the commander of the U.S. army that occupied and controlled Japan after World War II

Major, John—the British prime minister, 1990 to 1997

Mandela, Nelson—the president of South Africa, elected in 1994

Manley, Michael—the prime minister of Jamaica, 1972 to 1980 and 1989 to 1992, who eliminated censorship and lifted the ban on civil liberties

Mao Zedong—a leader of the Chinese Communist Party from 1931 to 1976; chairman of the People's Republic of China from 1949 to 1959

Marconi, Guglielmo—an Italian physicist and inventor who developed the wireless telegraph; received first transatlantic signal in 1901

Marcos, Ferdinand—the president of the Philippines who fled his country after the military deserted him in 1986

Marshall, George—a general of United States army during World War II; later became U.S. secretary of state (1947 to 1949) and secretary of defense (1950 to 1951); proposed the 1947 European recovery program, which became known as the Marshall Plan

Martin, Paul—a prime minister of Canada, 2003 to 2006

Martinelli, Ricardo—the president of Panama, elected in 2009

McCarthy, Joseph—a United States senator who led a hunt for communism within the United States itself

Medvedev, Dmitry—the president of Russia, elected in 2008

Meir, Golda—prime minister of Israel, chosen by Labor Party in 1969

Mendel, Gregor—an Austrian monk who studied genetics

Mengistu, Haile Mariam—a communist leader of Ethiopia, who fled the country in 1991

Merkel, Angela—the chancellor of Germany, elected in 2005

Mills, John Atta—the president of Ghana, beginning in 2009

Milosevic, Slobodan—a Serbian leader and president of Yugoslavia

Mitterrand, François—the president of France, 1981 to 1995

Mubarak, Hosni—the president of Egypt, 1981 to 2011

Mugabe, Robert—the prime minister of Zimbabwe, who came to power in 1980

Mulroney, Brian—the Canadian prime minister, 1984 to 1993

Mussolini, Benito—the head of Italy's Fascist Party and Italian premier from 1922 to 1943

Nagy, Imre—the premier of Hungary's revolutionary government in 1956

Nasser, Gamal Abdel—the president of Egypt from 1956 to 1970; created the United Arab Republic

Nehru, Jawaharlal—the first prime minister of the Republic of India from 1950 to 1964

Ngo Dinh Diem—an authoritarian leader of South Vietnam

Nicholas II—the tsar, or emperor, of Russia from 1894 to 1917

Nixon, Richard M.—the U.S. president, 1969 to 1974, when he resigned from office

Nkomo, Joshua—the leader of Rhodesia's National Democratic Party

Nkrumah, Kwame—the leader of Ghana, 1952 to 1966

Noda, Yoshihiko—prime minster of Japan, beginning in 2011

Noriega, Manuel—a leader of Panama who profited from drug trade

Obama, Barack—the president of the United States, elected in 2008

Obasanjo, Olusegun—the president of Nigeria, 1999 to 2007

Ojukwu, Odumegwu—a military leader of Biafra, 1967 to 1970

Ortega, Daniel—the president of Nicaragua from 1985 to 1990, re-elected in 2006

Pahlavi, Mohammad Reza—the shah of Iran, 1941 to 1979

Park Chung Hee—a military leader of South Korea, who was assassinated in 1979

Pavlov, Ivan—a Russian biologist who explained conditioned reflex

Perón, Eva—the wife of Argentine president Juan Perón, also known as "Evita"

Perón, Juan—the popular dictator of Argentina from 1946 to 1955

Planck, Max—a German scientist who originated and developed quantum theory

Pol Pot—the leader of the communist Khmer Rouge in Cambodia

Pompidou, Georges—the president of France, 1969 to 1974

Ponce de León, Ernesto Zedillo—a president of Mexico who worked to ease border conflicts with United States

Portillo, Jose López—the president of Mexico, 1976 to 1982, who made popular changes

Putin, Vladimir—the president of Russia, beginning in 2000

Rabin, Yitzhak—the prime minister of Israel, 1974 to 1977 and 1992 until his assassination in 1995

Rawlings, Jerry—a leader of Ghana who came to power in 1979

Reagan, Ronald—the U.S. president, 1981 to 1989

Rivera, Miguel Primo de—a Spanish military dictator from 1923 to 1930

Romero, Oscar—the popular bishop in El Salvador who worked for human rights and was assassinated in 1980

Rommel, Erwin—a general of the German army during World War II; also known as "The Desert Fox"

Roosevelt, Franklin D.—a U.S. president who implemented the New Deal; in office from 1933 to 1945

Rousseff, Dilma—the president of Brazil, elected in 2010

Rutherford, Ernest—an English scientist who discovered the nuclear nature of atoms

Sakharov, Andrey—a Russian physicist arrested for criticizing the government

Sarkozy, Nicolas—the president of France, elected in 2007

Sarney, José—Brazil's first civilian president

Saud, King—the ruler of Saudi Arabia, 1953 to 1964

Schmidt, Helmut—the German chancellor, 1974 to 1982

Schröder, Gerhard—the German chancellor, elected in 1998

Seaga, Edward—the prime minister of Jamaica in 1980s who cut ties with Cuba

Sein, Thein—the president of Burma, beginning in 2011

Seko, Mobutu Sese—a leader of Zaire (now the Democratic Republic of the Congo), who was in power from 1965 to 1997

Selassie, Haile I—the emperor of Ethiopia, 1930 to 1936 and 1941 to 1974

Sharon, Ariel—the prime minister of Israel, beginning in 2001

Sihanouk, Norodom—a leader of Cambodia until 2004

Smith, Ian—a leader of Rhodesia's Front Party; prime minister of Rhodesia, 1965 to 1979

Somoza, Anastasia—a military dictator of Nicaragua from 1936 to 1956

Stalin, Joseph—the secretary general of the Communist Party of the Soviet Union from 1922 to 1953, and leader of the Soviet state from 1941 to 1953; transformed the Soviet Union into a major world power during his dictatorial rule

Suharto—the leader of Indonesia for more than 30 years

Sukarno, Achmed—the first president of Indonesia

Thatcher, Margaret—Britain's first female prime minister, 1979 to 1990

Thomson, J. J.—an English scientist who discovered the electron in 1897

Tito, Josip Broz—a leader of Yugoslavia, 1943 to 1980

Torrijos, Omar—an authoritarian leader of Panama from 1968 to 1981

Touré, Sékou—the first president of Guinea

Trudeau, Pierre—a Canadian prime minister, 1968 to 1979 and 1980 to 1984

Trujillo, Cesar Gaviria—the Colombian president who helped to weaken drug cartels

Truman, Harry—the 33rd president of the United States, 1945 to 1953

Tudjman, Franjo—the president of Croatia

U Nu—a leader of Burma

Ulbricht, Walter—the communist leader of East Germany 1946 to 1971

Villa, Pancho—a Mexican bandit and revolutionary leader

Walesa, Lech—the Solidarity leader and president of Poland, elected in 1990

Watson, John—an American psychologist who developed the theory of behaviorism

Wilson, Harold—the prime minister of Great Britain, 1964 to 1970 and 1974 to 1976

Wilson, Woodrow—U.S. president, 1913 to 1921

Wright, Wilbur and Orville—American brothers who made the first powered and sustained airplane flight in 1903

Yar'Adua, Umaru Musa—the president of Nigeria, 2007 to 2010

Yeltsin, Boris—the president of the Russian Federation, 1991 to 1999

GLOSSARY

Aborigines (a-buh-RI-juh-neez) natives of Australia

AIDS (AYDZ) Acquired Immune Deficiency Syndrome, an incurable and fatal disease of the immune system

alliance (uh-LY-unts) a formal agreement made between two or more nations to help one another in times of conflict or war

Allied Powers (A-lyd POW-urz) the alliance made between France, Russia, Great Britain, and Italy at the start of World War I

Allies (A-lyz) the alliance made by Great Britain, France, the Soviet Union, China, and the United States during World War II

ally (A-ly) a country that agrees to come to the aid of another country in times of conflict or war

al-Qaeda (AL-KY-duh) terrorist network linked to many attacks against the West, especially United States-linked targets

anarchist (A-nur-kist) a person who wants an end to all government

ANC (AY EN SEE) African National Congress

annexation (a-nek-SAY-shun) when one country joins another country or territory to itself

apartheid (uh-PAR-tayt) the South African policy of strict separation of races; lasted from 1948 to 1990

PRONUNCIATION KEY

CAPITAL LETTERS show the stressed syllables.

a	as in m**at**	f	as in **f**it
ay	as in day, **say**	g	as in **g**o
ch	as in **ch**ew	i	as in s**i**t
e	as in b**e**d	j	as in **j**ob, **g**em
ee	as in **e**ven, **ea**sy, n**ee**d	k	as in **c**ool, **k**ey

appeasement (uh-PEEZ-munt) to give in to the demands of an aggressor, even if it violates one's principles

Arab League (AR-ub LEEG) a union formed in 1945 by Egypt, Iraq, Transjordan, Syria, Lebanon, Saudi Arabia, and Yemen to promote cooperation among these Arab nations and to prevent the formation of a Jewish state in Palestine

Arab Spring (AR-ub SPRING) a series of pro-democracy protests and uprisings in the Middle East and North Africa that began in 2011

armistice (AR-muh-stus) a temporary agreement to stop fighting a war; precedes a treaty

Armistice Day (AR-muh-stus DAY) the day that commemorates the end of World War I; the first was celebrated on November 11, 1919.

atomic age (uh-TO-mik AYJ) the nuclear age; started with the dropping of the world's first atomic bomb in 1945

atomic bomb (uh-TO-mik BOM) a new deadly weapon used during World War II; these powerful bombs are dropped from planes, causing massive destruction.

authoritarian (uh-thor-uh-TER-ee-un) having complete power

autocrat (O-tuh-krat) an absolute ruler

autonomy (o-TO-nuh-mee) the right of self-government

Axis Powers (AK-sus POW-urz) the alliance made by Germany, Italy, and Japan during World War II

PRONUNCIATION KEY

CAPITAL LETTERS show the stressed syllables.

ng	as in running	u	as in but, some
o	as in cot, father	uh	as in about, taken, lemon, pencil
oh	as in go, note	ur	as in term
oo	as in too	y	as in line, fly
sh	as in shy	zh	as in vision, measure
th	as in thin		

ayatollah (y-uh-TOH-luh) a high clergyman in the Shia branch of Islam

Balfour Declaration (BAL-fur   de-kluh-RAY-shun) a 1917 foreign-policy statement in which Great Britain expressed sympathy for the creation of a "national home for the Jewish people" in Palestine

Balkan (BOL-kun) refers to the Balkans; an area in southeastern Europe

Baltic states (BOL-tik   STAYTS) Latvia, Lithuania, and Estonia

Basic Treaty (BAY-sik   TREE-tee) a 1972 agreement that formalized relations between East and West Germany, giving East Germans greater access to West Germany

Battle of Britain (BA-tul   UV   BRI-tun) a four-month period during World War II in which German planes dropped bomb after bomb on British cities

Battle of Jutland (BA-tul   UV   JUT-lund) the only large naval battle in World War I

Battle of Stalingrad (BA-tul   UV   STA-lun-grad) the turning point in World War II, when Soviet troops defeated German troops; took place in 1942–1943

Battle of the Atlantic (BA-tul   UV   THUH   ut-LAN-tik) an ongoing battle during World War II in which German U-boats targeted North American ships delivering supplies to Allied ships

Battle of the Marne (BA-tul   UV   THUH   MARN) a 1914 battle near Paris in which French troops stopped the German advance; the second

---

PRONUNCIATION KEY

CAPITAL LETTERS show the stressed syllables.

a	as in m**a**t	f	as in **f**it
ay	as in d**ay**, s**ay**	g	as in **g**o
ch	as in **ch**ew	i	as in s**i**t
e	as in b**e**d	j	as in **j**ob, **g**em
ee	as in **e**ven, **ea**sy, n**ee**d	k	as in **c**ool, **k**ey

battle of the Marne, in 1918, marked the turning point of World War I in favor of the Allies.

Battle of Verdun (BA-tul   UV   vur-DUN) a battle in World War I in which 300,000 French and German soldiers were killed

behaviorism (bi-HAY-vyuh-ri-zum) a theory developed by John Watson in the 1800s; suggests that all human behavior is a response of the nervous system to stimuli

Biafra (bee-A-fruh) breakaway state of Nigeria, 1967–1970

black market (BLAK   MAR-kut) illegal selling of goods

blitzkrieg (BLITS-kreeg) the name given to the swiftness and force of Hitler's army and air force during World War II; means "lightning war"

blockade (blo-KAYD) a lining up of navy ships to prevent other ships from getting to a country's ports

Bolsheviks (BOL-shuh-viks) a party in the Russian Revolution; later took the name Communist Party

boycott (BOY-kot) noun: a refusal to buy a certain type of goods; verb: to cease normal trade with another country

Brezhnev Doctrine (BREZH-nev   DOK-trun) proclaimed the right of the USSR to intervene in other communist countries

Brown v. Board of Education of Topeka (BROWN   VER-sus   BORD UV   e-juh-KAY-shun   UV   tuh-PEE-kuh) the 1954 U.S. Supreme Court case in which the court said that segregation of schools by race was illegal

---

PRONUNCIATION KEY

CAPITAL LETTERS show the stressed syllables.

ng	as in running	u	as in but, some
o	as in cot, father	uh	as in about, taken, lemon, pencil
oh	as in go, note	ur	as in term
oo	as in too	y	as in line, fly
sh	as in shy	zh	as in vision, measure
th	as in thin		

Camp David Accords (KAMP   DAY-vud   uh-KORDZ) agreement Menachem Begin and Anwar el-Sadat produced in 1978 with the help of U.S. President Jimmy Carter

capitalism (KA-puh-tul-iz-um) open market system in which industry is privately owned

cartel (kar-TEL) a group formed to regulate the prices and supply of a product

censorship (SEN-sur-ship) government control of information, such as literature, news, and motion pictures

Central Powers (SEN-trul   POW-urz) the alliance made between Germany, Austria-Hungary, the Ottoman Empire, and Bulgaria at the start of World War I

chador (CHUH-dur) an outer garment that covers almost all of a woman's body; this is the term used for the garment in Iran.

chancellor (CHAN-suh-lur) title of the leader of the West German (and, later, German) government

Charter 77 (CHAR-tur   SE-vun-tee   SE-vun) document signed by Czechoslovakian dissidents in 1977

Chinese Soviet Republic (CHY-neez   SOH-vee-et   ri-PUH-blik) a communist government set up by Mao Zedong in China

Civic Forum (SI-vik   FOR-um) Czech political party formed in 1989

civilian (suh-VIL-yun) a person who lives in a country but is not a member of that country's military forces

---

PRONUNCIATION KEY

CAPITAL LETTERS show the stressed syllables.

a	as in mat	f	as in fit
ay	as in day, say	g	as in go
ch	as in chew	i	as in sit
e	as in bed	j	as in job, gem
ee	as in even, easy, need	k	as in cool, key

civil liberties (SI-vul   LI-bur-teez) individual rights, such as freedom of speech, that the government cannot interfere with

coalition (koh-uh-LI-shun) a group of different parties that agree to take joint action

Cold War (KOHLD   WOR) a long period of political and military tension between the United States and the Soviet Union in which both sides competed for allies and influence but did not engage in armed conflict

collective (kuh-LEK-tiv) a cooperative unit or organization made by collecting a number of things into one large whole; for example, a group of small farms joined into one large farm

colony (KO-luh-nee) a region that is controlled by a distant country

Comintern (KO-mun-turn) an organization that intended to spark communist revolutions all around the world

commonwealth (KO-mun-welth) government based on the common consent of the people; each member nation in a commonwealth is a self-governing territory.

Commonwealth of Independent States (CIS) (KO-mun-welth   UV in-duh-PEN-dunt   STAYTS) organization of republics of the former Soviet Union

Commonwealth of Nations (KO-mun-welth   UV   NAY-shunz) a group of countries, each of which is self-governing but pledges loyalty to the British ruler; has included Canada, Australia, New Zealand, and South Africa

---

PRONUNCIATION KEY

CAPITAL LETTERS show the stressed syllables.

ng	as in running	u	as in but, some
o	as in cot, father	uh	as in about, taken, lemon, pencil
oh	as in go, note	ur	as in term
oo	as in too	y	as in line, fly
sh	as in shy	zh	as in vision, measure
th	as in thin		

commune (KO-myoon) a community, usually rural, in which people live together in common buildings and share the use of the community's property

communism (KOM-yuh-ni-zum) a system of economic organization in which the individual, all property, and the means of producing goods are controlled by the state

Communists (KOM-yuh-nists) members of the Communist Party; people who believe that all industry should be owned by the government

constitutional monarchy (kon-stuh-TOO-shuh-nul MO-nur-kee) a country whose head of state is a king or queen, but whose government is run by a parliament and prime minister, or premier

Contras (KAN-truhs) anti-Sandinista group in Nicaragua supported by the United States

cooperative (koh-AH-pruh-tiv) a small group or organization in which members work together and share resources and the results of their work

corruption (kuh-RUP-shun) dishonest or evil behavior

coup (KOO) sudden overthrow of a government

Cultural Revolution (KUL-chuh-rul re-vuh-LOO-shun) when Mao Zedong sent millions of Chinese intellectuals to the countryside to be reeducated; began in 1966

Cyclone Nargis (SY-klohn NAR-GIS) a tropical cyclone that landed in Burma on May 2, 2008

PRONUNCIATION KEY

CAPITAL LETTERS show the stressed syllables.

a	as in mat	f	as in fit
ay	as in day, say	g	as in go
ch	as in chew	i	as in sit
e	as in bed	j	as in job, gem
ee	as in even, easy, need	k	as in cool, key

Dayton Peace Accord (DAY-tun   PEES   uh-KORD) the 1995 plan to end hostilities in Bosnia-Herzegovina

D-Day (DEE-DAY) the name given to June 6, 1944, the day Allied armies made a landing on the beaches of Normandy, in northern France, and began to push German troops back to the east

death squads (DETH   SKWODZ) groups hired by conservatives in El Salvador to kill people who opposed them

denounce (di-NOWNS) to accuse someone of a crime, especially a political one

depression (di-PRE-shun) a period of low economic activity and high unemployment

deregulation (dee-re-gyuh-LAY-shun) lessening of government control of industry

détente (DAY-tont) easing of tensions between nations

dictator (DIK-tay-tur) a ruler who has complete authority over the government and its people

discrimination (dis-kri-muh-NAY-shun) prejudice that affects the legal standing of an individual

disputed border (dis-PYOOT-ed   BOR-dur) a border on which two countries cannot agree

dissidents (DI-suh-dunts) people who disagree with government policies

---

PRONUNCIATION KEY

CAPITAL LETTERS show the stressed syllables.

ng	as in runni**ng**	u	as in b**u**t, s**o**me
o	as in c**o**t, f**a**ther	uh	as in **a**bout, tak**e**n, lem**o**n, penc**i**l
oh	as in g**o**, n**o**te	ur	as in t**er**m
oo	as in t**oo**	y	as in l**i**ne, fl**y**
sh	as in **sh**y	zh	as in vi**s**ion, mea**s**ure
th	as in **th**in		

"dollar diplomacy" (DO-lur   duh-PLOH-muh-see) a pattern of diplomacy in which the United States would lend money to a Latin American country and, when the country could not pay it back, U.S. forces would take control of that country's policies

dominion status (duh-MI-nyun   STA-tus) state of being self-governing but united with other nations

"Don't Ask, Don't Tell" (DOHNT   ASK   DOHNT   TEL) the official U.S. policy from 1993 to 2011 that banned openly gay people from serving in the military

Dunkirk (DUN-kurk) a small seaport in northern France

East Germany (EEST   JUR-muh-nee) the half of Germany occupied by the Soviet Union after World War II

Easter Rebellion (EE-stur   ri-BEL-yun) an armed uprising of Irish nationalists during World War I

economic sanctions (e-kuh-NO-mik   SANG-shunz) bans placed on trade with a certain country or group of countries

EEC (EE   EE   SEE) the European Economic Community; created by France, West Germany, Belgium, Luxembourg, the Netherlands, and Italy in 1957; known today as the European Union, or EU

Eisenhower Doctrine (Y-zun-how-ur   DOK-trun) a U.S. policy announced by President Dwight Eisenhower in 1957; declared that the United States would give military help to any country in the Middle East that was threatened by communism

---

PRONUNCIATION KEY

CAPITAL LETTERS show the stressed syllables.

a	as in m**a**t	f	as in **f**it
ay	as in d**ay**, s**ay**	g	as in **g**o
ch	as in **ch**ew	i	as in s**i**t
e	as in b**e**d	j	as in **j**ob, **g**em
ee	as in **e**ven, **ea**sy, n**ee**d	k	as in **c**ool, **k**ey

embargo (im-BAR-goh) refusal to buy or sell a country's products

entente (on-TONT) a friendly understanding between two or more nations to help one another in times of war or conflict

ethnic group (ETH-nik   GROOP) people belonging to a particular culture

euro (YUR-oh) the common currency of Europe as of 2002

European Union (EU) (yur-uh-PEE-un   YOON-yun) group of nations in Europe united for economic benefit

exile (EG-zyl) to drive someone out of his or her country, usually for political reasons

exiles (EG-zylz) people living in a foreign country who were forced from their own country

expansionist policy (ik-SPAN-shuh-nist   PO-luh-see) situation in which one country tries to expand its land area by using force to take neighboring territory

export (ek-SPORT) product sold to another country

faction (FAK-shun) group within a country with different loyalties from other groups

Fascist party (FA-shist   PAR-tee) a political party headed by Benito Mussolini in Italy

federation (fe-duh-RAY-shun) a group of states or republics recognizing a central authority

---

PRONUNCIATION KEY

CAPITAL LETTERS show the stressed syllables.

ng	as in running	u	as in but, some
o	as in cot, father	uh	as in about, taken, lemon, pencil
oh	as in go, note	ur	as in term
oo	as in too	y	as in line, fly
sh	as in shy	zh	as in vision, measure
th	as in thin		

"Final Solution" (FY-nul　suh-LOO-shun) Hitler's decision in 1941 that all Jews in Germany and in German-occupied lands were to be killed

Five-Power Treaty (FYV-POW-ur　TREE-tee) a pact in which the United States, Great Britain, Japan, France, and Italy agreed not to build any warships for ten years; made in 1922 during the Washington Naval Conference

Five-Year Plan (FYV-YEER　PLAN) the Communist government's plan, begun in 1928, to take complete control of the Soviet economy; followed by a second Five-Year Plan in 1933

Five-Year Plans (FYV-YEER　PLANZ) several attempts made by the Chinese government to gain total control of China's economy in the 1950s

fluorocarbons (flor-oh-KAR-bunz) chemicals used in refrigerators, air conditioners, and aerosol cans; known to destroy Earth's ozone layer

Fourteen Points (for-TEEN　POYNTS) a speech given by President Woodrow Wilson in 1917 that outlined 14 goals for reconstructing Europe after World War I

Gang of Four (GANG　UV　FOR) four hard-line communists of China, including Mao's widow

General Assembly (JEN-rul　uh-SEM-blee) the delegates of the United Nations; operates like a legislature

genocide (JE-nuh-syd) the deliberate and systematic destruction of a group of people

---

PRONUNCIATION KEY

CAPITAL LETTERS show the stressed syllables.

a	as in m**a**t	f	as in **f**it
ay	as in d**ay**, s**ay**	g	as in **g**o
ch	as in **ch**ew	i	as in s**i**t
e	as in b**e**d	j	as in **j**ob, **g**em
ee	as in **e**ven, **ea**sy, ne**e**d	k	as in **c**ool, **k**ey

ghettos (GE-tohz) special sections in German cities and eastern European cities for Jewish people; set up by Germany's Nazi government during the 1930s

glasnost (GLAZ-nost) the Gorbachev policy of openness

Goddess of Democracy (GO-dus   UV   duh-MOK-ruh-see) a statue set up by students in Tiananmen Square in 1989

Good Neighbor Policy (GOOD   NAY-bur   PO-luh-see) a U.S. policy in the 1930s that declared the United States would no longer interfere in the affairs of Latin America, but would promote cooperation with Latin American countries

Great Depression (GRAYT   di-PRE-shun) a worldwide period of low economic activity and high unemployment in the 1930s

Great Leap Forward (GRAYT   LEEP   FOR-wurd) an effort to force Chinese farmers to form farming communes and to run small industries; took place from 1958 to 1960; China's second Five-Year Plan

green revolution (GREEN   re-vuh-LOO-shun) new methods of cultivation, including better seeds and the proper use of fertilizers and pesticides—resulting in bigger and better crops

guerrilla (guh-RI-luh) a fighter who does not engage in standard warfare but slips in and out of a country or an area to attack people and destroy buildings

Gulf War (GULF   WOR) the war between Iraq and the United States, with its allies, in 1991

PRONUNCIATION KEY

CAPITAL LETTERS show the stressed syllables.

ng	as in runni**ng**	u	as in b**u**t, s**o**me
o	as in c**o**t, f**a**ther	uh	as in **a**bout, tak**e**n, lem**o**n, penc**i**l
oh	as in g**o**, n**o**te	ur	as in t**er**m
oo	as in t**oo**	y	as in l**i**ne, fl**y**
sh	as in **sh**y	zh	as in vi**s**ion, mea**s**ure
th	as in **th**in		

hard-liners (HARD-LYN-urz) Communists who wanted to follow the party line exactly

Hebrew (HEE-broo) the official language of Israel

Hindus (HIN-dooz) along with Muslims, one of the two main religious groups of India

Hitler-Stalin Pact (HIT-lur-STO-lin   PAKT) an agreement made between Adolf Hitler and Joseph Stalin in 1939; a nonaggression pact in which the Soviet Union and Germany agreed to split up lands in the nations of Eastern Europe

Holocaust (HOH-luh-kost) the name given to the destruction of European civilians and especially Jews during the Nazi era

Horn of Africa (HORN   UV   A-fri-ka) part of East Africa that juts into the Arabian Sea

illiteracy (i-LI-tuh-ruh-see) the inability to read

impeachment (im-PEECH-munt) accusation of misconduct against a public official

imperialism (im-PEER-ee-uh-li-zum) the process of building an empire by controlling colonies on foreign lands

imports (IM-portz) products bought from another country

incentives (in-SEN-tivz) rewards

Indochina (in-doh-CHY-nuh) a region in Southeast Asia that includes Vietnam, Laos, and Cambodia

---

PRONUNCIATION KEY

CAPITAL LETTERS show the stressed syllables.

a	as in m**a**t	f	as in **f**it
ay	as in day, s**ay**	g	as in **g**o
ch	as in **ch**ew	i	as in s**i**t
e	as in b**e**d	j	as in **j**ob, **g**em
ee	as in **e**ven, **ea**sy, n**ee**d	k	as in **c**ool, **k**ey

indoctrinating (in-DOK-truh-nayt-ing) teaching people to think a certain way

inflation (in-FLAY-shun) a situation in which prices rise and the value of money goes down

intellectuals (in-tul-EK-chuh-wulz) educated people

interest (IN-trust) amount paid to borrow money

intifada (in-tuh-FO-duh) Palestinian uprisings within the West Bank and Gaza that began in the late 1980s

investors (in-VEST-urz) people who commit money in order to make more money

Iraq War (i-RAK   WOR) war fought by the United States and its allies against Iraq in the early 2000s

Irish Free State (Y-rish   FREE   STAYT) Southern Ireland, after a 1921 agreement between the Irish Republic and Britain; a self-governing and Catholic part of Ireland

Irish Republican Army (IRA) (Y-rish   ri-PUH-bli-kun   AR-mee) Roman Catholic group in Northern Ireland

Islam (IZ-lom) a major religion of the world, founded by Muhammad

isolationism (y-suh-LAY-shuh-ni-zum) a policy of staying out of international affairs

Israel (IZ-ree-ul) the Jewish part of Palestine; proclaimed as an independent nation in 1948 by the United Nations

---

PRONUNCIATION KEY

CAPITAL LETTERS show the stressed syllables.

ng as in runni**ng**	u as in b**u**t, s**o**me
o as in c**o**t, f**a**ther	uh as in **a**bout, tak**e**n, lem**o**n, penc**i**l
oh as in g**o**, n**o**te	ur as in t**er**m
oo as in t**oo**	y as in l**i**ne, fl**y**
sh as in **sh**y	zh as in vi**s**ion, mea**s**ure
th as in **th**in	

junta (HUN-tuh) a group of leaders

kamikaze attacks (ko-mi-KO-zee   uh-TAKS) a war tactic used by Japanese troops in World War II; Japanese fighter pilots would crash their planes into U.S. vessels, blowing up themselves and at least parts of the American ships as well

Kellogg-Briand Pact (KEL-og   BREE-and   PAKT) a treaty signed by 62 countries that condemned war as a way of settling disputes between nations; signing began in 1928 and continued for several years

Khmer Rouge (kuh-MER   ROOJ) a communist group that seized control of Cambodia

Kuomintang (KWO-min-tang) Chinese nationalists

labor productivity (LAY-bur   proh-duk-TI-vuh-tee) the amount of work done

League of Nations (LEEG   UV   NAY-shunz) an organization formed by many of the world's countries after World War I; created at the Paris Peace Conference

Lend-Lease Act (LEND   LEES   AKT) an act that allowed U.S. President Franklin D. Roosevelt to supply arms and other supplies on credit to Great Britain and other nations involved in World War II; passed by Congress in March 1941

"Long March" (LONG   MARCH) the 6,000-mile march of Chinese Communists from southern to northern China; started in 1934 and ended in 1936

PRONUNCIATION KEY

CAPITAL LETTERS show the stressed syllables.

a	as in m**a**t	f	as in **f**it
ay	as in day, s**ay**	g	as in **g**o
ch	as in **ch**ew	i	as in s**i**t
e	as in b**e**d	j	as in **j**ob, **g**em
ee	as in **e**ven, **ea**sy, n**ee**d	k	as in **c**ool, **k**ey

machine gun (muh-SHEEN GUN) a type of gun that can rapidly fire many bullets, one after another

Maginot Line (MA-jin-oh LYN) the chain of fortifications built by France for protection after World War I

Manchuria (man-CHUR-ee-uh) the northern region of China

mandate (MAN-dayt) requirement

Maoris (MOW-rees) natives of New Zealand

March Revolution (MARCH re-vuh-LOO-shun) the Russian Revolution of 1917 that took Tsar Nicholas II out of power

market socialism (MAR-kut SOH-shuh-li-zum) the mix of economic policies practiced in Yugoslavia

Marshall Plan (MAR-shul PLAN) a long-range recovery plan to help Europe after World War II; set up by the nations of Western Europe under U.S. Secretary of State George Marshall

martial law (MAR-shul LAW) use of military force to govern citizens in time of a national crisis

Maya (MY-uh) a native people of Mexico and Central America

militancy (MI-luh-tun-see) state of being aggressively active in a cause

militarist (MI-luh-tuh-rist) one who favors a buildup of a country's military forces

---

PRONUNCIATION KEY

CAPITAL LETTERS show the stressed syllables.

ng	as in running	u	as in but, some
o	as in cot, father	uh	as in about, taken, lemon, pencil
oh	as in go, note	ur	as in term
oo	as in too	y	as in line, fly
sh	as in shy	zh	as in vision, measure
th	as in thin		

militia (muh-LI-shuh) an armed group of fighters not under the control of the army

monarchy (MO-nur-kee) country led by a member of royalty, such as a king or queen

Monroe Doctrine (mun-ROH   DOK-trun) a policy that said the United States would not allow European meddling in the affairs of the Americas

mulattoes (muh-LO-tohz) people of mixed black and white ancestry

multinational corporations (mul-tee-NA-shuh-nul   kor-puh-RAY-shunz) large companies with branches in many nations, making and selling their products all over the world

Muslims (MUZ-lumz) followers of Islam; along with Hindus, one of the two main religious groups of India

National Guard (NA-shuh-nul   GARD) a Nicaraguan army trained by the United States

nationalism (NA-shuh-nul-i-zum) pride in one's own country above all others

nationalization (na-shuh-nul-uh-ZAY-shun) the process of a government taking over private industries

NATO (NAY-toh) the North Atlantic Treaty Organization; formed in 1949 by the United States, France, Great Britain, Italy, and eight other nations

Nazi Party (NOT-see   PAR-tee) a nationalist political party formed in Germany in the early 1920s, led by Adolf Hitler

---

PRONUNCIATION KEY

CAPITAL LETTERS show the stressed syllables.

a	as in m**a**t	f	as in **f**it
ay	as in d**ay**, s**ay**	g	as in **g**o
ch	as in **ch**ew	i	as in s**i**t
e	as in b**e**d	j	as in **j**ob, **g**em
ee	as in **e**ven, **ea**sy, n**ee**d	k	as in **c**ool, **k**ey

neutral (NOO-trul) not supporting or favoring either side in a war, conflict, or contest

New Deal (NOO DEEL) a group of reforms started by U.S. President Franklin D. Roosevelt in the 1930s; aimed at changing American economic policy

Nine-Power Treaty (NYN-POW-ur TREE-tee) a pact in which the United States, Great Britain, Japan, France, Italy, and others agreed not to take any more land or rights from China; made in 1922 during the Washington Naval Conference

nonaggression agreement (NON-uh-GRE-shun uh-GREE-munt) a document signed by countries promising not to attack one another

nonaligned nation (non-uh-LYND NAY-shun) in the context of the Cold War, a nation not allied with either the United States or the USSR

Northern Ireland (NOR-thurn YR-lund) the Protestant-dominated counties in the northern part of Ireland that have remained part of the United Kingdom

November Revolution (noh-VEM-bur re-vuh-LOO-shun) the coup d'état by which the Bolsheviks took control of the Russian Revolution, seizing all government buildings

Nuclear Nonproliferation Treaty (NOO-klee-ur non-pruh-li-fuh-RAY-shun TREE-tee) a treaty designed to limit the number of nations that could test and possess nuclear weapons

---

PRONUNCIATION KEY

CAPITAL LETTERS show the stressed syllables.

ng	as in runni**ng**	u	as in b**u**t, s**o**me
o	as in c**o**t, f**a**ther	uh	as in **a**bout, tak**e**n, lem**o**n, penc**i**l
oh	as in g**o**, n**o**te	ur	as in t**er**m
oo	as in t**oo**	y	as in l**i**ne, fl**y**
sh	as in **sh**y	zh	as in vi**s**ion, mea**s**ure
th	as in **th**in		

nuclear physics (NOO-klee-ur   FI-ziks) the study of the nuclear structure of atoms

Nunavut (NU-nuh-vut) the self-governing homeland of the Inuit in Canada

Occupy Wall Street (OK-kyoo-py   WAL   STREET) a series of demonstrations against financial corruption beginning in 2011 in the United States

oligarchy (O-luh-gar-kee) government by a small group of wealthy landowners and business owners

OPEC (OH-pek) Organization of Petroleum Exporting Countries, made up of many of the largest oil producers in the Middle East, Africa, South America, and Asia

Organization of American States (OAS) (or-guh-nuh-ZAY-shun   UV uh-MER-uh-kun   STAYTS) an alliance formed in 1948 by 21 American nations; its members met regularly to discuss mutual policies and problems in the Americas.

Ostpolitik (OST-pol-uh-tik) the German chancellor Willy Brandt's policy of openness toward East Germany and the Soviet Union

ozone (OH-zohn) a layer of upper atmosphere that helps shield Earth from ultraviolet radiation

PAC (PAK) Pan-Africanist Congress

Pan-Africanism (pan-A-fri-kuh-ni-zum) belief that all Africans can unite, no matter what country they come from

---

PRONUNCIATION KEY

CAPITAL LETTERS show the stressed syllables.

a	as in m**a**t	f	as in **f**it
ay	as in d**ay**, s**ay**	g	as in **g**o
ch	as in **ch**ew	i	as in s**i**t
e	as in b**e**d	j	as in **j**ob, **g**em
ee	as in **e**ven, **ea**sy, nee**d**	k	as in **c**ool, **k**ey

Pan-Slavism (pan-SLA-vi-zum) a movement to unite the Slav peoples of eastern and east central Europe as a means of promoting common cultural and political goals

Paris Peace Conference (PAYR-us PEES KON-fruns) world conference held in 1919 to discuss the terms of peace after World War I

parliament (PAR-luh-munt) a lawmaking body

pass law (PAS LAW) in South Africa, a law requiring all nonwhites to carry a pass that showed their race and where they had permission to live and work

passive resistance (PA-siv ri-ZIS-tuns) a type of political protest that is based on nonviolence

Pathet Lao (PATH-et LOW) people from Laos who were pro-communist

peace treaty (PEES TREE-tee) a signed agreement that sets out the terms of peace after a war is over

peaceful coexistence (PEES-ful koh-ig-ZIS-tuns) a policy adopted by the Soviet Union and the United States that both East and West would exist side by side without war

Pearl Harbor (PURL HAR-bur) the site of a U.S. navy base; attacked by Japan in 1941, initiating U.S. involvement in World War II

People's Liberation Army (PEE-pulz li-buh-RAY-shun AR-mee) the Chinese army; fought the Red Guards during the Cultural Revolution

perestroika (per-uh-STROY-kuh) Gorbachev policy of restructuring

---

PRONUNCIATION KEY

CAPITAL LETTERS show the stressed syllables.

ng	as in runni**ng**	u	as in b**u**t, s**o**me
o	as in c**o**t, f**a**ther	uh	as in **a**bout, tak**e**n, lem**o**n, penc**i**l
oh	as in g**o**, n**o**te	ur	as in t**er**m
oo	as in t**oo**	y	as in l**i**ne, fl**y**
sh	as in **sh**y	zh	as in vi**s**ion, mea**s**ure
th	as in **th**in		

physics (FI-ziks) the study of matter and energy

PLO (PEE EL OH) Palestine Liberation Organization

Popular Front (PO-pyoo-lur FRUNT) a French coalition formed by the leftists

Prague Spring (PROG SPRING) a 1968 reform movement in Czechoslovakia

preemptive strike (pree-EMP-tiv STRYK) an attack against an opponent to keep the opponent from attacking first

privatize (PRY-vuh-tyz) to sell state-owned businesses to private individuals

propaganda (pra-puh-GAN-duh) information (often false) that is spread to support a cause

proxies (PROK-seez) substitutes

psychoanalysis (sy-koh-uh-NA-luh-sus) the study of the unconscious parts of the human mind; developed by Sigmund Freud in the early 1900s

psychology (sy-KO-luh-jee) the study of the human mind

recession (ri-SE-shun) a period of declining economic activity

Red Army (RED AR-mee) China's Communist army

Red Guards (RED GARDZ) mobs of students and other Chinese who terrorized citizens, 1966 to 1968

Reds (REDZ) term used for the Bolsheviks during the civil war following the Russian Revolution

---

PRONUNCIATION KEY

CAPITAL LETTERS show the stressed syllables.

a	as in m**a**t	f	as in **f**it
ay	as in day, s**ay**	g	as in **g**o
ch	as in **ch**ew	i	as in s**i**t
e	as in b**e**d	j	as in **j**ob, **g**em
ee	as in **e**ven, **ea**sy, ne**e**d	k	as in **c**ool, **k**ey

refugees (RE-fyoo-geez) people who flee to another country to escape from war or bad times

regimes (ri-ZHEEMZ) governments

regionalized (REE-juh-nul-yzd) divided and dominated by different political parties in different regions

religious fundamentalist (ri-LI-jus   fun-duh-MEN-tul-ist) one who believes in the strict interpretation of religious law

reparations (re-puh-RAY-shunz) payments for war damages

Republic of Ireland (ri-PUH-blik   UV   YR-lund) an independent country, also called Eire; formerly the Irish Free State

Republic of Turkey (ri-PUH-blik   UV   TUR-kee) a Western-oriented nation formed from the Ottoman Empire in the early 1900s

restrictions (ri-STRIK-shunz) limitations

Rhineland (RYN-land) German territory on either side of the Rhine River

right-wing (RYT-WING) conservative or reactionary

Roaring Twenties (ROR-ing   TWEN-teez) the 1920s; a period of peace and prosperity in the United States

Rome-Berlin-Tokyo Axis (ROHM   bur-LIN   TOH-kee-oh   AK-sus) a 1940 agreement between Italy, Germany, and Japan that said they would support one another

---

PRONUNCIATION KEY

CAPITAL LETTERS show the stressed syllables.

ng	as in runni**ng**	u	as in b**u**t, s**o**me
o	as in c**o**t, f**a**ther	uh	as in **a**bout, tak**e**n, lem**o**n, penc**i**l
oh	as in g**o**, n**o**te	ur	as in t**er**m
oo	as in t**oo**	y	as in l**i**ne, fl**y**
sh	as in **sh**y	zh	as in vi**s**ion, mea**s**ure
th	as in **th**in		

Roosevelt Corollary (ROH-zuh-velt   KOR-uh-ler-ee) a 1903 addition to the Monroe Doctrine; stated that the United States had the right to take "police action" in Latin America

SALT I (SALT   WUN) agreement between the Soviet Union and the United States to limit nuclear weapons

samizdat (SA-meez-dat) dissidents' self-published criticisms of the Soviet Union

sanction (SANG-shun) a heavy penalty, such as a fine or a restriction

Sandinistas (san-duh-NEES-tus) a rebel group in Nicaragua opposed to rule by the Somoza family and its allies

satellite (SA-tul-yt) a country that was controlled by the Soviet Union but was not part of the USSR; plural: also known as "people's republics" (included Poland, East Germany, Czechoslovakia, Hungary, Romania, Bulgaria, and Albania)

SEATO (SEET-oh) Southeast Asian Treaty Organization, a defensive alliance of Pacific nations formed in 1954; original members were the United States, Great Britain, France, Australia, New Zealand, Pakistan, Thailand, and the Philippines; formed to help prevent the forceful spread of communism

secede (si-SEED) to declare independence

secular state (SE-kyuh-lur   STAYT) a nation in which there is no official religion

---

PRONUNCIATION KEY

CAPITAL LETTERS show the stressed syllables.

a	as in mat		f	as in fit
ay	as in day, say		g	as in go
ch	as in chew		i	as in sit
e	as in bed		j	as in job, gem
ee	as in even, easy, need		k	as in cool, key

Securitate (si-KYUR-uh-tayt) the security police in Romania

Security Council (si-KYUR-uh-tee   KOWN-sul) a group of 15 members of the United Nations that works to keep peace in the world

separatist movement (SEP-ruh-tist   MOOV-munt) an effort for independence or separation from a greater unit

September 11 attacks (sep-TEM-bur   i-LE-vun   uh-TAKS) terrorist attacks in the United States with hijacked airplanes on September 11, 2001

Siegfried Line (SIG-freed   LYN) the chain of fortifications built by Germany for protection prior to World War II

Sikhs (SEEKS) a religious group in India; often associated with a military tradition

Six-Day War (SIX-DAY   WOR) the Israeli-Arab war of 1967

socialism with a human face (SO-shuh-li-zum   WITH   UH   HYOO-mun   FAYS) Alexander Dubcek's reform policies in Czechoslovakia

social reforms (SOH-shul   ri-FORMZ) changes in government programs to improve a country

Solidarity (so-luh-DAR-uh-tee) an independent trade union in Poland

sonar (SOH-nar) a type of weapon that uses sound waves to find and track submarines underwater

soviet (SOH-vee-et) a revolutionary council of workers

Soviet bloc (SOH-vee-et   BLOK) nations allied with the Soviet Union

---

PRONUNCIATION KEY

CAPITAL LETTERS show the stressed syllables.

ng	as in runni**ng**	u	as in b**u**t, s**o**me
o	as in c**o**t, f**a**ther	uh	as in **a**bout, tak**e**n, lem**o**n, penc**i**l
oh	as in g**o**, n**o**te	ur	as in t**er**m
oo	as in t**oo**	y	as in l**i**ne, fl**y**
sh	as in **sh**y	zh	as in vi**s**ion, mea**s**ure
th	as in **th**in		

Spanish Civil War (SPA-nish SI-vul WOR) a civil war in Spain that pulled in many other European nations; lasted from 1936 to 1939

spheres of influence (SFEERZ UV IN-floo-uns) regions within a nation in which other nations have special rights

stock market (STOK MAR-kut) a place where people buy and sell shares, called stocks, in companies

subcontinent (sub-KON-tun-unt) a large area of land that is smaller than a continent, for instance, a subdivision of a continent

submarine (SUB-muh-reen) a ship that operates underwater

summit conferences (SUH-mut KON-fuh-runs-ez) gatherings of the highest leaders of the United States, Great Britain, and France

superpower (SOO-pur-pow-ur) a nation capable of influencing international events and acts and policies of less powerful nations

supply-side economics (suh-PLY-SYD e-kuh-NO-miks) a policy of tax cuts designed to bring new income and economic growth

Taliban (TAL-uh-ban) a Muslim group that ruled Afghanistan under very strict Islamic law in the 1990s

tank (TANK) an armored vehicle that can break through enemy lines during war

tariff (TAR-uf) a tax on goods that come into a country from other nations

---

PRONUNCIATION KEY

CAPITAL LETTERS show the stressed syllables.

a	as in m**a**t	f	as in **f**it
ay	as in day, s**ay**	g	as in **g**o
ch	as in **ch**ew	i	as in s**i**t
e	as in b**e**d	j	as in **j**ob, **g**em
ee	as in **e**ven, **ea**sy, n**ee**d	k	as in **c**ool, **k**ey

theory of evolution (THEER-ee UV e-vuh-LOO-shun) a theory developed by Charles Darwin in the mid-1800s; explains why living creatures change over thousands of years

theory of relativity (THEER-ee UV re-luh-TI-vuh-tee) a theory developed by Albert Einstein; explains atomic events in terms of motion, space, and time

Third Reich (THURD RYK) Adolf Hitler's period of rule in Germany, from 1933 to 1945

Third World (THURD WURLD) a term that refers to the underdeveloped, non-Western countries of the world

Tiananmen Square (CHAN-un-men SKWAYR) site of student massacre in Beijing, China, in 1989

totalitarian (toh-ta-luh-TER-ee-un) a system in which a strong leader takes nearly absolute power, and people do not have the right to vote, speak freely, or oppose the leader

trade deficit (TRAYD DE-fuh-sut) the result when a country imports more than it exports; the amount of the deficit is the difference between those two numbers.

trench (TRENCH) a deep ditch

tribunal (TRY-byoo-nul) a court

Triple Alliance (TRI-pul uh-LY-unts) an agreement made between Germany, Austria-Hungary, and Italy in 1882; under this agreement, each country agreed to help the other countries in case of an attack by France.

PRONUNCIATION KEY

CAPITAL LETTERS show the stressed syllables.

ng	as in runni**ng**	u	as in b**u**t, s**o**me
o	as in c**o**t, f**a**ther	uh	as in **a**bout, tak**e**n, lem**o**n, penc**i**l
oh	as in g**o**, n**o**te	ur	as in te**r**m
oo	as in t**oo**	y	as in l**i**ne, fl**y**
sh	as in **sh**y	zh	as in vi**s**ion, mea**s**ure
th	as in **th**in		

Triple Entente (TRI-pul on-TONT) an understanding between Russia, France, and Great Britain in 1907; under this understanding, each country agreed to help the other countries in case of an attack by the Triple Alliance.

Truman Doctrine (TROO-mun DOK-trun) a U.S. policy that stated the United States would help any country that faced a threat by communists; announced by President Harry Truman in March 1947

tsar (ZAR) an absolute ruler, such as a king or an emperor; a term used in Russia, Serbia, and Bulgaria, where it originated

U-boats (YOO-bohts) German submarines

unconscious (un-KON-shus) thought processes that go on without a person being aware of them

unilaterally (yoo-ni-LA-tuh-rul-ee) only one party to an agreement making a decision

Union of Soviet Socialist Republics (YOON-yun UV SOH-vee-et SOH-shuh-list ri-PUH-bliks) the name given Russia in 1922 after the Bolsheviks took power; also called the USSR

United Arab Republic (UAR) (yoo-NY-tud AR-ub ri-PUH-blik) the union of Egypt and Syria; arranged by Gamal Abdel Nasser in 1958

United Nations (yoo-NY-tud NAY-shunz) an organization of the world's nations united to keep peace and help one another; officially started in 1945

universal suffrage (yoo-nuh-VER-sul SUH-frij) a situation in which every adult can vote

---

PRONUNCIATION KEY

CAPITAL LETTERS show the stressed syllables.

a	as in m**a**t	f	as in **f**it
ay	as in d**ay**, s**ay**	g	as in **g**o
ch	as in **ch**ew	i	as in s**i**t
e	as in b**e**d	j	as in **j**ob, **g**em
ee	as in **e**ven, **ea**sy, n**ee**d	k	as in **c**ool, **k**ey

UNRRA (YOO EN AR AR AY) the United Nations Relief and Rehabilitation Administration, an agency that provided emergency aid to Europe after World War II; started in 1943

urban (UR-bun) of or relating to a city

V-E Day (VEE-EE DAY) the name given to May 8, 1945, the day the German army surrendered; stands for "Victory in Europe Day"

Velvet Revolution (VEL-vut re-vuh-LOO-shun) 1989 overthrow of the Czechoslovakian Communist Party

Versailles Treaty (vur-SY TREE-tee) an agreement signed by Germany after World War I (1919); Germany agreed to do the following: pay for all civilian damage during the war; transfer large parcels of land to other nations; give up all its overseas colonies; shrink its military forces; and admit that the Central Powers were responsible for starting the war.

Vichy France (vee-SHEE FRANS) the area in southern France ruled by Marshal Pétain during World War II in collaboration with the Nazis

Viet Cong (vee-ET KONG) communist rebels who fought in South Vietnam

Vietnam War (vee-ET-nam WOR) a war fought between North Vietnam and South Vietnam in the 1960s and 1970s, with large numbers of U.S. troops fighting in support of South Vietnam

V-J Day (VEE-JAY DAY) the name given to August 15, 1945, when Emperor Hirohito announced the surrender of Japan; stands for "Victory in Japan Day"

PRONUNCIATION KEY

CAPITAL LETTERS show the stressed syllables.

ng	as in runni**ng**	u	as in b**u**t, s**o**me
o	as in c**o**t, f**a**ther	uh	as in **a**bout, tak**e**n, lem**o**n, penc**i**l
oh	as in g**o**, n**o**te	ur	as in t**er**m
oo	as in t**oo**	y	as in l**i**ne, fl**y**
sh	as in **sh**y	zh	as in vi**s**ion, mea**s**ure
th	as in **th**in		

war of attrition (WOR UV uh-TRI-shun) the wearing down of a country by constant small attacks

Warsaw Pact (WOR-saw PAKT) an agreement between the USSR and Eastern European countries in 1955 to provide troops for mutual use in case of war

Watergate (WO-tur GAYT) a scandal in which Republicans broke into Democratic Party headquarters in the 1970s

Weimar Republic (VY-mar ri-PUH-blik) a democratic government created in Germany in 1919, just after the end of World War I

West Germany (WEST JUR-muh-nee) the half of Germany occupied by the United States, Great Britain, and France after World War II

Whites (WYTS) anticommunists during the civil war following the Russian Revolution

Yom Kippur War (YOM ki-PUR WOR) Israeli-Arab war of 1973

Young Turks (YUNG TURKS) a group of Turkish nationalists who rebelled against the Ottoman ruler in 1908

ZANU (ZA-noo) Zimbabwe African National Union (black Rhodesian party)

ZAPU (ZA-poo) Zimbabwe African People's Union (black Rhodesian party)

Zimmermann telegram (ZI-mur-mun TE-luh-gram) the telegram in which German foreign minister Alfred Zimmermann outlined his country's secret plan to get Mexico's help in World War I; stated that Germany would give back parts of the southwestern United States to Mexico if it agreed to help Germany in the war

INDEX

Abacha, Sani, 243
Abbas, Mahmoud, 24
King Abdullah (of Jordan), 189
Abdullah (of Saudi Arabia), 181
Aborigines, 238, 254
Adenauer, Konrad, 89, 243
Aegean Sea, 10–11
Afghanistan, 216
    British participation in military action
      in, 153
    Canadian troops in, 125
    Soviet Union invades, 119, 173–174
    terrorist training camps in, 122
    U.S. troops in, 123
Africa, 194–209. *See also specific countries*
    AIDS epidemic in, 210
    colonialism in, 27
    at end of World War II, 97–100
    issues and trends in, 209–210
    unequal resources in, 201
    World War I in, 13, 15
African Americans, 110, 118, 123
African National Congress (ANC),
    207–209, 254
Afrikaners, 100
Ahmadinejad, Mahmoud, 185, 243
AIDS (Acquired Immune Deficiency
    Syndrome), 210
airplanes
    become military weapons, 62
    hit World Trade Center and Pentagon, 122
Albania, 11, 86, 159, 165
    becomes Soviet satellite, 76
    invasion of, 66
Alemán, Arnoldo, 243
Alexander (king of Yugoslavia), 46–47
Algeria, 98–99
    during 1940s and 1950s, 89
    war in, 89
alliances, 9–10
Allied Powers, 11, 12
    new territories desired by, 19
    strengths of, 12
    win propaganda war, 13
allies, 9

Allies, 63, 70–74
    control Middle East, 66
    set up Berlin airlift, 77
All-India Muslim League, 35–36
anarchists (Spain), 45
Anatolia, 34
animists, 209
annexation, 59–60
Anschluss, 59
apartheid, 100, 207, 209
Apollo 11, 118
appeasement, 60
Aquino, Benigno, 237
Aquino, Benigno III, 237
Aquino, Corazon, 237
Arab League, 94, 93
Arab Spring, 192–193
Arabs, 94
    conflicts between Jews and, 32, 33, 92,
      93, 185, 186, 187
    nationalism of, 38
    receive eastern Palestine from United
      Nations, 92–93
Arab Union, 94
Arafat, Yasser, 187
Argentina, 1121, 142–143, 147
    dispute over Falkland Islands, 152
Aristide, Jean-Bertrand. *See* Duvalier,
    Jean-Claude
armistice, 17, 19, 103
Armistice Day, 17
Armstrong, Neil, 118
Aryans, 34, 67
Asia. *See also specific countries*
    economic slump in, 236
    Japan moves in, 69–70. *See also* Japan
    World War I in, 15
al-Assad, Bashar, 190
al-Assad, Hafez, 190
assembly line, 4
Aswan High Dam, 92
Atlantic, Battle of the, 71
atomic bomb, 4, 62, 73, 84, 225, 234
    effects of, 73
Attlee, Clement, 88–89

Germany invades, 66
royal dictatorship in, 47
Burma, 70, 107, 218–219
Bush, George H. W., 120, 182
orders invasion of Panama, 132
Bush, George W.
challenges faced by, 123
election in 2000 of, 121–122
war in Iraq and, 123
Buthelezi, Mangosuthu, 209

Calderón, Felipe, 129
Cambodia, 105, 107, 217–220
Cameron, David, 153
Campbell, Kim, 125
Camp David Accords, 195–196
Canada
from 1960s to present, 123–126
effect of September 11 attacks on, 125
issues and trends in, 126–127
native peoples of, 125
political parties in, 124
regionalization of, 124
capitalism, 79, 225–226, 229
Caribbean, 135. *See also specific countries*
Carol II (king of Romania), 47
Carter, Jimmy, 119, 140, 186, 195
castes, 35
Castro, Fidel, 112, 136–137
programs of, 136
Castro, Raúl, 137
Catholic Church, in Spain, 45
el Caudillo. See Franco, Francisco
cease-fire, 26, 92, 131, 152, 182, 185, 195, 201, 206, 215
Ceausescu, Elena, 166
Ceausescu, Nicolae, 166, 170
censorship, 137, 180
Central America, 129–134. *See also specific countries*
civil wars in, from 1960s to 1980s, 130
Central Intelligence Agency (CIA), 132
Central Powers, 11–12, 14, 18, 22
and reparations, 20
Chad, 191, 197

chador, 184
Challenger, 120
Chamberlain, Neville, 60
Chamorro, Violeta Barrios de, 131
chancellor, 155
Charlottetown Accord, 125
Charter 77, 162
Cheonan, 233
Chernobyl, 73
Chiang Kai-shek, 37, 101
China, 36–37
capitalism in, 266
changes in, after Mao, 226
civil war in, 101
Cultural Revolution, 224
explodes first atomic bomb, 225
and Hong Kong, 228
Japan invades, 37, 48, 57
Nixon visits, 119
People's Liberation Army, 224
Red Guards, 224
relations between Soviet Union and, 102, 225
resumption of relations between United States and, 225
revolution in, 224–225
and Taiwan, 101, 228–229
Tiananmen Square, 226–227
Chinese Soviet Republic, 37
Chirac, Jacques, 154
Chrétien, Jean, 125–126
Christian Democratic Union, 89
Christianity
in Lebanon, 96
spread through imperialism, 8
in Sudan, 209
chromosomes, 5
Churchill, Winston, 65, 75, 86, 88
at Yalta, 75
Civic Forum, 162–163
civilians
become targets in World War II, 62, 74
killed in World War I, 13, 17
civil liberties, 137, 152
Civil Rights Act, 118
civil rights movement, 36, 110–111, 118

Clinton, Bill, 121, 182
    scandal during second term of, 121
coalition, 20, 40, 90, 95
coca, 141, 144
cocaine, 144
Cold War, 79, 80, 83–84
    Afghanistan and, 216
    and Cuba, 113
        crisis in, 113
        U.S. embargo on Cuban sugar, 136
    conflict on Grenada, 135
    effect on U.S. foreign policy, 109
    end of, 120
    fought in Central America, 129
    game played by Sukarno, 235
    in Middle East, 179
    Nasser refuses to take sides in, 92
    NATO, 84
    Nehru refuses to take sides in, 104
    politics, Korea and, 109
    protests in Japan, 230–231
    revival of, 119–120
    rivalry reflected in U.N., 80
    Southeast Asia as field of battle in, 105
    Vietnam and, 118
    Warsaw Pact, 84
collectives, 52, 102, 112
Collor de Mello, Fernando, 142
Colombia, 144
    drug trade in, 141, 144
    exports of, 144
colonialism, end of, 207, 213. *See also*
    colonies
colonies
    in British Empire, 27
    come under mandate system, 32
    demand self-rule, 32, 103–104
    and imperialism, 8
    independence for many, 91
    loss of Germany's, 15, 20
    lost by France, 89
    want self-rule after World War I, 19, 32, 35
Colon, Rafael Hernandez, 139–140
Comecon (Council for Mutual Economic
    Assistance), 84
Comintern, 52

Common Market, 84–85
commonwealth, 139
Commonwealth of Independent States (CIS),
    172, 175
Commonwealth of Nations, 137, 208,
    237–238
    South Africa withdraws from, 208
communes, 102, 223, 226
communism, 85
    aggressive spread of Chinese, 102
    barrier to spread of, 76
    basic idea of, 79
    Cuba's ties to, 113
    Eisenhower Doctrine, 109
    fear of, in United States, 110
    formation of alliances to counter
        NATO, 109
        SEATO, 109
    in Peru, 233
    Soviet desire to expand, 77, 83, 85
    stopping spread of, 22, 76, 83, 89, 105, 109
    struggle in Korea, 103
    Truman Doctrine, 109
    under Lenin, 50
    under Stalin, 52
Communist Party, 50–52, 90
    in China headed by Mao, 37, 101–102
    in U.S.S.R., 51
communists, 29
    blame assigned by Germans to, 42–43
    Bolsheviks, 16, 22
    in China, 37
    response of former Russian allies to, 22
concentration camps, 43, 67–68, 74
conditioned reflex, 5
Congo, 204–205
Conservative Party (Canada), 124
Conservative Party (Great Britain), 26,
    88–89, 151–152,
constitutional monarchy, 40, 45, 98
Contras, 131
cooperatives, 145, 223
Coral Sea, Battle of the, 72
corruption, 132, 138, 142, 146, 169,
    financial corruption, 193
    in Mexico, 128–129

coup(s), 47, 94, 95, 111, 112, 198, 203, 221, 237

Croatia, 21, 47, 165, 167, 169–171
  declares independence, 168

Croats, 21, 46, 169–170
  massacres by, 47

Cuba, 136–137
  exiles from, 117
  Soviet missiles in, 86, 113, 117
  and Soviet Union, 113, 117–118
  United States breaks off diplomatic relations with, 113
  U.S. embargo on sugar from, 136
  women in, 147

Cultural Revolution, 224

Curie, Marie, 4

Curie, Pierre, 4

Cyclone Nargis, 219

Czechoslovak Communist Party, 161–162

Czechoslovakia, 20, 21, 58, 92, 159, 161–163
  becomes Soviet satellite, 76, 86
  collapse of communism in, 162
  democracy in, 161
  dissolution of, 21
  Hitler targets, 44
  issues and trends in, 163–164
  taken over by Hitler, 59–60

Czech Republic, 21, 156, 159
  formation of, 263

Daimler, Gottlieb, 3

Daladier, Edouard, 60

Dalai Lama, 227

Danzig, 61

Darwin, Charles, 5

Dayton Peace Accord, 169

D-Day, 72

death squads, 133

de Gaulle, Charles, 65, 89, 99
  arranges settlement for Algerian war, 99

de Klerk, F. W., 208

democracy
  breakdown of, in new African nations, 98
  commmunism in U.S.S.R. calls for overturn of, 52
  "discipline-flourishing," 219

  in Eastern Europe, 46, 59
  failing, in many countries, 25
  Japan becomes, 78, 101
  limits on leaders in, 40
  parliamentary, 215
  promotion of by U.S., 83, 109

Democratic People's Republic of Korea. *See* North Korea

Democratic Republic of the Congo, 204–205

Deng Xiaoping, 226, 364

Denmark, invasion of, 64

Department of Homeland Security, 201

depression
  Great Depression, 29–31
  worldwide, 26, 40, 41, 43,

deregulation, 239

"The Desert Fox." *See* Rommel, Erwin

deserts, spread of, 201

détente, 173

Díaz, Porfirio, 37

dictators, 25, 30, 37, 40, 71, 72, 76, 79, 85, 87, 99, 101–102, 104, 120, 130, 192, 223, 225. *See also* specific dictators
  in Argentina, 112, 143
  in Austria, 46
  in Bulgaria, 47
  in Caribbean, 135
  Central American, 130
  in Cuba, 112, 136
  in Europe come to power in 1920s and 1930s, 40–43, 45–47
  in Romania, 47, 166
  in Spain, 90

discrimination, 118, 124
  sexual, 126

dissidents, 162, 173

Djibouti, 94

"dollar diplomacy," 39

Dominican Republic, 38–39

dominions, 137
  in British Empire, 27

dominion status, 137

"Don't Ask, Don't Tell," 123

drug trade, 129, 144, 146,

Druse, 189

Dubcek, Alexander, 162–163

becomes part of Soviet Union, 63
democracy in, 46
Ethiopia, 199–201
declared socialist state, 200
Italy's invasion of, 35, 41, 199
quarrel between Eritrea and, 200–201
"ethnic cleansing," 47
ethnic groups, 10, 168, 174
history of conflict between Balkan, 10, 165
hostilities between Balkan, 165, 171
movable holidays of, 301
in post-World War I countries, 21
in Yugoslavia, 46, 170
ethnic minorities, 21, 168, 235
in Indonesia, 235
euro, 157
Europe
alliances in, 9–10
democracies in Eastern, 46
divided, 75
East versus West, 76–77
Iron Curtain across, 86
military buildup in, 9
nations of Eastern and Central, 159–164.
See also specific countries
new borders in, 21
postwar, 75–77
"powder keg" of, 10
rebuilding of Western, 76
rise of dictators in, 30, 40
European Economic Community (EEC),
85, 238. *See also* Common Market
European Union (EU), 85, 156–157, 163
current members, 156
peacekeeping force in Balkans, 169
evolution, theory of, 5
exiles, Cuban, 113, 117, 136
expansionism
communism and, 77
of Hitler, 44
of Japan, 48–49, 69
expansionist policy, 235, 238
exports, 27–28, 136, 144, 145, 230, 238

King Fahd, 293
King Faisal, 179

Falange, 45
Falkland Islands, 143, 152
famine, 199–201, 203, 221, 223–224
farming, 6
in Asia, 7
in China, 102
collective, 52, 88, 102, 112
green revolution, 221
subsistence, in Africa, 97
in United States, 29, 30
in U.S.S.R., 52
Farouk I (king of Egypt), 91–92
Fascist Party, 41
fascists, 41, 45, 46, 47, 52, 57
Federal Republic of Germany. *See* West
Germany
Fernández de Kirchner, Cristina, 143
Ferrer, Luis, 139
"Final Solution," 67
Finland, 64, 156
financial crisis, worldwide, 157
Five-Power Treaty, 58
Five-Year Plan, of Russia, 52
Five-Year Plans, of China, 102
flappers, 29
flu epidemic, 17
fluorocarbons, 127
Ford, Gerald, 140
Ford, Henry, 3–4
Fourteen Points, 18–19, 22
France, 153–154
costs of World War I to, 27–28
declares war on Germany, 61
division of, 64–65
Dunkirk and fall of, 64
follows policy of appeasement with
Hitler, 60
gets mandates for lands in Middle East, 32
guerrilla campaign against, in Vietnam,
106
as imperialist power, 8
industrialization of, 6
loses colonies in Southeast Asia, 89
politics in, after World War I, 28
student strikes in, 154
"the resistance" inside, 65

Grenada, 135
Guatemala, 112
Guinea, 99
Gulf War, 121, 182, 189
Gypsies, 68

Haile Selassie I, 41, 199
Haiti, 39, 138–139
hard-liners, 226
Hariri, Rafik, 190
Harper, Stephen, 126
Hausa-Fulani, 202
Havel, Václav, 162–163
Hayes, Rutherford, 3
Hebrew, 188
Herzegovina, 11, 21, 168–169
highways, 6, 74, 196
Hindus, 35, 104, 213
    fighting between Muslims and, 104, 213
Hirohito, 48
Hiroshima, 62, 73, 84
Hitler, Adolf
    blitzkrieg of, 63
    death of, 72
    "Final Solution" of, 67–68
    foreign policy of, 44
    Germany and, 42–45
    invades Poland, 61
    makes pact with Stalin, 53, 60
    sends troops into Rhineland, 44, 57
    takes over Austria, 59
    takes over Czechoslovakia, 59–60
    ties between Mussolini and, 42, 44, 59
    turns Germany into police state, 43
Hitler-Stalin Pact, 60
HIV/AIDS, 210
Ho Chi Minh, 106, 217
Ho Chi Minh Trail, 219
Holness, Andrew, 137
Holocaust, 74
Holocaust Memorial Museum, 74
Honecker, Erich, 156
Hong Kong, 228
Hoover, Herbert, 30
Horn of Africa, instability of, 199
Humala, Ollanta, 146

human-rights abuses, 112, 128, 129, 130, 141, 143, 145, 181, 204
Hungary, 148
    becomes pro-Nazi and pro-Hitler, 46
    becomes separate nation, 19, 20
    becomes Soviet satellite, 76
    communist government in, 86, 88
    Germany invades, 66
Husák, Gustáv, 162–164
Hussein Ibn Talal, 188–189
Hussein, Saddam, 120, 122–123, 181–183
    capture and execution of, 183
Hutus, 205, 209–210

Ibo, 202
il Duce. See Mussolini, Benito
Iliescu, Ion, 167
illiteracy, 188
immigrants, illegal, 128–129
impeachment
    faced by Nixon, 119
    inquiry faced by Clinton, 121
imperialism
    ending of era of, 32
    reasons for, 8
    rivalries caused by, 8
    spheres of influence, 34
    spreading of Christianity through, 8
imports, 145, 147, 203, 227, 230, 231–232
incentives, 230
India, 35–36, 214, 227–228
    becomes atomic power, 227
    neutrality of, 103, 104
    problem of overpopulation in, 104
    relations between Pakistan and, 104–105, 213–214, 215
    tradition of parliamentary democracy in, 215
Indian National Congress, 35–36, 103
Indian Subcontinent, 213
Indochina, 102, 105
indoctrination, 223
Indonesia, 235–236
    becomes a republic, 108
inflation
    during Carter administration, 119

during World War I, 11, 12, 36
during World War II
    conquests of, 69–70, 101, 105
    leaders tried for war crimes, 74
    surrender of, 73
    tide of victory turns, 72–73
Jaruzelski, Wojciech, 161
jazz, 29
Jews
    Balfour Declaration and, 15, 33
    blame assigned by Germans to, 42
    conflicts between Arabs and, 15, 33, 93–94
        186–187, 195
    destruction of European, 74. *See also*
        genocide
    Hitler's "Final Solution," 67
    Italian, laws restricting, 42
    massacre of, 47, 67–68, 74
    migration of, to Israel, 93
    move to Palestine, 33, 92
    rights and property taken away from
        German, 43, 67
Jiang Qing, 226
Jiang Zemin, 227
John Paul II, 160
Johnson, Lyndon B., 118
Jonathan, Goodluck, 204
Jordan, 159, 303–304. *See also* Transjordan
    during 1940s and 1950s, 94, 96
    becomes mandate territory, 32
    formation of, 15
junta, 111, 143
Jutland, Battle of, 15

Kabila, Joseph, 205
Kabila, Laurent, 205
kaiser, 17
Kalahari Desert, 201
kamikaze attacks, 73
Karzai, Hamid, 216
Kashmir, 104, 215
Kellogg-Briand Pact, 58
Kellogg, Frank, 58
Kemal Atatürk, 21, 34, 97. *See also*
    Mustafa Kemal

Kennedy, John F., 86, 113, 117–118
    assassination of, 118
Kennedy, Robert, assassination of, 118
Kenya, 99–100
Kenyatta, Jomo, 100
King Khalid, 180
Khatami, Mohammad, 185
Khmer Rouge, 219–220
Ayatollah Khomeini, 180, 181
Ayatollah Ruhollah Khomeini, 184–185
Khrushchev, Nikita, 85–86, 118
    de-Stalinization under, 225
Kikuyu, 99
Kim Dae-jung, 233
Kim Il Sung, 234
Kim Jong Il, 234
Kim Jong Un, 234
Kingdom of Serbs, Croatia, and Slovenes.
    See Yugoslavia
King, Martin Luther, Jr., 36, 118
    assassination of, 118
    civil rights movement and, 111, 118
Kirchner, Nestor, 143
Kissinger, Henry, 225
Kohl, Helmut, 155
Korea
    division of, 102–103. *See also* Korean War;
        North Korea; South Korea
    map of, 230
Korean War, 102–103, 109
    armistice ends, 103
Kosovo, 153
Kovác, Mihal, 163
Kuomintang, 36, 101
Kurds, 182
Kuwait, 158
    Iraq claims, 95
    Iraq's invasion of, 95, 120, 180, 182, 189,
        190
    joins Arab League, 94

Labor Party, 186
labor productivity, 152
Labour Party, 26, 88–89, 151, 152
Laos, 105, 106–107, 221

Latin America. *See also specific countries*
farming in, 7
issues and trends in, 146–147
problems in, after World War II, 111
United States and, 38–39
United States control of areas in, 9
Latvia
becomes part of Soviet Union, 63
creation of, 22
democracy in, 46
Lawrence of Arabia. *See* Lawrence, Thomas E.
Lawrence, Thomas E., 15
League of Communists of Serbia, 168
League of Nations
condemns Germany, 44, 57
countries joining, 43, 53, 58
countries leaving, 44, 48
creation of, 20
Danzig run by, 61
Haile Selassie asks for help from, 41–42
inaction of, 57, 59
Japan and, 48, 57
lack of power of, 20
oversees Allies' governing of colonies, 32
places economic sanctions on Italy, 57
Great Britain sponsors Egyptian membership in, 35
successes of, 58
U.S. dislike of, 22
Lebanon, 305
during 1940s and 1950s, 96
attacks Israel, 93
becomes mandate territory, 32
civil war in, 96
formation of, 15
Lebensraum, 44
Lee Myung-bak, 233
Lend-Lease Act, 110
Lenin, V. I., 50
death of, 52
launches New Economic Policy (NEP), 51
Lesser Antilles, 135
Liberal Democratic Party (LDP), 230
Liberal Party, 124, 125
Libya, 94, 98, 192, 196–198

Lithuania, 22
becomes part of Soviet Union, 63
democracy in, 46
part of European Union, 156
Little Red Book (Mao), 225
Locarno Pact, 58
"Long March," 37
López Portillo, Jose, 128
Low Countries, fall of, 64
Loyalists, in Spain, 45
Lula da Silva, Luiz Inacio, 142
Lusitania, 15
Luxembourg, fall of, 64

MacArthur, Douglas, 73, 103
commands army in postwar Japan, 78
Macedonia, 165, 167, 168, 170
machine guns, 13, 62
Macmillan, Harold, 207
Maginot Line, 63, 64
Major, John, 152
Malaya, 70, 107
Malcolm X, 118
Manchukuo, 48
Manchuria, 53, 69, 101
Japan takes over, 37, 48, 57
Russia invades, 73
mandate system, 32, 96
Mandela, Nelson, 208, 209
becomes president of South Africa, 209
Manley, Michael, 137
Manrique, Alejandro Toledo, 146
Maoris, 238, 239
Mao Zedong, 37, 101, 223, 225
Great Leap Forward, 223–224
turns on intellectuals, 224
March Revolution, 50
Marconi, Guglielmo, 3
Marcos, Ferdinand, 236–237
marijuana, 144
market socialism, 168
Marne, Battle of the, 14
Maronite Christians, 189
Marshall, George, 76
Marshall Plan, 76, 88, 109
Martin, Paul, 126

Martinelli, Ricardo, 133
Marxists, 50, 131
Marx, Karl, 50
Mau Mau, 99–100
Mauritania, 94
Maya, 129
McAuliffe, Christa, 120
McCarthy, Joseph, 110
Medvedev, Dmitry, 176
Meech Lake Accord, 125
Mein Kampf (Hitler), 43
Meir, Golda, 186
Mendel, Gregor, 5
Menem, Carlos Saul, 143
Mengistu Haile Mariam, 200
Merkel, Angela, 156
Mexican Revolution, 38
Mexico, 16, 37–38, 121, 128–129
    native peoples of, 128
Middle East, 32. *See also specific*
    countries
        under Allies' control, 66
        Arab-Jewish conflict in, 33. *See also* Arabs;
            Jews
        Arab Spring, 192–193
        effects of Cold War on, 179–180
        issues and trends in, 191–192
        lands become mandate territories, 32
        World War I in, 13, 15
Midway Islands, 72
militarists, 41, 42
Mills, John Atta, 199
Milosevic, Slobodan, 168, 169
    charged with war crimes, 169
U.S.S. *Missouri*, 73
Mobutu Sese Seko, 204–205
Model T, 4
Mohammad Reza Pahlavi. *See* Reza Shah
    Pahlavi
Mohammed, 214
monarchy, 20
    constitutional, 40, 45
Monroe Doctrine, 38
Monroe, James, 38
Montenegro, 10, 21, 153, 165, 167, 168, 170
Montgomery, Bernard, 70

moon
    first person walks on, 118
    Soviet rocket reaches, 86
Morocco, 94, 98, 195
Moscow Summer Olympics, 120
Mossadegh, Mohammed, 96
movies, 4
Mubarak, Hosni, 192, 196
    resigns as a result of protests, 196
Mugabe, Robert, 206, 207
mujahideen, 216
mulattoes, 138
Mulroney, Brian, 124–125
multinational corporations, 221
Muslim League, 35
Muslims, 214. *See also* Islam
    in Afghanistan, 173
    Berber, 98
    in Bosnia, 47, 169, 170
    fighting between Hindus and, 213
    in India, 35, 104–105
    in Indonesia, 235
    in Iran, 184
    in Lebanon, 96, 189
    in Nigeria, 202
    in the Philippines, 236, 237
    in Sudan, 209
    in Turkey, 34
Mussolini, Benito
    death of, 72
    declares war on France and Britain, 64
    forced to resign, 71
    foreign policy of, 41–42
    invades Ethiopia, 57
    rise of, 41
    ties between Hitler and, 42, 44, 59
Mustafa Kemal, 21, 34. *See also*
    Kemal Atatürk
Myanmar, 218. *See also* Burma

Nagasaki, 62, 73
Nagy, Imre, 88
Namib Desert, 201
Nasser, Gamal Abdel, 92, 179, 195
    belief in Arab unity of, 94
    and war of attrition against Israel, 194

National Assembly for Wales, 153
national debt, 120
National Democratic Party, 206
National Guard (Nicaragua), 130
National Guard (Panama), 132
National Socialist German Workers' Party.
   See Nazi Party
National Transitional Council, 198
nationalism, 8, 91, 132
   Arab, 33, 93, 98, 188
   in colonies, 32, 91, 154
Nationalist Party, 36–37
Nationalists, in Spain, 45–46
nationalization (of private industries), 38,
   89, 96, 131, 136, 152, 154, 157, 196, 200,
   204
NATO (North Atlantic Treaty Organization),
   84, 109, 159, 238
   peacekeeping force in Balkans, 169
   Romania joins, 167
   Turkey joins, 97
   West Germany joins, 89
Nazi Party, 43
   depression feeds, 43
   in France, 65, 72
   groups targeted by, 43, 68
   murder conducted by, 67
   "racial purity" idea of, 67
   racism of, 42, 68
   in Sudetenland, 59
   takes control of Danzig, 61
Nehru, Jawaharlal, 104, 215, 227
neo-Nazi hate groups, 158
Netanyahu, Benjamin, 187
Netherlands, 64, 69, 85, 108, 151, 156
neutrality
   of Belgium, 11
   of Cambodia, 107, 219
   of Denmark and Norway, 64
   of Germany and the Soviet Union, 53
   of India, 103, 104
   of Jordan in Middle Eastern conflicts, 189
   of Spain during World War I, 45
   of Turkey, 66
   of United States, 15, 65–66
New Deal, 30–31

New Democratic Party, 124
New Economic Policy (NEP), 51
New Guinea, 70
New York Stock Exchange, 29
New Zealand, 27, 73, 237, 238–239
Ngo Dinh Diem, 106, 217
Nicaragua, 39, 129, 130–132
   women in, 147
Nicholas (tsar of Russia), 49
Nigeria, 202–204
   civil war in, 202–203
Nine-Power Treaty, 58
Nixon, Richard M., 119, 173
   resignation of, 119
Nkomo, Joshua, 206
Nkrumah, Kwame, 99, 198
Noda, Yoshihiko, 232
nonaggression agreement, 373
nonaggression pact, 66, 69
nonaligned nations, 167, 170
Noriega, Manuel, 132–133
Normandy, invasion of, 72
North Africa
   Arab nations in, 98
   Axis Powers expelled from, 70
   Egypt, 91–92, 194
   Free French in, 65
   Italy and Germany in, 66
   World War II in, 62, 70
North American Free Trade Agreement
   (NAFTA), 121
Northern Ireland, 26, 151, 152–153, 158
Northern Ireland Assembly, 153
North Korea, 102, 103, 122, , 233–234
   development of nuclear power in, 234
   invasion of South Korea by, 103
North Vietnam, 106, 118, 217, 218, 219
Northwest Territories, 125
Norway, invasion of, 64
November Revolution, 85
Nuclear Nonproliferation Treaty, 249
nuclear physics, 4
nuclear power, 73, 215, 234
Nunavut, 125
Nuremberg trials, 74

Obama, Barack, 123
Obasanjo, Olusegun, 203
Occupy Wall Street, 193
oil, 33, 34, 38, 42, 51, 71, 92, 95, 98, 120,
  126, 128, 160, 179, 180, 181, 182, 183,
  184, 191, 195, 196, 197, 203, 220, 227, 239
Ojukwu, Odumegwu, 202
Okinawa, return of, 231
oligarchy, 133
Oman, 94, 195
OPEC, 180, 181
Organization of American States (OAS), 111
Ortega, Daniel, 131, 132
Ostpolitik, 155
Ottoman Empire, 33–34, 35. *See also* Turkey
  lands in, become mandate territories, 32
  loss of land by, 20
  weakening of, 10
  in World War I, 11
ozone layer, 127

Pacific Ocean, 15, 38, 48, 154, 232
  islands, 48, 70
  United States control of areas in, 9
  World War II in, 62, 72–73
Pakistan, 213, 214–215
  authoritarian military rule in, 215
  creation of, 104
  problem of overpopulation in, 104
  relations between India and, 215
Palestine, 15
  becomes mandate territory, 32–33
  becomes nation of Israel, 33
  and Israel, 92–93, 185
  Transjordan annexes Arab portion of, 96
  United Nations splits, 92
Palestine Liberation Organization (PLO), 33,
  188
pan-Africanism, 198
Pan-Africanist Congress (PAC), 207–208
Panama, 38, 129, 132–133
  U.S. invasion of, 132–133
Panama Canal, 38, 132
  Panama receives control of, 133
Pan Am jet explosion, 197
"Papa Doc." *See* Duvalier, François

Paris Peace Conference, 19
  separate peace treaties made at, 20–21
Park Chung Hee, 233
parliament, 28
passive resistance, 36
pass law, 207
Pathet Lao, 106
Paul, Alice, 127
Pavlov, Ivan, 5
peaceful coexistence, 86, 102, 110
peace treaties, 17. *See also* specific treaties
  World War I, 19–21
Pearl Harbor, 69–70
Pentagon, attack on, 122
People's Liberation Army, 224
perestroika, 174
Perez, Alan Garcia, 145
Perón, Eva, 112
Perón, Isabel, 143
Perón, Juan, 112, 142
Persia, 32, 34, 96. *See also* Iran
Peru, 141, 145–146
  drug trade in, 145, 146
Pétain, Philippe, 65
Petrograd Soviet of Workers' and Soldiers'
  Deputies, 50
Philippines, 70, 107, 236–237
  Muslim separatists in, 236
  taken back by MacArthur, 73
phonographs, 4
photography, 4
physics, 4
Pilsudski, Josef, 47
Planck, Max, 5
poison gas, 13, 62, 67
  used by Iraq, 181–182
Poland, 21, 259–260
  becomes Soviet satellite, 76
  complete takeover of, 63
  demand for reform grows in, 88
  Hitler invades, 61, 63
  Hitler targets, 44
  issues and trends in, 163–164
  military dictator in, 47
Polish Communist Party, 160, 161
pollution, 126, 221

exits World War I, 16
fall of tsarist government of, 16
Germany invades, 66–67
leadership of Lenin in, 50–51
leadership of Stalin in, 52–53
loss of land by, 21
March Revolution, 50
November Revolution, 50
renaming of, 51
revolution in, 49, 50, 51
Russian Federation, 175–176
organized crime in, 175
Rutherford, Ernest, 4
Rwanda, 205, 209

el-Sadat, Anwar, 186, 187, 189, 191, 195
Sahara Desert, 97, 98, 201
as-Said, Nuri, 95
Sakharov, Andrey, 173, 174
Salinas de Gortari, Carlos, 128
samizdat, 173
Sandinista National Liberation Front (FSLN).
See Sandinistas
Sandinistas, 131, 132, 146
Sandino, Augusto, 130, 131
Sarkozy, Nicolas, 154
Sarney, José, 142
satellites, 75
King Saud, 179
Saudi Arabia, 94, 179–181
formation of, 15
SAVAK, 184
Schmidt, Helmut, 155
Schröder, Gerhard, 155
science, breakthroughs in, 4–5
Scotland, 151, 153, 197
Scottish Executive, 153
Scottish Parliament, 153
Seaga, Edward, 137
SEATO, 109, 238
secession, 125
secular state, 215
Securitate, 165, 166
Security Council, 80, 103, 190
economic sanctions imposed by, 80
raises combat force against North Korean
agression, 103

veto power in, 80
segregation, 36, 110
actions taken against, 110–111
Sein, Thein, 219
separatist movement, 124–125
September 11 attacks, 122, 125, 153, 197,
216
effect on Canada of, 125
Qaddafi condemns, 197
Serbia, 10, 11, 21, 153, 165, 167–171
independence of, 10–11
Serbs, 21, 46, 47, 168, 169, 170
massacre of, 47
17th parallel, 106
Sharon, Ariel, 187
Shiite Muslims, 189
Shining Path, 145
Siegfried Line, 63, 72
Sierra Leone, 153
Sihanouk, Norodom, 107, 219
Sikhs, 214
Sinai Peninsula, 92, 93, 195
Singapore, 107, 220
Six-Day War, 186, 187, 188
slave labor, 68
Slavs, 10, 11, 67, 68
Slovakia, 21, 156, 159, 161–163
formation of, 159, 163
Slovenia, 21, 156, 165, 167, 168, 170
declares independence, 168
Smith, Ian, 206
socialism, 31
African, 97, 198
in Great Britain, 88
in Hong Kong, 229
with a human face, 162
socialists, 41, 45
blame assigned by Germans to, 42
in Russia, 49
social reforms, New Deal, 31
Social Security Act, 31
Solidarity, 160, 161, 164
Solomon Islands, 70
Somalia, 94
violence in, 200, 209
Somoza, Anastasio, 130
overthrow of, 131

sonar, 71
South Africa, 27, 100, 206, 207–209
    during 1940s and 1950s, 100
    apartheid in, 100, 207, 209
South America, 141–147. *See also specific countries*
    human-rights abuses in, 141, 143
Southeast Asia, 105–108, 217–222. *See also specific countries*
    as field of battle in Cold War, 105
    France loses colonies in, 89
    impact of World War II on, 105
South-East Asian Defense Treaty. *See* SEATO
South Korea, 102–103, 233–234
    North Korea invades, 103
South Vietnam, 106, 118, 217, 218
Soviet bloc, 84, 159
soviets, 50–51
Soviet Union, 85–86, 172, 173–175. *See also* Russia; Union of Soviet Socialist Republics (U.S.S.R.)
    advances in rocket science of, 86
    Baltic states become part of, 63
    blockade of Berlin by, 77
    break-up of, 159
    conflict with United States, 78–79, 109–110
    countries invaded by, 63–64
    and Cuba, 113, 117, 136–137
    invades Afghanistan, 119–120, 216
    Japan signs nonagression pact with, 69
    under Khrushchev, 85–86
    Nixon visits, 119
    policy of peaceful coexistence, 86, 110
    power struggle in, 85
    relations between China and, 102
    satellites of, 75–76
    as a superpower, 109, 117, 173
space exploration, 86, 118, 120
Spain, 90
    and Franco, 45–46
Spanish Civil War, 42, 45–46, 90
    as mini-European war, 45–46, 57
spheres of influence, 34, 36
Sputnik, 86
SS, 44

Stalingrad, 70–71
Stalin, Joseph, 52–53, 71–72, 85
    controls Eastern Europe, 83
    disagreements between Tito and, 167–168
    Five-Year Plan of, 52
    makes pact with Hitler, 53, 60
    purges of, 52
    turns U.S.S.R. into police state, 52
    at Yalta, 75–76
standard of living
    in Asia, 239
    U.S., 117, 119
stimulus, 5
stock market, 29–30, 121
    collapse of, 30
stocks, 29
Strategic Arms Limitation Treaty (SALT I), 119, 173
strikes
    air, 153, 183
    hunger, 36
    labor, 40, 41, 43, 45, 49, 154, 160, 163, 207
    student, 154
submarines, 13
    attacks from German, 15, 16, 66, 71
    blockades by, 14–15
Sudan, 94, 195, 209
    violence in, 200, 209
Sudetenland, 59–60
Suez Canal, 35
    in Allied hands, 70
    crisis, 92, 93
    refusal to allow Israeli goods through, 93
Suharto, 235–236
Sukarno, Achmed, 108, 235
summit conferences, 85
Sunni Muslims, 189
Sun Yat-sen, 36–37
superpowers, 109, 117, 173
supply-side economics, 120
"The Swamp Fox." *See* Marion, Francis
Syria, 189–192
    during 1940s and 1950s, 95
    attacks Israel, 93, 186
    becomes mandate territory, 32

formation of, 15
France puts down revolts in, 33

Taiwan, 101
and China, 228–229
Chinese threats against, 102
Taliban, 122, 216
and Osama bin Laden, 216
tanks, 13
tariffs
affect U.S. overseas trade, 30
disruption of world trade by, 27
effect on Great Britain of, 25
technology
advances in, 3–4
needs in Latin America, 146–147
North American, 126–127
telephones, 3
television, 163, 184, 200, 226
Tennessee Valley Authority, 31
terrorism
in Egypt, 196
in India, 214
in Indonesia, 236
in Israel, 187
in Northern Ireland, 26, 152
in Puerto Rico, 140
Qaddafi's support of, 197
in the United States, 122, 216
Terry, Fernando Belaúnde, 145
Thailand, 108, 220–221
Thatcher, Margaret, 152, 157, 206
theory of evolution, 5
theory of relativity, 5
Third International, 52
Third Reich, 44
Third World, 104
38th parallel, 103
Thomson, J. J., 4
Tiananmen Square, 226–227
Tibet, 102, 227
Marshal Tito, 76, 87, 167, 170
disagreements between Stalin and, 167–168
Tlatelolco Massacre, 128
Tokyo war crimes trial, 74

Tontons Macoutes, 138
Tories. *See* Conservative Party
Torrijos, Omar, 132
totalitarianism. *See also* dictators; fascists
life under, 40
Touré, Sékou, 99
trade
barriers lowered by NAFTA, 121
dependence of Great Britain on, 25
disruption of, due to tariffs, 27
expansion of Japan's postwar, 101
Panama Canal, as boost to U.S., 38
tariffs affect U.S. overseas, 30
trade deficit, 231
Transjordan. *See also* Jordan
annexes Arab portion of Palestine, 96
attacks Israel, 93
as British mandate, 96
transportation, 3–4
changes brought by advances in, 6
Transylvania, 167
trenches, 13, 14, 62, 63
tribunal, 169, 183
Triple Alliance, 9, 10
Triple Entente, 9, 10
Trotsky, Leon, 52
Trudeau, Pierre, 124
Trujillo, Cesar Gaviria, 144
Truman Doctrine, 77, 83, 94, 109
Truman, Harry, 73
tsar, 16, 49, 50, 51
tsunami,
in Indonesia. *See* earthquake
in Japan. *See* earthquake
Tudjman, Franjo, 169
Tunisia, 94, 98, 192, 195
protests in. *See* Arab Spring
Turkey, 33–34
during 1940s and 1950s, 97
joins NATO, 97
neutrality of, 66
as possible Soviet target, 77
societal changes in, 34
Tutsis, 205, 209–210
twentieth century
breakthroughs in science, 4

inventions of, 3–4
new industrial world of, 6–7
new knowledge about humans, 5–6
transportation changes, 3–4

Ubico, Jorge, 112
U-boats, 71
Ukraine, 66, 73, 160, 175
Ulbricht, Walter, 87
ultraviolet radiation, 127
Ulyanov, Vladimir Ilyich. *See* Lenin, V. I.
UN. *See* United Nations
unemployment
in Germany after World War I, 43
during Great Depression, 30
Union of Soviet Socialist Republics
(U.S.S.R.), 51. *See also* Russia; Soviet Union
break-up of, 172
turns into police state, 52
United Arab Emirates, 94
United Arab Republic (UAR), 94
United Kingdom, 151–153, 157–158. *See also*
Great Britain
United Nations, 79–80
acts against Libya, 197
arranges Middle East truce, 93
cease-fires, 92, 195, 201, 215
Congo peacekeeping force, 204
creation and purpose of, 79–80
in East Indies, 108
and East Timor, 236
economic sanctions imposed on Iraq, 182
General Assembly, 79
peace plan for Cambodia, 220
powers of, 80
sanctions on Rhodesia, 206
Security Council, 80, 103
sends peacekeeping force to Suez Canal
area, 92
splits Palestine, 92–93
Taiwan holds "China seat" in, 228–229
troops in Croatia, 169
UNRRA (United Nations Relief and
Rehabitation Administration), 76
United Nicaragua Opposition, 131

United States
in the 1960s, 117–119
in the 1970s and 1980s, 119–120
in the 1990s, 120–121
after World War II, 117
assassinations in, 118–119
attacks Iraq, 123
breaks off diplomatic relations with
Cuba, 113
changes in society and politics, 31
comes under attack, 69–70, 122
conflict with Soviet Union, 78–79, 109–110
"dollar diplomacy" of, 39
domestic policy, 110–111
embargo on Cuban sugar, 136
enters World War I, 15–16
enters World War II, 69–70
fails to agree to Versailles Treaty, 22
foreign policy in late 1940s and 1950s,
109–110
gives aid to Franco, 90
imperialism of, 9
industrialization of, 6–7
isolationism and the Roaring Twenties, 29
issues and trends in, 126–127
and Japan, 231–232
and Latin America, 38–39
and Mexico, 37–38
neutrality of, 66
postwar policy in Japan, 78
and Puerto Rico, 139–140
resumption of relations between China
and, 225
as a superpower, 117
universal suffrage, 220
UNRRA (United Nations Relief and
Rehabitation Administration), 76
U Nu, 218
U.S. Senate
investigation of Watergate break-in, 119
refuses to ratify Versailles Treaty, 22
U.S. Supreme Court
landmark decision of, 110
and presidential election of 2000, 121–122

V-E Day (Victory in Europe Day), 72

World War II

attempts to keep peace before, 58
Battle of the Atlantic, 71
Battle of Stalingrad, 70
beginning of, 61
brings Mexico and United States back
    together, 38
difference between World War I and, 62
Dunkirk and the fall of France, 64–65
Germany invades Russia, 66–67
Great Britain and the United States,
    65–66
impact on Southeast Asia of, 105
invasion of Italy, 71
Japanese conquests during, 69
Mussolini's foreign policy and, 41
nations involved in, 63
nature of, 62–63
new international order after, 78–79
North Africa, 70
peace treaty signed for, 78
price of, 74
role of airplanes in, 62
steps leading to, 49, 57–58
trials held for war crimes after, 74
United States enters, 70
victory in Europe, 71–72
war in the east and south, 66
war in the Pacific, 72–73
war in the west, 63–64
years between World War I and, 25

Wright, Orville, 4
Wright, Wilbur, 4

Yalta conference, 75–76
Yalu River, 103
Yar'Adua, Umaru Musa, 203–204

Yeltsin, Boris, 174–175
as president of Russian Federation,
    175–176
Yom Kippur, 186
Yom Kippur War, 186, 195
Yoruba, 202
Young Turks, 34
Yugoslav Federation, 168
Yugoslavia, 20, 167–170
becomes pro-Hitler, 47
begins to fall apart, 168
civil war in, 47
communism in, 159
countries comprising former, 167
countries formed by collapse of, 21, 165
dissolution of, 21
ethnic conflicts in, 46
Germany invades, 66
issues and trends in, 170–171
under Tito, 76, 87

Zapatistas, 128, 146
al-Zarqawi, Abu Musab, 183
Zedillo Ponce de León, Ernesto, 129
Zimbabwe, 205–207
continuing unrest in, 207
**Zimbabwe African National Union
(ZANU)**, 206
**Zimbabwe African People's Union
(ZAPU)**, 206
Zimmermann, Arthur, 16
Zimmermann telegram, 16